PAUL

GÜNTHER BORNKAMM

PAUL

Paulus

TRANSLATED BY D. M. G. STALKER

1817

HARPER & ROW, PUBLISHERS

NEW YORK AND EVANSTON

Translator's Note

The translator wishes to acknowledge his great indebtedness to Mrs. Anne C. Leader, of Washington, D.C., who read through the manuscript and made many corrections and improvements.

CONTENTS

PART TWO: GOSPEL AND THEOLOGY

PREFACE

This book makes a certain demand on its readers, though perhaps less on the professional theologian *au fait* with current research than on the "layman," for whom it is equally designed. The reader will look in vain here for much that from the beginning has been a familiar part of the church's tradition, deriving above all from the Book of Acts. The reasons for this slight, and critical, use of Acts are given in the Introduction. In the matter of Paul's own epistles, too, this book often goes ways of its own. If we are to think Paul's theology along with him and follow it, we certainly need to prepare ourselves and to persevere. At the same time, with a thinker of Paul's stature, it is impossible to make him seem easier than he is. I have tried not only to give some account of his life and thought but also to let the reader share in the process of questioning and discovery.

In Paul's theology many topics and ideas are so interrelated that the reader should not in every case expect exhaustive treatment of a particular subject under the relevant heading. For more detailed discussion he must refer to other related ideas and key words.

The character and limited compass of the book made it impossible in every case carefully to discuss the pros and cons of interpretations differing from my own. My indebtedness to the work of other men, including those not mentioned here, and the extent to which joining issue with earlier and present-day research has been a formative factor in my own understanding and of judgments on Paul will be obvious to the expert on page after page. The nonexpert may count himself happy not to be required to retraverse their tracks, both right and wrong.

—GÜNTHER BORNKAMM

Heidelberg

CHRONOLOGICAL TABLE

The only certain date in Pauline chronology follows from the mention in Acts 18:12 of the governor L. Junius Gallio, a brother of Seneca's. On the basis of an inscription found at Delphi, his period of office as proconsul of Achaia can be calculated as being from the spring of 51 to the spring of 52 (less probably 52–53). All further relative dating has to be conjectured by calculation both forward and backward from this point, following incomplete and, in some cases, not very precise information found in Acts and the Pauline Epistles; in details we sometimes have to allow for a margin of error. The most recent thorough investigation of Pauline chronology is to be found in D. Georgi, *Die Geschichte der Kollekte des Paulus für Jerusalem* (1965), pp. 91–96 (further bibliography given there). The chronological table which follows is in general agreement with his findings. It gives no more than a few of the most important dates between which the other events described in the present study are to be placed.

Crucifixion of Jesus	*c.* 30
Paul's date of birth	unknown (probably about the beginning of the century)
Conversion and call	*c.* 32
Apostolic assembly	48 (49?)
Paul in Corinth	18 months; winter of 49/50 until summer of 51

Paul in Ephesus	about 2½ years; probably 52 to 55
Last stay in Macedonia and Achaia	probably winter of 55/56
Journey to Jerusalem and arrest	spring of 56
Taken prisoner to Rome	probably 58
Two years' imprisonment in Rome	probably 58–60
Martyrdom under Nero	probably 60

INTRODUCTION

A brighter light shines on Paul than on any other figure in primitive Christianity. Even so, he still stands in the twilight of history. Of many others, even the disciples closest to Jesus, we know just a little—at best their names and some facts in their life story. With the majority we are completely in the dark, in spite of all the efforts of legend to illuminate them. Even with Jesus, the historian is in a worse case than with Paul, since Jesus left no writings of his own behind. What we know of him goes back behind the Gospels to the oral tradition of the post-Easter church and is so deeply embedded in the church's witness to its faith that it is often difficult to distinguish between historical account and expression of the earliest Christians' faith. As a result, our knowledge of the historical Jesus is to a large extent uncertain and far from complete.

With Paul the sources are much more plentiful, and of a different kind. The most important are his own letters, a large number of which the church has preserved in the New Testament. Of the twenty-seven books in the canon no fewer than thirteen bear his name. Present-day scholarship does not, of course, believe that all of them come from Paul himself, some being later imitations, written in his name in order to preserve his apostolic legacy or even to confer authority upon the authors themselves. The reasons for and against the authenticity of a particular letter cannot be gone into here (see Appendix I). At this point I merely specify those I regard as genuinely Pauline. Taking them in their most probable chronological order—though this is not in every case certain—they are 1 Thessalonians, the apostle's letters to the church at Corinth (probably a collection of his extensive correspondence with it ranging over a considerable period), Galatians, Philippians, Philemon, and finally, the great letter to the Romans. All of these will be discussed later as we try to describe the apostle's life and work. Among the Deutero-Pauline letters, that is to say, those composed under his name, we agree with the majority of present-day scholars in including the so-called Pastoral Epistles (that is, directions in letter form to Timothy and Titus concerning their "pastoral office" and the right ordering of the church) and—although these are much more disputed—Colossians, Ephesians, and 2 Thessalonians. Thus, even after criticism has sifted out a certain number, we are still left with a considerable and important body of genuine, authoritative material. These letters put us into direct contact with Paul and his message, furnish an extremely vivid picture of the apostle's activity and struggles, his successes and failures, his experiences and ideas, and at the same time afford us unique glimpses into the history of primitive Christianity. Written in the fifties of the first century, they are also historical sources of the first rank; indeed, they are the oldest and, for the historian, the most trustworthy of all the earliest Christian writings; they are decades earlier than the Gospels which tell us of the life and preaching of Jesus.

Paul's letters are the primary and normative source not only for his message and theology, but also for the first subject to be discussed in this book, his life. All that we are told of Paul elsewhere will need to be measured against them. They are, of course, in no sense autobiography, but arose out of the apostle's work. This work therefore, and not Paul himself, is in the forefront. Moreover, they are conditioned by the events which gave rise to them, and were all written within a short space of time in the last phase of his life, when his work was at its peak but was also already drawing to its end. In principle, therefore, we may not expect from them equal fullness of information about all the chapters of his life. For long stretches of it the letters leave us in the dark, and for much of the detail casual allusions are often the only clue.

These deficiencies might appear to be offset by the fact that the New Testament offers a second important source, the Book of Acts (in the Latin canon, *Acta Apostolorum*). More than half of this, the most extensive New Testament writing, by the same author as Luke's Gospel and explicitly linked with it as one historical work (see the prologue, Acts 1:1 ff.), deals exclusively with the work and fortunes of Paul. It is little wonder then that Acts has come to be regarded in all essentials as *the* source for Paul's life, the letters being utilized only for his teaching. The result is that the usual picture of Paul in the church's tradition has derived the vast majority of its features from Acts.

Present-day research rules out this traditional way of treatment. Its foundations have been shaken by the clear evidence that Luke's history is to be understood primarily as a document of his own time, the post-apostolic age. It was during, and for, this time that Luke wrote, at the earliest toward the end of the first century, more than forty years after Paul's letters were written. To us this may seem a relatively short interval. But it must be realized that the conditions and events, the controversies and conflicting views, of the earlier period, to which Paul's letters bear ample testimony, were already quite alien to the age of Acts. By the time Acts was written, all these matters were largely things of the past, settled and forgotten; accurate memory of them had faded, some of the tradition been suppressed, and in many respects the earlier conception of the gospel of salvation, of Christian faith, of the church and its relationship to the world, had given way to new questions, new views, new tasks.

There is, of course, good reason for Acts' particular interest in Paul. Without Paul the position represented by its author and his age would be inconceivable. Luke writes as a Greek and a Gentile Christian. By his day the gospel has long since finally broken down the once hard-contested and stubbornly defended boundaries between the privileged people of the Jews and the Gentiles. The church has spread over the nations making up the Roman empire—Paul as seen in the last verse of Acts (28:31) preaches the gospel in its capital city "unhindered." The ground on which Luke stands was prepared by Paul. His book has all kinds of echoes of Pauline ideas, although he often changes and simplifies them. At the same time, it is everywhere apparent that the tensions which prepared this soil were over by Luke's time, and the story of their causes, of which we have glimpses in the letters, forgotten. Thus in Acts, even where Paul's accent lasts on, the old saying holds true: when two people say the same thing, it ceases to be the same thing. History seen in retrospect and history still open to the future and awaiting its issue are not just one and the same thing. What emerges from comparison between Acts and the authentic Pauline Epistles is like a river which has not only deposited much during its course, but also been replenished by new sources and tributaries.

Against such considerations it may be urged that Luke manifestly wrote as a historian and, moreover, as one who for a considerable time was a fellow worker of Paul's and accompanied him on journeys (Philemon 24; Col. 4:14; 2 Tim. 4:11); consequently, as an eyewitness Luke guarantees the truth of what he says. But there is an answer to this objection; Acts itself nowhere mentions its author by name, and recent research has furnished good reasons for challenging the church's tradition, which after all was established only at the end of the second century. But even if tradition were correct, such simplistic conclusions are in any case unwarrantable for assessing the historical value of Acts; of this there is hardly any question today. Of course Luke wrote as a historian (his traditional name is retained for simplicity's sake). But his is ancient, not modern, historiography, and we can never apply to him Ranke's now accepted dictum that the historian has "only to tell what in fact took place." In the ancient world a narrator had much more free play in the matter of literary art, and precisely as a historian he made use of particular ways of presenting his subject which are not at the disposal of the present-day historian. His contribution consisted not only in transmitting the tradition, but in reproducing it in such a way as to make things vivid and meaningful. He worked it into scenes and tableaux, thereby interpreting it. He made a unity out of the multiplicity, and brought out the "sense of direction" in events (Dibelius). That he worked up traditions, if these were available, is not in dispute, but naturally he did not do so according to the methods and principles of critical analysis and examination: these evolved only in modern historiography. In no case, then, is he to be measured against the norm of dead accuracy in matters of historical fact.

These considerations apply also to Luke; even a person without much scholarly equipment can satisfy himself of this by noting the great differences in the various portions of the book. These show at once that the question as to the historical value of Luke's account cannot be answered in the round. Along with brief, dry notes, found particularly in Paul's journeys, about dates, people, and places, we also have stereotyped formulas relating, for example, to the growth and life of the churches and either marking a transition or pointing out a connection. Again, we find grand, vivid tableaux to illustrate main topics—the miraculous powers of Christ's witnesses, the healing and conversion of individuals, the superiority of the gospel over the idolatry and superstition of the heathen, the steadfastness of witnesses before hostile tribunals, their preservation by God's power, and so on. A particularly prominent element in the whole book is formed by numerous speeches, some of them lengthy, which set forth the basic truths of the gospel to Jews or Gentiles, to a crowd or the governing classes. In view of the abundant material from ancient historiography that shows a preference for this kind of presentation, there can be no doubt that the speeches—twenty-four in number, and forming almost a third of the whole book—are not transcripts of or excerpts from speeches actually delivered, but are compositions by the author of Acts. He has no interest in characterizing the various speakers as individuals: Paul, Peter, or others. By his use of all these devices at his disposal for painting his picture Luke shows himself to be a "historian" in the sense of his own day, and therefore, paradoxical though it may seem, he is least to be regarded as an authentic witness: instead, he is only a reporter at second hand (Dibelius).

To remember Luke's place in time and his method of presentation is a help toward seeing why there are considerable discrepancies between his picture of Paul and Paul's life and that found in the letters. From its very beginnings the church is depicted in Acts

as the community of believers concerned for the Gentile world and
with all its members living in perfect concord. It was led by the
mother church in Jerusalem, represented by the twelve apostles,
and, from Christ's resurrection and exaltation onward, was power-
fully guided in unity by the Spirit of God. In it the Old Testament
promises were fulfilled, and to it was transferred the heritage of
salvation history forfeited by the unbelieving Jews. Thus, in pur-
suance of its Lord's promise (Acts 1:8), and in spite of all adver-
sity and persecution, it steadily spread with power from Jerusalem
through the Gentile world. While it is easy to see that this total
picture, even if it is a very much simplified and idealized one,
preserves a Pauline heritage, the considerable historical and theological differences are equally clear. The two things are bound up
together and, as will later be made clear in detail, bear on fundamental and not just marginal questions. Here it may be enough to
indicate just one or two particularly noticeable features which are
also characteristic of all of Luke's work. Luke is emphatic in
representing Paul, even after he has become a Christian and missionary, as still the convinced Pharisee, continuing faithful to the
Law of his fathers and to belief in the resurrection of the dead, a
belief held particularly by the Pharisees and now confirmed by
Jesus' resurrection, whereas the Jews, by rejecting Jesus, have
betrayed their own most holy traditions (cf., e.g., Acts 26:2 ff.).
The real Paul was completely different from this. Philippians in
particular shows that he abandoned his former Pharisaic zeal for
righteousness based on the works of the Law and counted everything as "loss" and "refuse," finding salvation solely in faith in
Christ (Phil. 3:5 ff.). From this obvious difference one may not,
of course, conclude that Acts has a primitively Judaistic tendency.
The approach of Acts became possible once the battle between
Jews and Christians over the validity of the Law had been settled
and the Law, freed from its former particularism, had come to be
thought of as a permanently valid divine dispensation for all men.
No less characteristic is the fact that Acts denies Paul the status
and title of apostle; this designation it reserves exclusively for the
Twelve. There is, of course, no thought of demoting Paul. Rather,
the distinction reveals a fundamental change in the understanding
of the church and the apostolate. As distinct from Paul's view,

Acts regards the apostolic office, as instituted by Jesus while on earth, confined to the Twelve as his most intimate companions and eyewitnesses, and as guaranteeing correct tradition, which was tied to the mother church in Jerusalem. Paul, on the other hand, is not himself an apostle, but the great missionary to the Gentiles legitimated by Jerusalem. If we remember from the evidence in his letters how fiercely, in many of his churches, the real Paul had to contend with adversaries, and certainly with the authorities in Jerusalem, in order to be recognized as an apostle, we can see the significance of this further difference between the letters and Acts. As a consequence, Luke also gives a picture of the relationships between Paul and Jerusalem different from the one which we find in Paul, particularly in Galatians and Romans. Further examples of such differences are to be found in points which Luke never mentions at all: Paul's clashes with the Judaizers or the "enthusiasts," or the importance of his message of the cross, which was the decisive factor in his understanding both of himself and of Christianity in general. Acts no longer has anything of this, replacing it by the picture of the triumphant witness. A similar picture could be drawn of Luke's eschatology and of other theological questions.

The discrepancies just enumerated do not in the least imply that Acts has no historical value at all. Doubtless Luke had many trustworthy accounts to work from, and no portrayal of Paul can do without them. We can be most sure of them where we find least traces of obviously legendary embellishment, of the overriding interests of the book, and of the literary artistry of its author. In many cases these are the least striking passages, and the reader passes quickly over them. Unfortunately, Luke never divulges his sources: we are thrown back on conjecture. For Acts he quite certainly did not have literary predecessors, as he tells us he had for his Gospel (Luke 1:1-4). What he attempted in Acts was pioneering work. He may possibly have followed the practice of many other classical historians and made visits to the most important of Paul's church foundations. Or he may have learned stories in circulation about him from others. Here and there style and content suggest that he may have used records already in written form, of whatever origin. By and large, however, these cannot have been continuous complexes of any length. For a long time critics have claimed that some such fairly extensive written source lay behind certain passages in which the third-person narrative suddenly changes to the first person plural, and the speaker seems to be an actual traveling companion of the apostle (16:10–17; 20:5–15; 21:1–18; 27:1–28:16). But even here there is no clear evidence of the use of a source; in addition to the stylistic characteristics already mentioned, the vocabulary and the way in which the story is told have nothing to mark them off from the rest of the book. Further, the delimitation of the "we passages" is not certain. Above all, however, parallels in other ancient historians show that this change of person, too, was a favorite literary device, to add vividness. Dibelius was therefore correct in substituting for the hypothesis of the "we source" the much more plausible conjecture that here and there Luke made use of an "itinerary," that is to say, a brief diary of the journeys. Even if we can only make out fragments of it, this itinerary must be regarded as a very valuable source. This is not to deny that at places in Acts one can discover clear traces of unexceptionable oral or written tradition. Nevertheless, in the question of sources no universally assured results have thus far been arrived at: nor will they be in the future.

It is a matter of great surprise that not a single passage in Luke's whole book shows either knowledge of the apostle's own letters or use made of them. We must conclude from this that at the time when Acts was composed, there was still no representative collection of Paul's letters distributed over the church's major areas. No doubt from quite early on, single letters were exchanged among neighboring churches. There are references to a collection in certain early Christian writings, but they are isolated; they do, however, increase in number from the nineties of the first century onward. Even if Acts shows no knowledge of the letters, this is also the approximate period to which it is to be assigned. Since before writing Acts, Luke wrote his Gospel, which is the latest of the Synoptics—all of them after A.D. 70—and probably composed in the eighties, we may best put Acts in the nineties.

Confined though it was to the main features of Acts, the critical analysis just given makes evident that this second source for Paul is not simply a supplementation and confirmation of our basic source, the letters: instead, it raises certain difficulties. These compel us to abandon the widespread practice of uncritically combining Acts and the letters, and to use great restraint in drawing upon the former. This procedure may seem odd to those who read the Bible uncritically and are used to the traditional view; more often than not, conservative critics as well may feel it overdone. But both must come to realize that it will not do confidently to make Acts the basis of Paul's life and to assign to the letters merely the role of an occasional welcome supplement or illustration; nor may we uncritically fill in gaps in the letters from the copious material in Acts. In other words, when the one source is silent, it will not do uncritically to listen to the other. The great service done by recent research is that it has revealed the questionable character of this current combination of sources. Combining and harmonizing have been disastrous. They have resulted in the blurring of the contours of the picture of Paul as he was and in seriously damaging the understanding of the historical and theological problems connected with his gospel and work. My own critical caution will, I hope, prove to be no more than the other side of a well-founded trust in Paul's letters as authoritative evidence not only for his gospel and theology but also for his life.

The apostle's literary legacy is composed exclusively of letters. This is not merely an accident of history: rather, it is of considerable material significance. There is absolutely nothing to suggest that it ever occurred to Paul to tell the story of Jesus of Nazareth in, for example, a Gospel, as was done decades later, first by Mark and then by others. Again, he would hardly have thought of writing, say, commentaries on single books of the Old Testament such as we have from the hand of his Jewish contemporary Philo of Alexandria and other early Christian writers. Nor would he have had any idea of composing regulations for the churches, or theological tractates, or treatises on dogmatics, which can be found in abundance from the time of the early church. Even what might be called, and has often been regarded as, the nearest approximation to a kind of treatise, Romans, cannot be classified as such. The reasons for this state of affairs are quite obvious. Paul was, as we say with some truth, a man engaged in missionary work, not a

writer; indeed, as many would add, this time very unjustly, he was
not even strictly a theologian, but an envoy and preacher, striving
to complete his grandiose missionary program before Christ's
imminent return, and harassed by specific tasks, questions, and
conflicts. How could he possibly ever have found time for theological reflection and authorship? This explanation is, however, a
hopeless confusion of true and false, and can be completely misleading. Taken by itself, the usual contrast between "theory" and
"practice," in Paul's case between life and theology, is absolutely
absurd. And, above all, such recourse obscures the very close way
in which Paul's exclusive use of the letter form is related to the
content and characteristics of his theological thinking.

These letters are real letters. But because the present-day reader
is accustomed to hearing them in church and used in the liturgy,
he is often completely unaware, or insufficiently aware, of their
true character. For the church they are, by and large, simply holy
texts for readings and prayers. Of course, they are not private
letters, but were designed for the larger audience of Paul's
churches, and intended to be read aloud at the meeting for worship (1 Thess. 5:27), as is shown by the liturgical turns of phrase
and the prayers and benedictions at beginning and end. Nonetheless, this does not disqualify them from being real letters. They are
not collections of pious maxims and religious meditations, nor are
they products of literary artistry in the garb of letters (a practice
for which there are plenty of examples beginning with the classical
world). Like all real letters, they were written on and for a particular occasion, for specific reasons, for particular people. In this
sense they are occasional writings—and often enough the occasion
was unhappy. The author himself often saw them as makeshifts,
an unsatisfactory substitute for a personal meeting which was no
longer, or not yet, possible. This he says more than once, deplor-
ing the adverse circumstances which prevented him from coming
to a church and made a letter necessary (1 Thess. 2:17 f.; Rom.
15:22 ff.).

His letters make it equally clear, of course, that the very fact of
his being detained and obliged to set down his ideas in peace and
quiet on paper lent depth and conviction to his thoughts and

allowed him to organize what he had to say in a way only occasionally possible in the cut and thrust of face-to-face encounter. His opponents in Corinth were well aware of this and stirred up the church against him by saying that while his letters were weighty and strong, his bodily presence was weak and his speech clumsy (2 Cor. 10:1, 10; 11:6). This malicious criticism is, of course, to be judged in the light of the lofty standards of discourse as represented by the "enthusiasts," which Paul utterly repudiated (1 Cor. 2:3 ff.). Paul's success as a missionary shows that he made good use of preaching, yet it would be true to say that often he effected more by means of his letters than by the spoken word. At the same time, what was said above remains true: communication by letter is a second-best and a substitute, inferior to what may be achieved by direct encounter, as Paul found out.

Thanks to these at first tiresome and apparently chance circumstances, nearly two thousand years later we are able to enter into the apostle's exchange with his churches, though the lapse of time prevents us from at once understanding everything he says and refers to, and leaves much of what then was perfectly clear a matter of conjecture for today. In letters from the past an obscurity often simply indicates that the original readers, who were familiar with the situations and questions discussed and with certain individuals, particularly the author himself, and at home in the same realm of ideas and concepts, at once understood what was said. Our distance in time from the documents is therefore to be given due consideration, and not overhastily ironed out. This does not, of course, alter the fact, as anyone knows who has worked with such historical sources, that it is letters that convey better than anything else the feeling of direct proximity. Provided their writers do not conceal themselves behind clichés and conventional flowery expressions but—and with Paul this is very much the case—know how to express their personalities, letters bear the . unmistakable stamp of a particular man better than any other documents. We feel, so to speak, his breath, and at the same time we are brought very close to those to whom he wrote. Thus, carried back over the centuries, we become eyewitnesses of an encounter, partners in that original conversation. We, too, are

addressed, questioned, and appealed to. We shall do well to remember these general experiences when we approach the letters of
Paul.

More needs to be said, however, because in kind the Pauline
letters are unique. Despite the impress of Paul's own personality
and the limitation to particular situations, they are more than just
private letters in respect of author, recipients, and subject matter.
The apostle's task and his responsibility and passionate concern
for the gospel and the churches entrusted to him give them their
hallmark, and not any personal friendship with particular individuals.

Originating in the apostle's missionary work and designed to
promote this work from a distance, the Pauline letters became the
oldest literary genre in primitive Christianity. Classical literature
has nothing similar. Their distinctiveness lies in their being still
close to the living voice of the gospel, that is to say, the gospel
proclaimed by word of mouth and aimed at gaining both a hearing
and obedience in faith. They do not move in the realm of abstract,
theoretical reflection, but always include the hearers' own actual
situations as a determining factor. It was Paul who created this
primitive Christian genre, letters, as a means of communication,
and they remain its model, often imitated but never matched. He
no doubt made use of the fixed conventionalized forms of Hellenistic letter writing, most obviously in the salutations at the
start, the thanksgivings and assurances of intercession for the
readers, and the greetings and wishes at the end. Yet quite often
he modifies these to suit the purposes of his letter: for example,
when he introduces himself as called to be an apostle and a servant of Jesus Christ and his fellow workers as joining him in
sending the letter (without, however, implying joint authorship),
when he characterizes the churches spiritually in the greetings,
thanksgivings, and intercessions and substitutes the normal wish
for the recipient's welfare by the promise of salvation ("grace and
salvation be with you"), also found in Jewish letters from the
east. The differences in the length and content of the various
sections show how much Paul gave an individual stamp to the set
forms. This makes clear that he does more than merely use external forms: rather, thoughts and words follow an intrinsic pat-

tern dictated by the subject matter. In particular, the major sections of the letters have no parallel in the traditional forms. They link up with entirely different forms, those of the sermon, of theological argumentation, of exhortation, and of the liturgy (confession, the hymn, doxology, blessing and cursing, etc.). This explains why the letters were passed to other churches (Col. 4:16), why they were collected at a relatively early period, and why use was made of them later. But their own peculiar character helps us to understand as well the great influence they exerted and the preeminence of the epistle as a literary genre in primitive Christian literature. Letters to churches were written in the name of Paul, or ascribed to some other apostle, to assure a like authority for themselves.

Paul's letters differ from countless other church treatises and pastoral epistles both early and late in that their author's person and work are an indissoluble unity. The modern reader will often feel their strangeness, nor should he try to gloss it over. But he should also be conscious that here the power of the spirit is united with the power of the heart and finds expression in language which is often quite amazing in its mastery. Very often it is difficult, impenetrable, and overloaded; it shifts and changes, being wooing and gracious, but abrupt and harsh as well. In every case, however, it is dictated by the apostle's work and gospel. It is a tool used by a man who is himself a tool in the hand of his master. Never does Paul let his concerns harden into empty formulas; he never becomes a pious functionary; nor are those whom he addresses ever simply people to be preached at. Anyone who studies the letters should never let himself become oblivious of this. The reason why this does in fact often happen is not only the remoteness of our world from his; it is also because of the widespread yet incomprehensible use we are accustomed to make of the ideas and words of the apostle within the church's tradition. To put it another way, a coating of dust has for centuries now lain on the holy writings like a pall.

We spoke above about the two opposed impressions which the letters convey—they bring us very close to Paul, but they also make us feel strangely remote from him. This brings us to the subject of his distinctiveness. These contradictory impressions are

by no means due only to our distance in time from the composition of the letters. Of greater importance are the tremendous tensions and contrasts that Paul unites in his own person, to a degree
without parallel in the primitive church. They make shipwreck of
any attempt to speak of him at all adequately; an orthodox Jew
hostile to Christ who became his Lord's bondslave and a preacher
of the justification vouchsafed to the godless, one "untimely born"
among the apostles (1 Cor. 15:8) who could yet say: "But by the
grace of God I am what I am, and his grace toward me was not in
vain" (1 Cor. 15:10). The element of the mysterious even goes
as far as his physical life. He tells us more than once that he
suffered from an illness—to use his own words, was afflicted with
a "thorn in the flesh," "was buffeted by a messenger of Satan," a
suffering not removed even after much prayer (2 Cor. 12:7 ff.).
Attempts to define its precise nature in medical terms have led
nowhere, for the simple reason that Paul's descriptions are manifestly metaphorical and reveal the ancient popular idea that ill-
nesses of any kind were the work of demonic powers. However,
this sick, delicate man was not only enabled to bear inconceivable
physical hardships (2 Cor. 11:23 ff.): in addition to all his other
labors, in less than ten years and more than once in most adverse
circumstances he found it possible to journey through the eastern
half of the Roman empire and founded churches capable of main-
taining their existence in Asia Minor, Macedonia, and Greece; he
even planned to visit Rome and the west as far as Spain. Moreover, the intellectual range of his gospel, too, soared to incom-
parable heights—today still unconquered. Small wonder that
many readers are left gasping at his letters—loaded to the line
with a heavy cargo of thought—and that not a few who yield
themselves to his gospel are left feeling like a traveler overcome
by vertigo in an Alpine region surrounded by steep, cloud-covered
peaks, who often does not know how to follow on and how he is
going to last the journey.

Even in the primitive church Paul was a controversial figure—
revered and loved, feared and hated. The status the church now
accords him should not blind us to the fact that down to the
present day Christianity has generally drawn its life from sources
very other than his gospel, even if it has conferred the innocuous

dignity of sainthood on Paul himself and accorded his once revolutionary teaching an assured but ineffectual place in dogmatics. It is equally true, however, that the great moments in the church's history and the revolutions which have been of benefit to her have always taken place at times when Paul's gospel again burst forth like a supposedly extinct volcano. In many respects its influence is seen at work as early as the second century, in the movement started by Marcion, more of a Paulinist than Paul himself. Appealing without right to Paul, this founder of a heretical counter-church called in question the unity of God and his revelation in the Old and New Testaments and, by a dualistic disruption of the link between creation and redemption, distinguished between the "unknown" God of righteousness in the Old Testament and the "known" gracious God revealed in Christ. This summoned the church to battle and to a fresh concern for the legacy of the apostle. It must of course be confessed that often the church appropriated only parts of Paul's work, and with considerable modifications. The Paul who became an authority for the church had largely been domesticated. The powerful, revolutionary influences of his person and theology can best be seen in their effects on other figures and movements in church history. One cannot conceive of Augustine's theology apart from his rediscovery of Paul, and the same is particularly true of the breakthrough to new insights on the part of Luther and Calvin at the Reformation and, centuries later, of John Wesley's movement in England. Finally, we have also to remember that the so-called dialectic theology, without which the church's struggle against the deranged heresies of national socialism is unthinkable, stemmed from Karl Barth's rousing new exposition of Romans. At the same time we must not forget the vigorous anti-Pauline movements which still persist both inside and outside the church. Within, an ally is to be found in the unreflecting zeal which, in Jesus' saying, builds and adorns tombs for the prophets. But equally, voices are still raised complaining that Paul blocks access to the gospel taught by Jesus, and he is even called the perverter of Christianity.

Our discussion of the sources, particularly the letters, has revealed a constant and radical interrelationship between Paul's life history—what he experienced in his own person and the response to his words and work—and his gospel and theology. The result is that any account of his life must constantly refer to his theology. But *per contra*, there can be no study of Paul's theology divorced from Paul himself and his churches. This is not meant to imply that his theology is thus given second place and may be understood as, let us say, simply a derivative, accidental or inevitable, of his own particular path of life, which would involve a serious misjudgment of the crucial importance of his theology. The historian who wanted only to write Paul's life would have constantly to be reminded that, in the eyes of the apostle himself, the work to which he knew himself commissioned was more important than his person or the outward circumstances of his life. At the same time, it would be equally beside the mark to try at this point to present a sketch of Paul's theology with a biographical introduction as mere preface. For his theology is as little a system of universal timeless truths and religious experiences as his life was simply a series of favorable or adverse events. One of the most marked features in his character is that the insights granted him by faith mapped out the path he was to follow, and that he himself pondered very deeply—independently, sometimes indeed in a self-opinionated way—on his life's experiences.

It is hoped that this unity will become clear in the following account, even if it first traces the story of Paul's life before coming to its proper theme, the body of ideas constituting Paul's theology.

PART
ONE
LIFE
AND
WORK

I

PAUL'S DESCENT

AND ENVIRONMENT

BEFORE CONVERSION

Paul came from a strict Jewish family living in the Diaspora. The city of Tarsus, where he was born about the beginning of our era (Acts 21:39; 22:3), was the capital city of the region and Roman province of Cilicia. It is situated close to the Mediterranean at the foot of the Taurus Mountains, on the road leading over high passes from Asia Minor to Syria. Although it is insignificant today, in Paul's time its favorable situation for trade and commerce had made it a flourishing Hellenistic city. Tarsus was also particularly renowned as a center of Greek culture; the geographer Strabo (XIV, 673) sometimes even mentions it in the same breath as Athens. Luke, who had been given what is certainly reliable information about Paul's birthplace (Acts 22:3: cf. 23:34), says in the same context that Paul spent his childhood and received his education in Jerusalem; this would imply that while he was still young his parents moved to that city. However, this all too clearly reveals Luke's inclination to make Paul an out-and-out Jew and connect him with Jerusalem as closely and early as possible. One fact of itself makes Luke's statement less plausible—had such been the case, Paul would certainly have mentioned Jerusalem in his account of himself in Philippians 3:5. He himself never names his birthplace. However, provoked by his opponents, he proudly speaks of his Jewish ancestry: "Are they

3

Hebrews? So am I. Are they Israelites? So am I. Are they descendants of Abraham? So am I" (2 Cor. 11:22; cf. Rom. 11:1). Paul was also fighting on a similar battlefront in the passage just mentioned in Philippians, where he enumerates all the gains and glories that were his before his conversion in virtue of his birth and chosen way of life: "circumcised on the eighth day, of the people of Israel, of the tribe of Benjamin, a Hebrew born of Hebrews; as to the law a Pharisee" (Phil. 3:5). These accumulations of terms convey not only his own Jewish descent as a matter of race but also his people's unique religious standing in the world. This comes out in the archaic honorific name "Hebrews," just as the other terms, "Israelite" and "descendants of Abraham," declare the religious priority of place in which the Jew glories as a member of God's chosen people. As such, Paul bore the age-old sign of the covenant, circumcision, and was proud of his descent from one of the twelve tribes, whose first king is also recalled by his Jewish name Saul (Acts 7:58; 8:1, 3; 9:1, 8).

The enumeration given in letters to Gentile Christians of the advantages he once enjoyed is of more than biographical importance. It discloses that this was a form of introduction also used by his opponents on presenting themselves to the churches in order to make an impression. Their proud appeal to their descent was obviously intended to assure for themselves a higher authority and more likelihood of being listened to, and to checkmate Paul. This sheds light on the high esteem in which Jews were then held even in an originally heathen milieu. We today are liable to have entirely wrong ideas on this subject. To be a Jew, a Hebrew, a son of Abraham, by no means branded those who appealed to such facts as belonging to an inferior "race" and as members of a despised, outcast nation. All these modern associations of ideas must be firmly set aside. Furthermore, had not Jews been respected, the amazing spread and enormous increase of their communities in the Hellenistic age would have been impossible.

Our sources are so sparse and incomplete as to make it impossible to give exact numbers for the Jews in the Roman empire. Nevertheless, scholars are fairly well agreed that at the time of Augustus and his successors they must have amounted to about 4,500,000, if not more. This made up 7 per cent of the total population of the empire: outside Palestine they were concentrated chiefly in Egypt and Syria, where they lived above all in the great cities (Alexandria, Antioch, Damascus, etc.). On the basis of notices in Philo and Josephus, hardly likely to be exaggerated, we may reckon with a million in each of them. Various references also give high numbers for Asia Minor, Cyprus, Cyrenaica, and many other districts and cities throughout the seaboard of the Mediterranean. Over and above this—the numbers are not certain —they spread into the Euphrates Valley and farther east (cf. the list of the nations represented at Pentecost, Acts 2:9-11, and also many extrabiblical references). There can be no doubt that the Jewish population of the Diaspora was many times greater than that of Palestine. For this there were various reasons: there is repeated testimony to planned settlements of Jews for purposes of colonization beginning with the Diadochoi, and also to voluntary emigration and immigration; only seldom were there still deportations by force, such as those of earlier times at the hands of the Assyrians and Babylonians. Before the Roman period the Hellenistic rulers had granted the Jews extensive rights of incorporation, protection at law, and special privileges, and the Romans took up the same attitude. The Jews had thus been expressly confirmed in the right of practicing their cultus without molestation, and of the organization (political as well as religious) of their communities, the management of their own property, and most important of all, even self-jurisdiction to the extent that this did not infringe on the common law of the empire. The rights went as far as exemption from emperor worship and as a rule—in consideration of their strict laws about the Sabbath—from military service.

In keeping with the Jews' favorable legal status, many of them were citizens of their cities and, as was true of Paul from birth (Acts 16:37; 22:28), possessed Roman citizenship. As we know, the apostle's status as *civis Romanus* repeatedly played an important role in his later life. He is also marked out as a Roman citizen by his good Roman name, which is the one he uses throughout his letters. It is commonly thought that he assumed it only at the time of his conversion—just as those who enter certain orders in the church give up their baptismal name for a spiritual one—but this is not so. Not even Acts maintains it. On the first missionary journey he appears as "Saul, who is also called Paul" (13:9); there is no connection here with the story told of his meeting with the proconsul Sergius Paulus in Cyprus, and thereafter Luke uses Paul, the name by which he is generally known. His Jewish name Saul was probably a more familiar additional name (*signum* or *supernomen*) in use among the members of his faith. All that has just been said may show that Paul did not grow up in a ghetto, but was born into a family with just the same social and civic rights as the rest.

Nevertheless, dispersion, toleration, and privileged status are not enough to explain the enormous increase in the number of Jews in the heathen Diaspora. It would be wrong to attribute it to biological reasons, a population explosion among the Jewish race. What it actually represents is the extraordinary missionary force of Judaism even among the Gentiles. In Paul's time, Diaspora Judaism was more than any other faith imbued with an extremely strong consciousness of world-wide mission in accordance with Deutero-Isaiah's prophecy during the exile in Babylon—Israel was appointed to be "a light to the nations" (Isa. 42:6, etc.). The literature of Hellenistic Judaism, though far from completely preserved, is not inconsiderable, and it affords quite a body of evidence for this. Paul himself furnishes what may almost be called classic testimony, in Romans, in the context of his extremely sharp attack on the Jews. He enumerates the many advantages claimed by the Jew and taken as the basis of the Jewish mission: "But if you call yourself a Jew and rely upon the law and boast of your relation to God and know his will and approve what is excellent, because you are instructed in the law, and if you are sure that you are a guide to the blind, a light to those who are in darkness, a corrector of the foolish, a teacher of children, having in the law the embodiment of knowledge and truth . . ." (Rom. 2:17–20). At this point the series of "if" clauses breaks off abruptly to continue in a counterseries of devastating questions (2:21–24) which show the Jew the discrepancy between his claim and his God-dishonoring conduct. The passage ends with words taken from the Scriptures, the Jew's supreme authority, but here turned against him: "for because of you God's name is despised among the Gentiles" (Isa. 52:5). For us the interest lies in the proud self-consciousness and awareness of mission which, as the typically Greek formulation makes clear, was characteristic of Diaspora Judaism.

The intensive propaganda carried on both within and outside the synagogue was not without success. Philo proudly says that the laws of the Jewish people attract and win the attention of all, of barbarians, of Greeks, of dwellers on the mainland and islands, of nations of the east and the west, of Europe and Asia, of the whole inhabited world from end to end (De Vita Mosis II 20, Colson's translation: cf. also Josephus, Contra Apionem II 39). And pagan writers, too, including geographers, historians, and poets (Strabo, Suetonius, Seneca, Dio Cassius, Tacitus, Horace, Juvenal), confirm, though often with ridicule or disgust, the attractions and seductiveness of the Jewish mission.

Why was the Jewish faith so pervasive and attractive? Let us recollect some of the main features of the late classical world. Religiously and philosophically it was in a state of profound confusion. The old, sheltered environment of the *polis* was a thing of the past; the world had expanded to a degree hitherto unknown: men were thus thrown back upon themselves. Temples were still erected for the old gods, priests continued to serve and sacrifice to be offered, but these were obsolete; and the myths about the gods were a spent force, no longer capable of satisfying the individual's longing for protection and blessing, salvation and redemption, in this world and the next. Everywhere a process was afoot of syncretizing the old religions with new ones streaming in especially from the east, and the odder and vaguer these were, the greater their attraction. A whole host of mystery cults and doctrines of salvation promised eternal salvation and deliverance from the powers of fate and death. But this was also the time when there was a radical rationalistic criticism of the various religions, which, in the shape of diverse philosophies reaching even the man in the street, strove for a spiritualization of religion and therefore looked down on the rival miracle-workers and alleged purveyors of salvation bustling about in the market place.

This is the background against which we have to view Judaism with all its differences and strangeness, its belief in the one, invisi-

ble God, Lord of heaven and earth, the rigor of its law, its ethical
and ritual commandments (observance of the Sabbath, the dietary
laws, etc.), its uniform way of life throughout the whole world,
the venerable antiquity of its history, its call to turn away from all
idolatry and moral confusion, and its proclamation of the judgment about to overtake the impenitent and of the peace and righteousness which the Messiah, soon to come, would bring in his
train.

Hellenistic Judaism as practiced in the synagogues of the
Diaspora had long been prepared for entering on its mission to the
Gentiles, because, however much in theory it still regarded Jerusalem as the focal point of the saving history, it had asserted its
independence from Palestinian Judaism centered on the temple,
sacrifice, and priesthood. To all intents and purposes, the temple
had been superseded by the synagogue, sacrifice by the exposition
of the Torah, and the priests by the scribes and lawyers. In addition, in spite of all its separation from its heathen environment,
Hellenistic Judaism developed a way of thinking in terms of the
whole world and mankind, in which even the language and ideas
of Hellenistic pagan wisdom-teaching were accorded a place. This
is shown not only by the Jewish wisdom literature, Philo and
many others, but also by the Greek translation of the Old Testament (the Septuagint, after the legendary number—seventy—of
its translators). This became the sacred book of the synagogue
and the early church, just as Greek was the tongue used in worship, preaching, the liturgy, and prayer. Greek was also the means
of entry of a considerable body of Greek thought into Diaspora
theology—ideas taken from classical religious criticism of idolatry
and superstition, and also from Platonic and Stoic teaching on
reason and ethics. There was no fastidiousness in the choice of
material for propaganda and apologetic. For example, the theology of Hellenistic Judaism made good use of the allegorical
method of scriptural exposition, which it borrowed from the post-
classical interpretation of Homer. Again, the Diaspora had a
predilection for disguising its propaganda for the Jewish faith as
the works of Greek poets, wise men, and seers—there was even
imitation of the ancient Greek and Roman oracles of the fabled
Sibyl. Nevertheless, there can be no suggestion that the cultural

factors in the environment, the enlargement of Jewish theology to include Wisdom, and the adoption of contemporary ways and means of propaganda ever seriously brought Judaism into danger of becoming a syncretistic religion. Awareness of being something utterly different and unique, and strict maintenance of its own way of life while living among Gentiles, were, and continued to be, Judaism's prime characteristics. These are the reasons for the great attraction, and also, of course, for the frightful outbursts of ill will, slanders, and pogroms which it had to suffer from time to time in certain communities and regions at the hands of the pagans.

We can be sure that in his youth Paul was never trained in Greek philosophy and culture to anything like the same extent as his renowned contemporary Philo of Alexandria (died c. A.D. 50): in particular, Paul shows not the slightest trace of Philo's abiding interest in harmonizing the Old Testament Jewish heritage with the wisdom of the Greeks. Nevertheless, through the preaching and theology of the Diaspora synagogue, Paul did learn a considerable number of the elements of Greek culture. This is to be seen in his use of concepts and ideas originating in the popular philosophy of the Stoics (e.g., freedom, reason, nature, conscience, sobriety, virtue, and duty) and also in his often masterly command of the devices used in earlier rhetoric and in typical forms of contemporary popular teaching; these he often uses arbitrarily, adapting them to his own purpose, and occasionally giving them remarkably subtle nuances. The means of teaching adopted by the itinerant preachers of the time, which was also the form used by preachers in the Hellenistic synagogues, is the so-called diatribe (literally, pastime) discourse. It propounded philosophic, moral, or religious ideas without long-winded deductions or purely speculative arguments, and deliberately avoided elevated technical language. Taking the form of a lively conversation, its short sentences were enlivened by direct address, advancing an imaginary opponent's objections, making reader and hearer partners in a conversation, and never for a moment losing sight of them. All these characteristics are to be found in abundance in the Pauline letters. The great Greek scholar Wilamowitz-Moellendorf's verdict on the high quality of Paul's diction is absolutely correct: "But the

fact that this Jew, this Christian, thinks and writes in Greek . . .
that this Greek comes right from the heart but is nevertheless
Greek, not Aramaic in translation (like the sayings of Jesus),
makes his writing a classic of Hellenism. At long, long last, Greek
speaks out of a vivid spiritual experience."

This sketch of the Hellenistic synagogue shows that because of
his ancestry, education, and gifts, the youthful Paul, still a member of the Jewish faith, was eminently marked out to become a
missionary to the Gentiles. There is, indeed, something to be said
for the idea that he believed himself called to be a missionary of
the Jewish faith. The Diaspora synagogue's mission was fairly
liberal in its principles, being satisfied if the "God-fearers" drawn
from the heathen into adherence to the Jewish community pledged
themselves to confess belief in the one God and to observe a
minimum of ritual commandments (Sabbath observance, the
dietary laws, etc.) and the basic ethical commandments of the
Law. No demands were made for circumcision—not all were required to become "proselytes," full members of the Jewish people.
Orthodox Palestinian Judaism led by the Pharisees disapproved of
this and insisted on circumcision for all. Nevertheless Pharisees,
too, conducted a mission to the Gentiles, though certainly with
less success than the Diaspora. This is what Jesus refers to in his
words to the Pharisees, "Woe to you, scribes and Pharisees,
hypocrites! for you traverse sea and land to make a single proselyte, and when he becomes a proselyte, you make him twice as
much a child of hell as yourselves" (Matt. 23:15).

This shows us that even within the Jewish mission to the Gentiles there were two conflicting schools of thought on circumcision,
the one originating in the Diaspora and the other in Jerusalem. An
excellent example, from Paul's own time, both of the success of
the Jewish mission in general and of its differences is furnished by
the north Syrian king, Izates of Adiabene. Initially he was won
over to Judaism by a Diaspora Jew. But the latter was followed by
a Palestinian Jew of the Pharisaic school of thought who induced
the king to become a full Jew by submitting to circumcision.

Against this background we can see how significant it was that,
following perhaps a family tradition (Acts 23:6), the Diaspora
Jew Paul attached himself to the Pharisees, that is to say, to the

most strictly orthodox school of thought both in manner of life
and in mission (Phil. 3:5). As contrasted with the external tradi-
tionalism of the priestly aristocracy in Jerusalem, and also with
the laxness of popular conformity, the strictness of Pharisaism
made it a highly esteemed lay movement, with the Old Testament
laws about holiness as its binding standard. It survived even the
disastrous Jewish war and the destruction of Jerusalem, and
thereafter, when Judaism was reconstructed, became the sole determinative authority, the seedbed of Talmudic Judaism.

This movement, originating in the homeland, is not to be judged
on the basis of the criticism of it in the Gospels. At the time when
Paul joined, Pharisaism was not nearly as narrow and exclusive as
it became after A.D. 70. Its theology still had ample room for what
it rejected only toward the turn of the century, ideas and concepts
belonging to late Jewish apocalyptic which employed great cosmic
pictures and designs to describe and try to calculate the time of
the expected end of this old, evil aeon, and the dawn of a new
messianic age. Only at this later date, too, were Christianity and
the Jewish theology of Alexandria categorically and universally
branded as heresy. The strict Jewry of Palestine entered a ghetto
of its own choice. Thus, in electing for the Pharisaic school of
thought, Paul was by no means required to disavow his origins in
the Diaspora and to jettison the theological ideas he brought with
him from there. This explains why in his letters as an apostle there
are still traces of both Pharisaic and Hellenistic ways of thinking.

In any case, as evidenced by his decision to join the Pharisees,
Paul became a passionate devotee of the Law. Acts will be correct
in saying that he was trained in Jerusalem, the movement's spiritual home. This is the time he will be referring to when he says
that he advanced beyond many of his own age among his people
and was extremely zealous for the traditions of his fathers (Gal.
1:14), "as to righteousness under the law blameless" (Phil. 3:6).
He may or may not have been a pupil of Gamaliel the older, a
particularly renowned teacher of the Law (Acts 22:3). The information fits in rather too well with Luke's high esteem of
Pharisaism and the notoriously false idea that even as a Christian
Paul remained a Pharisee down to the very end.

With Paul, too, theological training in Judaism was combined with the learning and practice of an occupation. Acts tells us (18:3) that he was a tentmaker, something like our saddler. We often read how, on his subsequent missionary journeys, he supported himself by the work of his hands (1 Thess. 2:9; 1 Cor. 4:12; 2 Cor. 11:27).

The most important point, however, is this: we have good grounds for believing that when the Diaspora Jew Paul chose to become a Pharisee, he also decided to be a Jewish missionary to the Gentiles along the lines taken by orthodoxy, and was actually such before becoming a Christian. This is suggested by the fact that later on, when his Judaizing opponents in Galatia maintained the need for circumcision, they exploited the apostle's former activities against him. He said in reply: "But if I, brethren, *still* preach circumcision, why am I *still* persecuted? In that case the stumbling block of the cross has been removed" (Gal. 5:11). This most probably means that had he continued in the kind of missionary preaching that the Judaizers were now propagating afresh, but with which Paul had long also broken, he would have been spared persecution at the hands of the Jews—but at the cost of the gospel of the cross.

As long as Paul was an orthodox Jew and as such made "proselytes" among the Gentiles, it was only logical for him to be zealous in persecuting the church—and be it noted, the Hellenistic church (Damascus), which had severed itself from his people's basis of salvation. This alone explains the tremendous tensions between his Jewish past and his turning to Christ, his former zeal for the Law and his gospel of justification available for all men, not on the basis of doing what the Law commanded, but by faith alone. His later battles against the Law and circumcision were not a reversion to more liberal principles as these had already developed in the Diaspora synagogue, but the setting forth of the gospel of the Crucified One.

II

PAUL'S PERSECUTION

OF THE CHURCH AND

HIS CONVERSION AND CALL

The city of Damascus, closely associated with both the activities of Paul the Pharisee as persecutor of Christians and his conversion and call, draws attention to a momentous episode in the church's earliest history. How did the gospel spread far beyond the confines of Jerusalem and Judea into the Gentile territory of Syria even before Paul's day? The sources give no direct answer. But in all likelihood the beginnings go back to the time of the first great conflicts and crises within the mother church of Jerusalem. Unfortunately, Acts' account of them is defective and manifestly colored. Its author is obviously striving to impress his readers with the perfect harmony and accord of the early church. But at salient points his information was at odds with this idea and forced him to make changes. As early as Acts 6:1–6 we hear of clashes in the church between the "Hellenists" and the "Hebrews." Both parties consisted of Christians of Jewish descent. The former, however, came from the Diaspora, and their mother tongue was Greek, while the latter lived in Palestine and spoke Aramaic. Thus far the account is perfectly trustworthy. In the sequel, at first it is merely a matter of grievances in the rapidly growing church about the common meals and the provision for widows, and of the too heavy burden being imposed on the Twelve, preventing them from doing justice to their proper work of preaching the word and prayer. As a result, Luke says, seven men were chosen—significantly all with Greek names, among them Stephen and Philip—and by prayer and laying on of hands the apostles solemnly appointed them to a special charitable ministry. Thus the emergency that has arisen constitutes the reason for the now essential differentiation between (apostolic) evangelists and administrators.

Nevertheless, as shown by the vagueness of the report itself, and in particular by the way in which the story goes on, these dissensions, ostensibly only on matters of organization, conceal a much more serious cleavage, of whose magnitude Acts, composed much later, has obviously no real idea. Quite soon afterward Stephen, like the man named along with him, Philip, emerges not only as a kind of administrator but as evangelist and spokesman of the "Hellenists"; he preaches vehemently against the Jewish nation and dies as the church's first martyr, being stoned to death by the mob. Again, it is the "Hellenists" who, after his death, find themselves severely persecuted and forced to flee from Jerusalem. They scatter into non-Jewish areas and for the first time bring the gospel to the Greeks (11:20). The writer of Acts remarks (8:1) that with the exception of the Twelve, the whole of the Jerusalem church was persecuted and scattered. But here he contradicts himself, for in later accounts he assumes the presence of a church there as a matter of course. Obviously, the non-Hellenistic part of the mother church was left unmolested.

What was the reason for the Hellenists' plight? Quite certainly they represented an understanding of the gospel altogether revolutionary in the eyes of the rest of the church, in conflict with the orthodox Jewish view of the Law and calling in question the chosen people's hallowed traditions, the temple worship, and their exclusive claim to salvation.

As we have already seen, these are precisely the reasons which, according to Paul himself, impelled him as a Pharisee to persecute the Christians. They let us understand that his zeal was directed against a church of the Hellenistic Diaspora. More than once—and with no bad conscience whatsoever—he specifies persecution of the church as one of the proofs of his former righteousness according to the Law (Gal. 1:13; Phil. 3:6); he speaks of this, be it noted, as a logical outcome of his former irreproachable observance of the Law and not as a past wrong whose memory still torments him. This shows that his orthodoxy, and it alone, was the reason for his hostility to Christ and his zeal as persecutor. We must get away from the common, but false, idea that for an orthodox Jew like himself belief in Jesus as the Messiah was of itself sufficient reason for persecution. This belief would have made Paul and others think of Christians as an odd and deluded Jewish sect, but never as blasphemous heretics. Even before Jesus' day considerable bodies of peoples had regarded now one, now another, "prophet" as the Messiah without laying themselves open to the risk of persecution by the Jews and excommunication. As late as the thirties of the second century, in the time of the emperor Hadrian, the most highly esteemed contemporary teacher of the Law, R. Akiba, proclaimed the leader of the final Jewish revolt against the Romans, Bar Cocheba, as the Messiah.

There are therefore strong reasons against Acts' idea that, while still resident in Jerusalem, Paul persecuted the mother church, a church which in fact still observed the Law and so was not in the slightest exposed to the crucial charge of hostility toward it. Luke's picture is also clearly contradicted by the apostle's remark in Galatians 1:22, that he was personally unknown to the churches in Judaea—and therefore before this to the church in Jerusalem; they heard of him only later on, when the antagonist of the past had changed into the successful missionary in Syria and Cilicia. This is absolutely inconceivable in the case of a man who in Jerusalem had previously taken the prominent part in persecuting Christians ascribed to him by Luke (Acts 22:4 ff.). So Paul can hardly have been present at the stoning of Stephen: the connection is clearly of Luke's own making (Acts 7:58; 8:1). Nowhere does Paul himself speak of any persecuting in Jerusalem.

Acts' ideas of Paul's appearances in Damascus are also open to criticism. He is said to have gone there furnished with authority from the high priest to drag the Christians in bonds before the Sanhedrin in Jerusalem. But this is impossible, because under the Roman administration the supreme court never possessed such a sphere of jurisdiction—Damascus is far beyond the frontiers of Judaea! We must assume, then, that Paul the Pharisee was acting within the framework of the internal penal power (scourging, ban, excommunication) granted to synagogues. We have ample evidence that the front line of battle for and against Christ lay in and around the synagogues. Paul himself says in 2 Corinthians 11:24 that later on as a witness to Christ he more than once suffered the synagogue's gruesome punishment of scourging. We may suppose that in the synagogue of Damascus he appeared first as judge and later as witness to Christ's passion.

On the subject of his conversion and call to be an apostle Paul speaks surprisingly seldom. When he does so, it is, however, in important remarks and always in the context of the exposition of his gospel. This suggests that we should not follow the common practice of making Paul's own personal experiences and, specifically, Christ's appearances to him, central, partly on the basis of the vision on the way to Damascus repeatedly described at length in Acts and partly under the influence of pietistic tradition and modern psychology. We do best to keep our feet firmly on the ground, take our lead from what Paul himself says, and not let ourselves be sidetracked from what for him was the heart of the matter.

The importance and far-reaching effects of this decision for Christ—not strictly Paul's own, but one made for him—are particularly clearly set forth in the passage from Philippians quoted above. Passives are used, and this is significant: "I let myself suffer the loss of all things . . ." (3:8); ". . . because I was apprehended by Christ Jesus" (3:12, A.V.). Turning sharply on his opponents, Paul first enumerates the prerogatives he once could boast of. But then he goes on: "But whatever I gain I had, I counted as loss for the sake of Christ. Indeed I count everything as loss because of the surpassing worth of knowing Christ Jesus my Lord. For his sake I have suffered the loss of all things, and count them as refuse, in order that I may gain Christ and be found in him, not having a righteousness of my own, based on law, but that which is through faith in Christ, the righteousness from God that depends on faith" (Phil. 3:7–9).

There is no suggestion that, while Paul highly esteemed his former possessions, they did not mean everything to him; and that an intense longing was still unfulfilled. His former wealth changed into refuse, and he is filled with loathing for it: his former zeal to be accepted by God, his righteousness—simply an attempt at self-assertion. "In the depths, the height on which I stood; lost, the security in which I lived; darkness, my once-clear vision" (Barth). What Paul here illustrates by means of his own conversion is very much more than a personal confession of faith. It takes precedence over the hour when Christ appeared to him—of this there is not a word here—and becomes the most decisive statement about his whole life. But it goes further: it epitomizes his gospel of the revelation of God's righteousness which treats all men as lost, but now, for the first time, through the gospel, brings them under divine grace. Christ's coming and self-sacrifice betoken the turning point in the aeons, as is said in the great words in Romans: "For Christ is the end of the law, that every one who has faith may be justified" (10:4).

Galatians 1:15–16 is very much akin to Philippians 3 in subject matter, but yields more from the point of view of biography. Although the information is very terse—it comes only in a subordinate clause—and gives no description of his experience at conversion, Paul here sheds more light on his call to be an apostle to the Gentiles, taking as his model prophetic calls in the Old Testament (Jer. 1:5; Isa. 49:1). As in Philippians 3, this is immediately preceded by a glance back to his former zeal for the Law and his persecution of the church (Gal. 1:13 f.). But then comes the great change: "But when he who had set me apart before I was born, and had called me through his grace, was pleased to reveal his Son to me, in order that I might preach him among the Gentiles, I did not confer with flesh and blood, nor did I go up to Jerusalem to those who were apostles before me, but I went away into Arabia; and again I returned to Damascus" (Gal. 1:15–17).

The passage is of supreme importance not only as a remark of Paul's own about his calling to be an apostle to the Gentiles, but also because together with its context (Gal. 1 and 2)—this makes it unique—it gives an authoritative and exact account of a considerable space of time in his life and work, the period immediately after his conversion, long years of which Acts scarcely preserves a memory.

In order properly to understand the passage, a previous question has to be cleared out of the way. What was the cause of

Paul's giving such a lengthy account of himself? And what purpose did he hope to serve? The occasion of Galatians, written when Paul was working in Ephesus, was the trouble stirred up by Judaizing false teachers who had insinuated themselves into the churches in Asia Minor and driven them to the brink of apostasy. Their attack was directed against the gospel without the Law as preached by Paul among the Gentiles, to their thinking a crude abridgment of the gospel on grounds of expediency, because it meant superseding circumcision, taken to be the prerequisite of salvation, and the necessity for Gentiles, too, to obey the Law. This slur reflects the Judaizers' basic line of thought in all their varied attempts to undermine the apostle's mission to the Gentiles: "Of course we too are Christians, not simply Jews. But one can become a Christian only by incorporation into the chosen people, the Jews." This challenged not only Paul's gospel but also his work as an apostle, for which, they said, no one had given him authority. These two charges, of falsifying the gospel and of high-handed presumption in wanting to be an apostle, must have formed the substance of his opponents' slurs. Hence Paul rigorously defends both—and actually passes over to the attack—the truth of his gospel for the Gentiles and the divine origin of his commission. The two are quite inseparable: they form the two sides of the one coin bearing the impress of the authority of the one divine will.

Commentators often maintain that the troublemakers' taunt was that Paul was dependent on the original apostles in Jerusalem: what he taught he had received at second or third hand; he was therefore no original apostle commissioned by God himself. The object of his detailed proof of independence in Galatians 1 and 2, it is alleged, is to refute this. Now, it is quite true that throughout this almost formal sketch of his call, and conduct thereafter, Paul does in fact stubbornly assert his independence of all human authorities and, in consequence, the divine origin of both his gospel and his office. But surely his Judaizing opponents would have been the last people to join battle with him on the issue of dependence on Jerusalem: the church there had in no way broken with the Law, and was far from believing as a matter of course that Gentiles should have unconditional access to salvation. The opponents' presumptions being what they were, we must conclude that, whether justifiably or not, it was they themselves who appealed to Jerusalem, and that in their view a legitimate apostle had to be one who upheld the saving traditions of the chosen people as confirmed in the Law. If this conclusion is correct, then their charge must have run something like this: The original apostles had set Paul right, but to his shame he had cut adrift from what he had been taught—that Law, circumcision, and salvation must always go together—arbitrarily watering it down, in order to give him an easier approach to the Gentiles (Gal. 1:10). His preaching therefore meant betrayal of the national heritage; they, on the other hand, stood in the true line of continuity and presented the legitimate gospel.

In Galatians 1, Paul cuts this line of argument short by saying: Your very premises are wrong; the fact is that I had no relation whatsoever with Jerusalem, neither at the time of my call to be an apostle nor for some seventeen years after, apart from a short visit to Cephas (Peter) three years after that day on the road to Damascus. It was God who vouchsafed me my gospel and my mission to the Gentiles. The original apostles did not come into it. This is the reason why I no longer preach the necessity for circumcision, which once I did as a Pharisaic missionary to the Diaspora (Gal. 5:11), and which you say I ought to preach, alleging that the Twelve so instructed me. This is implied in the letter's very start: "Paul an apostle—not from men nor through man, but through Jesus Christ and God the Father, who raised him from the dead . . ." (Gal. 1:1; cf. 1:11 f.). Indeed, to checkmate his opponents, in his account of the apostolic assembly in Jerusalem, Paul goes on to add that on that occasion the Twelve, none other, themselves confirmed him in his freedom to preach his gospel for the Gentiles (Gal. 2:1–9). Thus, it all points not to Paul's opponents' having held up dependence on Jerusalem against him, but to Paul's having contested and demolished what they regarded as indispensable, the connection between the gospel and Jewish tradition.

At first sight, of course, the fervor with which the apostle states his case and illustrates it by reference to his own conduct is surprising and odd. For it creates the impression, and apparently confirms what in fact many presume, that the apostle disregarded the primitive church's tradition about Christ and took the appearance of the risen and exalted Lord to him in person as the one and only source and legitimation of his call and proclamation. Or, to put it another way, for the primitive church's traditions about Jesus, Paul substituted his own vision of Christ. If this idea were correct, it would follow from the passage before us that Paul's self-defense, and indeed his gospel and theology in general, exhibit oddly "enthusiastic" features. Imagine it: the former Pharisee and persecutor of Christians who had no personal acquaintance with Jesus while on earth (2 Cor. 5:16) refuses out of hand to have any dealings with Jesus' first disciples. And this not only immediately after his conversion: though obstinately at variance with the Jerusalem church and its leaders, he succeeds in doing missionary work in Gentile areas for many years on his own. As generally expounded, Galatians 1:15–16 would positively imply that he made that single experience on the way to Damascus the source of all that he was to go on to preach, and the basis on which he sought to authenticate his mission. In this case—and in his own day the charge was more than once brought against him—he would have been a disruptive, "enthusiastic" crank who, for the sake of his own experience, jeopardized the unity of the church.

All the same, ideas like these, which readily suggest themselves, though their logical consequences are seldom of course clearly stated, have led to misunderstanding and distortion of Galatians 1 and 2. In the case of Galatians 1, it is incorrect and misleading to lay down on principle a sweeping either-or: either tradition or special revelation vouchsafed the apostle as it were in utmost confidence as the basis of his mission and gospel. In Galatians 1 there is not one single word about mysterious ecstatic "promptings" allegedly more important and authoritative in his eyes than all traditions of the original apostles. The sole topics are the correctness of his gospel without Law for the Gentiles and his freedom to proclaim it. As in Philippians and Romans, its subject is that in sending Christ into the world God made an end of the Jewish way of salvation, righteousness on the basis of the Law, and inaugurated universal salvation on the sole basis of righteousness deriving from faith. That the way in which Paul realized this at the time when he was called as an apostle to the Gentiles was a most intimate and personal one—it changed his whole life—is not in dispute, and the fact is quite important. But all he says about himself personally only exemplifies and illustrates God's new action in Christ on behalf of and in transformation of the whole world, the action proclaimed in the gospel.

The principal factor in the subjectivist misconception just noticed, which affects the whole picture of Paul, is the meaning generally attached to the word "reveal" in Galatians 1:15–16. It is taken as vision and experience, and connected with the vision of the risen Christ which Paul most certainly had on the way to Damascus (1 Cor. 15:8; 9:1). That this was the occasion of the apostle's conversion and call is not in dispute. Nevertheless, to understand what he says about himself in Galatians 1, it is important to notice that he never makes the fact that he was one of those who saw the risen Christ the basis of a justification of his apostolic work with the Gentiles. Whenever he bears his Easter testimony, he ranges himself with *all* the apostles and in so doing endorses the gospel common to all. "Whether then it was I or they, so we preach and so you believed" (1 Cor. 15:11). In Galatians 1 and 2, however, the points at issue are his justification for having kept severely aloof from the original apostles and his preaching outside the Law among the Gentiles. Thus "revelation" in Galatians 1:15–16 must have another meaning. The word is taken from apocalyptic, and here as often elsewhere in Paul—and in the rest of Galatians itself, in fact—means an objective world-changing event through which God in his sovereign action has inaugurated a new aeon. This event is proclaimed in the gospel. Accordingly the apostle says: "Now before faith came, we were confined under the law, kept under restraint until faith should be *revealed* [make its appearance]. So the law was our custodian until Christ came, that we might be justified by faith" (Gal. 3:23–24; 28 f.). "But when the time had fully come, God sent forth his Son, born of woman, born under the law" (Gal. 4:4). Paul here uses the same honorific Christological title as in Galatians 1:15, "Son of God." With Paul especially this term transcends all the particularistic limitations of Jewish messianism and is one of his basic terms in speaking about the salvation now open to all, Jew and Gentile alike. In other words, it is part of the Pauline doctrine of justification (as well as Gal. 3:4, cf. also Rom. 8:2–4).

As in Philippians 3, then, Paul's testimony in Galatians 1 about his call shows that the lines of any understanding of his conversion and mission are entirely dictated by the subject matter of his preaching and theology, and not by any arbitrary claim to reception of *revelatio specialissima* (special revelation). The usual practice of introducing the formal either-or—in this case either promptings of the spirit in vision or the orderly transmission of received tradition—exposes the apostle to the charge of thinking in terms of general principles just like his opponents and ignores the objective contrast between Law and gospel affecting all men, and not just Paul himself.

What makes it all the more important to clear this matter up is the fact that even now such a misconception adversely affects our picture of Paul: a question mark is set against him, and he is stigmatized as an enthusiast and individualist. While Paul's studied aloofness to Jerusalem may in fact have brought this censure upon him, the theological and historical reasons for his attitude are fairly obvious. The earliest church was still very strictly tied to Jewish ways of thinking and to the expectation of the coming Messiah current in apocalyptic. In the earliest days, therefore, Paul could hardly have expected here any real appreciation of the gospel of free grace for all and of Christ as the end of the Law. To such a church the Hellenists' revolutionary questions and insights must have seemed alien and incomprehensible, though admittedly in the first fifteen years or so after Paul's call we are given no indication of any tendency on the part of the church in Jerusalem to excommunicate the Hellenistic churches and brand their missionaries as heretics. On the contrary, we are told that news of the missionary successes of the onetime persecutor came to the churches of Judaea and gave rise to joy and praise (Gal. 1:23 f.). Nevertheless the fundamental questions about the meaning of the gospel, which were bound to come up sooner or later, still lay dormant and unresolved beneath the surface. Some time was to elapse before the Jerusalem church had to face up to them, the day when the Gentile churches not founded by Jerusalem peremptorily knocked at the whole church's door. As we shall see later, this took place at the apostolic assembly.

In retrospect, a very obvious question is prompted: What prepared the way for Paul's conversion and what actually brought it about? In positive terms, the only simple answer is that as a result of arguments with the Hellenistic Christians in Damascus and elsewhere, whom he had originally hated and persecuted, it suddenly dawned on him who this Jesus really was whom hitherto he had regarded as a destroyer of the most sacred foundations of the Jewish faith and whom it had been right to crucify. He realized, too, the significance of Jesus' mission and death both for himself and for the world. We may be quite sure that this question, suggested by the faith and witness of Jesus' followers, had its effect on him and in him. Admittedly, he himself says nothing of this, but asserts unequivocally that the change was due not to any gradual process of maturing, but solely to the free and sovereign act of God. In all events, we must dismiss as fanciful the idea often put forward that his conversion was prepared long in advance: he had had a religious breakdown because, it is alleged, while still a devout Pharisee, he increasingly realized how shaky were the foundations of his faith and practice, and because he was more and more dissatisfied with his efforts to comply with the high ideals and strict demands of the Law. Paul's own words point in the opposite direction. When he was encountered by the crucified and risen Christ and called by God, he was the very reverse of one haunted by qualms of conscience and gone to pieces because of his own inadequacy (as we know Luther to have been): no, he was a proud Pharisee, whose unremitting boast was his membership in the chosen people, God's Law, and his own righteousness. Thus, when Paul was converted, it was not the case of a man without faith finding the way to God, but of one zealous for God, more in earnest than anyone else about his demands and promises. It was a devout man whose way God blocked through the Christ who had died a shameful death on the cross, and on whom he made that light shine of which Paul says elsewhere: "For it is the God who said, 'Let light shine out of darkness,' who has shone in our hearts to give the light of the knowledge of the glory of God in the face of Christ" (2 Cor. 4:6).

At this point there is no need of further justification of the method here adopted of telling the story of Paul's conversion and call—keeping to what he himself says and setting aside the descriptions of the road to Damascus given in Acts. Of the latter accounts there are no fewer than three, one in Luke's own narrative (9:1 ff.), the other two in the context of Paul's speeches (22:3 ff; 26:9 ff.). While there is some variation in detail, and the descriptions obviously draw on Old Testament and Jewish epiphanies and calls with legendary embellishments, they nevertheless form a magnificent and dramatic account. By means of them Luke has put a very deep stamp on the traditional picture of Paul, much deeper than the one from Paul's letters themselves. Without here examining the Acts accounts in detail, let us at least by comparison with the letters indicate some matters of importance. Common to both are God's overcoming of the man whose impassioned zeal for the Jewish faith made him a persecutor of Christ and his church: it was not therefore the conversion of a penitent sinner. Both sources agree that with sovereign authority the exalted Lord made the persecutor into his witness. At the same time there are not a few differences between Acts and the letter. Significantly, Luke's accounts are silent on Paul's call to be an apostle, ranged in equal status with the Twelve. Instead, blinded by Christ's appearance to him, and then in Damascus miraculously healed by the orthodox disciple Ananias, who also baptized him (9:18; 22:12 ff.), Paul comes back to Jerusalem. Only then, in the temple and by means of a fresh vision, is he given his vocation: Christ sends him away from the obstinate Jews to the Gentiles (22:17–21). Thus, Acts makes his missionary work in the Gentile world originate in Jerusalem; Acts 9:23 ff., in contradiction to Galatians 1, also says that directly after Paul's conversion Barnabas introduced him to the Jerusalem church and the Twelve. From this time on, he carries out his great work, not as an apostle, but as the authorized representative of the one apostolic church. In what he says, Luke was most certainly not just giving free play to fancy, but was working up traditions that had come to him orally, even if in the light of what Paul himself says we have to challenge their accuracy in detail. The total picture admittedly displays traits typical of Luke's understanding of history and of the church. Above all else, however, Luke knows nothing of what Paul himself says was the decisive factor in his conversion—and here the theological 'differences are at their deepest. To the end of his life Luke's Paul continues to be an orthodox Jew and Pharisee; for Christ's sake the real Paul gave up the Law as a means of salvation.

Paul himself has little to say about his conversion and call, and when he does mention them it is with reserve. But we can now see that this is not something to deplore. The power of the concern for the gospel which lighted upon Paul and became his own is also revealed in the way in which he speaks of his conversion. This again confirms that for him the one thing of importance was the gospel he was given, and not his own person.

III

FIRST MISSIONARY ACTIVITY

For more than fifteen years after his call outside Damascus, Paul worked as a missionary far away from Jerusalem before going up for the apostolic assembly. Only then did the basic questions between himself and the leaders of the Jerusalem church come to a head, questions for which his own labors for early Christianity were in no small measure responsible. We must pause for a moment and realize both how important these years were—they were the years immediately after Damascus—and also the considerable period of time involved, exactly noted by Paul himself: three years between his conversion and a first brief personal visit to Cephas (Peter) in Jerusalem (Gal. 1:18), and thereafter fourteen years of renewed independent work up to the meeting of the assembly (Gal. 2:1). Certainly, taking into consideration the ancient world's way of reckoning time—a fraction of a year counted as a full year—it can be made a little shorter. Even so, this gives, if not seventeen years, at least fifteen to sixteen. This is almost three times as much as the few later years which saw the writing of all of Paul's letters and about which we are very well informed from Acts as well. In the face of this, we can only deplore that we are so badly informed about these important early years. What we do know has to be gathered from Paul's all too brief statements in Galatians 1:16–24. Acts is completely silent about his missionary work at this time, and Paul's own statements show that the few notes it does give are unhistorical.

Still, brief though these statements are, they give exact information about times and places for the accuracy of which the apostle even vouched by an oath (Gal. 1:20), and they show us how much took place during this period. The one called to be an apostle among the Gentiles refrained from all consultation with the original apostles in Jerusalem and went off forthwith to Arabia, that is, to the Gentile district east of Jordan and southeast of Damascus (Gal. 1:17). It is wrong to imagine his stay of two and a half to three years there as time spent in monastic solitude during which he meditated on the work he was to do and prepared himself for it. This edifying but fanciful picture modeled on the anchorites of the early church finds no support in the letters, and is at odds with his clear and express commission to preach. Expecting as he was the end of the world and the imminent coming of Christ, how could he have put off the fulfillment of his task for such a long time? Further, Arabia was no solitary wilderness; it was settled country traversed as today by Bedouins, with well-known Hellenistic cities such as Petra, the residence of the Nabatean king Aretas IV (9 B.C.–A.D. 40) mentioned by Paul himself (2 Cor. 11:32), as well as Gerasa and Philadelphia (the present-day Amman). Thus, though it is not said in so many words, we must presume that what Paul did in this part of the present-day kingdom of Jordan was preach the gospel. Obviously, of course, he had no striking successes. He himself has no foundation of churches to tell of, and Acts' ignorance of this first missionary period is certainly no accident. It is also very probable that the fruitlessness of his labors and the persecutions with which he met forced him to break off his work abruptly and return to Damascus (Gal. 1:17). For in that city, too, an official of the Nabatean king plotted against him, and Paul had to flee posthaste, being let down in a basket through a window in the city wall (2 Cor. 11:32; and cf. Acts 9:23 ff.). Thus he certainly had notice taken of him in Arabia, though his preaching among the Palestinian nation bordering on Judaea mainly evoked hostility and persecution.

It was only then, two to three years after his conversion, that

Paul went for the first time to Jerusalem and got into touch with
Peter (Gal. 1:18). As he himself insists, however, it was only
with Peter and not with the church and the rest of the apostolic
body. The sole purpose of this fortnight's visit was to "make the
acquaintance" of Peter; Paul saw, he says, none of the rest of the
apostles except James the Lord's brother.

What would one not give for reliable information about what
happened at this first memorable meeting between Paul and Peter,
the first disciple called by Jesus! Little wonder that scholars have
gone to all possible lengths in trying to shed light on the darkness
and wrest some glimmer from every nuance in Paul's bare account. But the text has nothing to tell us, and forces us carefully
to examine what conjectures are justified and what not. It can be
said with certainty that even Paul's wanting to meet Cephas, the
then leader of the primitive church, is a fact of importance. There
was certainly also discussion of the understanding of the gospel on
which the Jerusalem church based its life and which Paul was
already preaching in his own way. We may perhaps further
presume that the conversations did not end in a quarrel, because
on an occasion when there was one between the two of them, Paul
was quite open about it (cf. Gal. 2:11 ff.). Thus, Peter can hardly
have put difficulties in the way of Paul's gospel. On the other
hand, of course, the meeting cannot have led to full agreement,
because had such been reached, Paul's remaining aloof, as he insists he did, from the rest of the apostles would be unintelligible.
Quite obviously Peter let the new evangelist go on doing as he
wished, without foreseeing the further issues which were only
gradually to come up. This, however, is the most we can conjecture, and it may even go too far. At any rate, one must reject the
fantastic idea that, at long, long last, Paul came to realize the
inadequacy of his own preaching of Christ and now—three years
afterward—obtained the information he hitherto lacked and put
his own apostolic office under the primacy of the apostles in Jerusalem. Ideas of the kind overlook the fact that everything in Galatians 1 and 2, including the mention of his short visit to Cephas,
comes under the rubric "for I did not receive my gospel from man,
nor was I taught it" (Gal. 1:12). A late catechumenate and a
crash course in missionary work with Peter are thus ruled out.

What we said about the two or three years before the apostle's visit to Jerusalem is equally true of the long years following, in the course of which he preached the same gospel, this time in Syria and his native Cilicia, and therefore certainly in the vicinity of Tarsus. Again we have only one piece of information (Gal. 1:21; but cf. Acts 9:30). But we can gather from the context that the work here was successful and led to the first founding of churches in the area. For news of the activity of the onetime persecutor had now reached the Christians in Judaea, to whom he was still unknown personally, so that they glorified God because of this turn of events (Gal. 1:22–24; cf. also Acts 15:23, 36, 41).

We know nothing of the duration of Paul's work in Syria and Cilicia. The one firm fact is that Barnabas, often mentioned in Acts and the letters, fetched him from Tarsus to work along with himself in Antioch (Acts 11:25 ff.). This introduces us to two important names in the history of primitive Christianity. Antioch on the Orontes, the capital of Syria, with a population of half a million, the largest city in the Roman empire after Rome and Alexandria, had already played a great part in early Christianity. The beginnings of its church go back to the Hellenistic Jewish Christians driven out of Jerusalem, whose faith was distinguished from that of the Palestinian church by its freedom in contrast to the Jewish Law. An old unimpeachable tradition found in Acts 11:19–26 preserves the memory of this important event. Thus, at Antioch, at a very early date and not owing to the preaching of Paul, Christianity burst its Jewish framework and reached the Greeks. Significantly, Antioch saw the first appearance of the new name for the believers, Christians (i.e., Christ's people) (11:26), a designation they would hardly have assumed of their own free will; it must have been conferred on them by their pagan neighbors, and marks them off as a third body alongside Jews and Gentiles.

Barnabas is to be reckoned as one of the founders of the church at Antioch. He was a Hellenistic Jewish Christian from Cyprus with property in Jerusalem. While for some considerable time he worked side by side with Paul, he also acted independently of him. Presumably he had been obliged to flee from Jerusalem along with Stephen's followers and so became a missionary. Acts, as is true,

gives him a different role to begin with: he was one of the delegates from the Jerusalem church sent to investigate the new Gentile church in Antioch. He approved of it, and immediately after
Paul's conversion was the means of bringing him to the Jerusalem
church and the Twelve (Acts 9:27). There is no need to say that
this combination of events, impossible to harmonize with Galatians, is typically Lukan. Furthermore, even on the showing of
Acts, let alone Galatians, the role played by Barnabas as Paul's
companion on missionary journeys and his fellow delegate from
Antioch at the discussions with the original apostles at the assembly in Jerusalem is at variance with Luke's reconstruction.

Barnabas will, however, probably have to be given the credit of
bringing the apostle of Christianity without the Law to Antioch
(Acts 11:26). The day was perhaps as momentous as the one
when Farel persuaded one greater than himself—as Paul was
greater than Barnabas—namely, the reformer Calvin, to come to
his home town of Geneva. Today we can only guess at what Paul's
arrival meant to the church at Antioch. But we also have to bear
the other side of the picture in mind. Up to now Paul had worked
at large without any church as base. Now, even if it was not to be
for long, for the first time he gained the support of one which
accepted his gospel. In all events, Antioch became the base of his
further work.

IV

THE APOSTOLIC ASSEMBLY

IN JERUSALEM

Had Christ's church been split apart? The rise of the Hellenistic churches and the line taken by Paul showed how serious was the threat to its unity even in its first ten years. What was the Jerusalem mother church to the vigorous new churches? Its eyes were on the past. It had not as yet really broken with Judaism and its restrictions. It had scarcely been affected by the persecution of the Hellenists. The basis of its life was apocalyptic expectation of the end of the world and the coming of the Son of Man from heaven. But equally, to the Jewish Christians in Jerusalem, must not the Hellenists have seemed heretics and dangerous fanatics? What was more likely than the mutual parting of the ways?

Amazingly enough, the church's unity did not break down, and neither section abandoned the other. This is demonstrated by the apostolic assembly in Jerusalem (c. A.D. 48), which may very well be described as the most important event in the history of the primitive church. Paul himself (Gal. 2:1–10) and Acts too (chap. 15) give a detailed account of it, and, though in different ways, each lets us see its significance: Paul's account both by the very space that he devotes to it in Galatians and by his noticeable personal interest in it, Luke's account because of its artistry and its placing in Acts. The account occupies a key position, right in the middle of the book, and, as has been aptly said, forms as it were a watershed; until the assembly everything turns on the Jerusalem church and its leading figures, Peter in particular; after it, these disappear, and the subject changes to the work of Paul.

Nevertheless, as a source the account in Acts has no independent value. Apart from a few quite important notes, confirmed in Galatians, about what gave rise to the assembly, the account proves to be a product of Luke's own, composed at a time when past conflicts had long been settled and now seemed no more than insignificant attempts from without to disturb what was in principle unassailable, the primitive church's unity. Luke could not, of course, avoid regarding the meeting as an impressive manifestation of the one united church led by Jerusalem, and in consequence he drew up his account on the basis of his own later idealized view of the church and its history.

Of course, in the nature of the case, no full and exact record is to be expected from Paul's account, either. The apostle is reviewing the assembly's proceedings a good five years later in a specific context, the troubles in Galatia. Thus, the whole purpose of his account is to serve the leading apologetic and polemical ideas he employed in order to combat his Judaizing opponents. Even if, as is the case, the main issue is stated correctly and the details merit credence, still the account is obviously condensed for the later situation, and in addition, Paul continuously adapts it. It is certainly no accident that statements about events in the past repeatedly alternate with others bearing on the matter at hand, the Galatians, and the troublemakers in the churches; yesterday's battlefront passes over into today's. All the same, there can be no doubt that Galatians 2 furnishes us with a trustworthy account of the assembly; indeed, it is the only source of any use.

The occasion of the apostolic assembly can be discerned from Paul's account, and this Acts confirms. Strictly orthodox Jewish Christians from Jerusalem forced their way into the church at Antioch and demanded that the Gentile Christians be circumcised. This gave rise to a dispute, and in order to clarify the question, it was resolved to send Paul and Barnabas to consult the original apostles in Jerusalem. This resolution itself as well as the whole course of the discussions indicates that the troublemakers are not to be thought of as official emissaries of the Twelve and the Jerusalem church, even if they made themselves out to be this. Had they been so, Paul would certainly have identified them as such; when speaking of his later confrontation with Cephas, he says explicitly, "certain men from James" (Gal. 2:12), and does not just call them "false brethren brought in" (Gal. 2:4). Further, supposing the trouble in Antioch had been stirred up directly by the highest quarters, the Jerusalem church, the only possible reason for sending Paul and Barnabas would have been to protest against unreasonable demands on the part of the Twelve, and of this there is no suggestion in the sources. Besides, had this been so, there would be no accounting for the fact that in the course of the assembly the people whom Paul designates as "pillars," James, Cephas, and John, approved of his preaching of a gospel without the Law among the Gentiles. It is absolutely impossible for them to have sent these Jewish Christians with official commission to Antioch, and then, shortly afterward, at the assembly, left them in the lurch. Paul at any rate, if not Luke, would certainly have mentioned this *volte-face* on the part of Jerusalem. Thus, the troublemakers in Antioch can only have been extremely orthodox Jewish Christians from Jerusalem, representing a particularly active school of thought opposed to the now considerable body of Gentile Christians. Galatians 2 leaves no doubt as to the purpose of their appearance: they forced their way into the church in order to "spy out our freedom which we have in Christ Jesus, that they might bring us into bondage" (Gal. 2:4); as such, therefore, they were of the same stamp as the Judaizers some time later in Galatia. As regards Antioch, the position was this: because of the views they held, the troublemakers wanted Gentile Christians to submit to the jurisdiction of the Jerusalem church which was still strictly tied to the Law: this failing, they should be excommunicated. But for Paul, this put at stake the "truth of the gospel" and the "freedom" of faith (Gal. 2:5).

This made the Old Testament and the Jewish requirement of circumcision the all-important confessional question. In all probability it had for long been smoldering under the surface, between Jewish and Gentile-Christian churches, without having broken out openly into flames. Now, at the assembly, it became the most important subject of debate, and Paul himself took it up as such in principle, by bringing with him to Jerusalem—provocatively enough—the person who was afterward to be his fellow worker, Titus, an uncircumcised Greek. Either as an ultimatum or as a compromise, it was at once urgently demanded of Paul that he should circumcise Titus. Paul, however, did not submit even for a moment (Gal. 2:5).

We today may find it hard to understand why, of all things, an archaic ritual prescription like this could have given rise to such a strong contention in the early church. As early as the post-apostolic generation it ceased to play any part: Acts itself only gives it as among the reasons for the assembly's meeting, a matter raised by one or two narrow-minded Pharisees; in the proceedings themselves there is no mention of it. Accordingly, Acts says nothing about Titus. How then, we may ask, was it possible for the retention or abandonment of this immaterial ancient rite, not even maintained by the liberal, Hellenistic Jews of the Diaspora, to have acted as the catalyst in the battle in the Christian church about gospel and faith? There can be only one answer: for strict Jews and Jewish Christians circumcision was the indispensable sign of the covenant which God made long ago with Abraham for his descendants and which assured the Jews that they belonged to the true chosen people. It stood as "the seal of election" (Rabbi Akiba), as a confession of faith and an act of obedience to God's holy law and to the requirement that the Jews should separate themselves from the heathen world around them. For the Jerusalem church, which still strictly observed the Law, circumcision involved nothing less than the physical continuity of the saving history and, in consequence, the question of the legitimation of its claim to be the true Israel as opposed to the Jews who had rejected their promised Messiah-king.

Comparative religion and church history both show that important and far-reaching questions of principle have often come to a head on the issue of ancient rites and symbols, the meaning of which later generations scarcely understood. In the early days of the church and its mission, the problem of the historicity of faith, vital for Judaism and Christianity alike, became focused on circumcision; both are essentially based on history. Thus, at no time have they been able to view themselves as religious societies which one can opt for and change to at will, as was perfectly possible in the Hellenistic and Oriental world round about, where people had recourse to several at the same time to be on the safe side.

Thus, the modern idea of "leaving one church and going over to another" cannot in principle be applied to the relationship then existing between Judaism or Christianity—any more than the category of "founder of a religion" can be applied to Jesus. To use Pascal's well-known words, this tells us that the Lord of Christian faith, too, is the "God of Abraham, Isaac, and Jacob," and not "the God of the philosophers." From this viewpoint we see that in this now long-obsolete dispute at the apostolic assembly the unity of the people of God and of its history, and, as a result, the question of salvation in general, was at stake. Seen in this light, Paul's opponents do not appear as dyed-in-the-wool ritualists, nor is he himself a headstrong innovator unwilling to make the slightest compromise in inessentials. He was obliged to put to himself the same questions as did his opponents, though he gave them a fundamentally different answer.

Before going on to the course of the proceedings at Jerusalem and their outcome, we must first look at the kind of meeting it was and the roles of the people who took part. As will at once be apparent, it dealt with important problems affecting the constitution of the early church, the apostolic office, tradition, and authority for doctrine, questions which ever since have remained crucial for the church and its understanding of itself. Galatians makes it perfectly possible to give these debated points an answer, though here again, admittedly, it will differ significantly from the account given by Luke. We have from the outset used the term "apostolic assembly" in preference to the traditional "apostolic council." This is deliberate, because as regards the summoning of the meeting and the way in which it was conducted, and also the publication of its resolutions, the latter term automatically imports wrong ideas about church law and hierarchy which obtained only later.

This traditional view of the assembly, still common in present-day scholarship, has some measure of support lent it in the account given in Acts. For there the authorities and speakers are in fact the Jerusalem apostles and elders, just as, at the end, it is in their name that the "apostolic decree," mentioned only in Acts, is sent to the churches in Antioch, Syria, and Cilicia (Acts 15:22 ff.). Speeches of Paul and Barnabas, on the other hand, are not given, and they come into the picture only as narrators of the wonders God did by means of them among the Gentiles. In this connection the report does no more than establish—and this is very significant for Luke's historical view—that Paul and Barnabas were not the first to take the important step of conducting a mission to the Gentiles: this was initiated by the Jerusalem apostle Peter. By his mouth, according to God's will, the gospel had long ago and for the first time been proclaimed to the heathen, as Peter expressly states in his earlier speech (Acts 15:7 f.) with reference to the miraculous conversion of the Gentile centurion Cornelius which has already been described at length in Acts as showing the future shape of events (Acts 10:1–11:18). Finally, Paul and Barnabas are mentioned along with other emissaries in the matter of the transmission of this "decree" to the Gentile churches: they act in the name of the apostles, but are not themselves such.

Here again we see at once how the leadership of the Jerusalem church and its apostles is exalted at the expense of the church at Antioch, a view quite impossible to harmonize with the authentic account given in Galatians 2. Acts too, of course, leaves no doubt that the initiative in the meeting was taken by Antioch, and that Paul and Barnabas were not, as has been asserted, in any sense officially "cited" before the superior court of the original Twelve (against Stauffer).

None of this can be read out of the Epistle to the Galatians. Paul's account of the assembly begins with the words: "I went up by revelation [to Jerusalem]" (Gal. 2:2). But this is certainly not to be taken as supporting any idea that (after roughly seventeen years of missionary work!) a divine revelation suggested to him that the authority of the apostles called before him was greater than his own apostolic office, and that now, at long last, he found himself ready to submit himself and his gospel, with the possibility of rejection, to the only people duly authorized to pronounce upon them, the leaders of the church in Jerusalem. Apart from all else, this view forgets that there is no break between the first and second chapters of Galatians. As we have seen, this implies, as shown by Galatians 1:12, that Paul's seventeen years' strictly maintained independence of Jerusalem and his gospel without the Law for the Gentiles were acknowledged by the Twelve at the assembly itself. True, he says: "I laid before them, and in particular [perhaps at a special meeting] before those who were of repute, the gospel which I preach among the Gentiles, lest somehow I should be running or had run in view" (Gal. 2:2). But the words most certainly do not imply any admission of readiness, should the authorities impose a veto, either completely to give up the gospel he had received from God and not from men or even to make such changes in it as they wished. Instead, they express the great store which he, too, had set on the unity of the church made up of Jews and Greeks, and his anxiety lest Gentile Christians might be denied fellowship. Nevertheless, for the sake of unity he was not ready to pay the price of the truth of the gospel (Gal. 2:5).

There is absolutely nothing to support the idea recently advocated by Stauffer that Paul's journey to the "council" represented a "going to Canossa," just as previously his fortnight's visit to Cephas had made him disloyal to his former principles, a fact (Stauffer says) none too successfully covered later by obscurities in language and appeal to a "revelation." Besides, it is alleged, his submission is proclaimed by a matter which he himself mentions, his undertaking to make a regulation "levy" from Gentile Christians on behalf of Jerusalem, the real, prescriptive nature of which was to be disguised by calling it a "collection" (Gal. 2:10).

This grossly distorts the whole point of the account and brands Paul himself as more or less a liar, at a time, furthermore, when he was confronting opponents in Galatia who undoubtedly could have cast any falsification of the true facts in his teeth. This interpretation even misconceives the term with which the account opens. In Galatians 2:2, as commonly elsewhere, "revelation" means a divine "direction" such as we find prophets giving at the church's meetings for worship (cf. Acts 13:2). Because of this, Paul felt himself summoned to take what was assuredly no easy road and go to Jerusalem. He says that the revelation was expressly directed only to himself, not to Barnabas. This does not, however, mean that he appeared in Jerusalem as a lone wolf, having taken a few like-minded people with him only for the sake of his very own theological ideas. His way of putting it is quite easy to explain. At the assembly he was obviously the principal speaker and the really controversial figure; furthermore, in the situation then obtaining in Galatia, he was having to defend himself and not the people who had gone along with him. However, as well as having business of his own, as envoy of the Gentile churches he had also to represent their desires (Acts 15:2 f.), as had also Barnabas, whom Galatians 2:9 names as joining in the conclusion of the agreement. Thus, there can be no question of their merely reporting to the apostolic office bearers as superiors who alone could take a decision. Rather, at the assembly Jewish Christian and Gentile Christian churches met on equal footing, even though the Antiochenes and Paul himself had no small regard for the special status accorded throughout the church to Jerusalem and the Twelve. But here we must be very careful to distinguish between the apostles' uncontested importance owing to their past and an unrestricted authority which Paul was not ready to concede to them. Thus, while, without any overtones of irony, he repeatedly uses terms like "those of repute," "who were reputed to be pillars" (Gal. 2:2, 6, 9), at the same time he flatly disallows them a formally constituted authority, as, for example, having been disciples who followed Jesus while on earth: "What they were makes no difference to me" (Gal. 2:6).

Paul tells a little about the course of the assembly's proceedings. Still, his account does let us see that although agreement was not reached at the first passage of arms, his exposition of his gospel of God's all-encompassing grace, doing away with the limitations imposed by the Law and the firmly drawn distinction between Jew and Gentile, prevailed upon the Twelve, and they added nothing to it for the Gentiles (Gal. 2:6). There is no reason to suppose that their agreement was simply a grudging acceptance, a church political concession. As Paul expressly adds, they acted as they did because they realized that God's grace had authorized him to preach among the Gentiles just as Peter had been made apostle to the Jews (Gal. 2:7). On these terms the church's unity was sealed by each party's giving the other the right hand of fellowship (Gal. 2:9).

We may be sure that the Jerusalem church did not adopt Paul's gospel in its entirety and all its logical implications. Apparently the direct realization of God's wondrous works played a larger part in the achievement of unity than did considerations of pure theology. Paul viewed the church as God's new creation in which there is neither Jew nor Gentile, but all are one in Christ (Gal. 3:28). This he can scarcely have doubted from the time of his conversion and call onward, and he subsequently developed the idea in his letters. We may not, however, suppose that it was accepted by Jerusalem without more ado. Instead, for the Jewish Christian churches and preaching to the Jews the *status quo* still remained in operation, and even the Antiochenes had obviously lacked either the will or the power to exact more. Nevertheless, their stand effectively freed the gospel from limitations imposed by Judaism, primarily for their own mission field, but also in some sense for the Jewish-Christian one too, since the Jewish view of salvation as being exclusively Law, saving history, and chosen people, was henceforward broken down.

The terse "we to the Gentiles, they to the Jews" (Gal. 2:9) undoubtedly keeps close to the express formula of the concordat. Its meaning is not at once apparent. Does it refer to a geographical delineation of missionary spheres? Hardly, for then the Jerusalem church would have had to confine its activities to Jerusalem and Judaea and yield up all the rest of the world, including the great Jewish Diaspora, to the Gentile-Christian mission. In this case, too, Peter would never have been able to cross the boundary and go to Rome. Yet, a purely ethnographical understanding of the words is not feasible, either: this would mean that henceforward Paul and his companions might preach only to Gentiles, and that for Jews a mission of a different nature, on the lines of Jerusalem's, would have to be provided. And what of the practical difficulties of such a solution? On his later missionary journeys Paul would have continuously and grossly infringed the agreement by preaching on numerous occasions in synagogues in the Diaspora. So we should not press the words too hard; they are best referred to the basic character of the missionary preaching of the two groups. In this case, they could simply mean that the Gentile Christian mission should go ahead unimpeded, each side abstaining from rivalry and competition in the other's sphere.

The agreement left important questions still open, as was to become apparent a little later when Paul and Peter came into conflict at Antioch. These related to social intercourse, specifically table fellowship, between Jewish and Gentile Christians in mixed churches, a matter which affected the very heart of their worship. Ritual prescriptions strictly forbade a Jew to sit at table with a Gentile, and these the Jewish Christians felt themselves still bound to observe. This problem had not been on the agenda at the assembly. Even so, without minimizing all the differences, the agreement represented an extremely important step forward in the history of the church. For the Jerusalem apostles in particular it was a brave decision which does them great honor. Just because the assembly modestly kept within its terms of reference, and was therefore necessarily provisional and limited in scope, the agreement deserves to be called a real decision on the part of the church.

Thus far nothing has been said of a further resolution made by the assembly. Acts passes it over in silence, but it is mentioned by Paul at the end of his account: "Only they would have us remember the poor, which very thing I was eager to do" (Gal. 2:10). The importance of this apparently trivial agreement is not at once obvious. But that it was important can be seen both from the terms in which it is couched and from Paul's subsequent letters to the Corinthians (1 Cor. 16; 2 Cor. 8 and 9) and the Romans (15:25 ff.), passages entering into great detail and highly charged with theology. In no sense was this "collection" a measure of public charity to be undertaken by all churches alike (as making provision for the needy in all the churches or even as "bread for the world"). Instead, it was aid to be given by the Gentile Christian churches specifically to the mother church in Jerusalem. How far exceptional social needs came into question is a matter of dispute. But the tremendous pains in the discharge of this duty taken by Paul himself and later by his churches in Galatia, Macedonia, and Greece suggest that the reason was not simply charity. Nor does the term "the poor" necessarily imply charity. In late

Judaism and early Christianity the word was not confined to the underprivileged. It was also an honorific religious title taken over from Judaism for the true Israel which looked to God for help in the end. Applied to the collection, it means that though the Gentile Christian churches' offerings were meant to alleviate want, they were also intended for the whole body of the Jerusalem mother church as token of her special status in secular and sacred history alike, a status which remained unchallenged; they were an expression of thanks for the blessings that had gone forth from Jerusalem into the world (Rom. 15:27). The collection has sometimes been regarded as an official tax on Jerusalem's behalf, like the temple tax collected annually from all Jews in the Diaspora. But this is a mistake. To think of it as a tax would again necessitate the idea of the mother church's having an official primacy. Again, it was never a regular import, and while Paul had various names for it—contribution, proof of grace, participation in relief, promised gift, acknowledgment of the gospel of Christ—he avoided terms taken from Law. In all likelihood, the purpose of the collection was to signal the unity of the church historically founded from Jews and Gentiles, the equal status of its members, and thereby also the legitimacy of the gospel without the Law. Only on these terms can we understand both the eagerness with which Paul's churches later threw themselves into it and, as shown in the letters, the extent of his efforts to organize it and reflect upon it theologically. There is also the fact that both the apostle's life and his death, which must be discussed later, were fatefully linked together with it.

The account in Acts shows no trace of what we learn from Galatians, neither with respect to the significance of the question of circumcision nor regarding Paul's battle for the truth of his gospel and its freedom. Instead, according to Luke, Peter and James at once resorted to lengthy well-turned speeches smacking of a later popular "Paulinism," and represented that it would be unfair to impose on Gentiles the yoke of a law that even Jews by birth were unable to bear. It would be quite sufficient, they said, to make some few minimal regulations affecting morals and ritual obligatory for both parties: there was to be no idolatry or unchastity, and all were to abstain from meat not ritually slaughtered and from blood. This is the content of the "apostolic decree" proposed here by James (Acts 15:23–29), at once resolved on by the apostles and others, and then transmitted to the churches in Antioch, Syria, and Cilicia. It gives regulations designed to enable Jewish and Gentile Christians to have real fellowship in the church. Luke also once or twice mentions a collection on behalf of Jerusalem (Acts 11:27 ff.; 24:17), but not in the context of the assembly and Paul's mission to the Gentiles; nor is there any hint of its importance. Past questions and decisions have now sunk into oblivion.

Paul's account makes it quite certain that the "apostolic decree" can never have been part of the resolutions of the assembly. Galatians 2:6 says categorically: "those who were of repute added nothing to me" (cf. also the word "only" in Gal. 2:10). Again, had there been such a resolution, a quarrel could not have arisen, as it did very soon in Antioch between Paul and Peter (or James), about table fellowship (Gal. 2:11 ff.). Finally: later, in Corinthians, Paul had to deal with questions of meat offered to idols and of unchastity: one would have expected him to appeal to a decree to which allegedly he himself was partner and which had been published. But this is never done. Thus, we have to make a choice. Either the resolution was taken without Paul's having any part in it, at a time when the question had already arisen of table fellowship in mixed churches, or else, as the evidence rather suggests, it reflects the practice which Luke found in the churches of his own day, at the end of the first century. In the context of Luke's account, the purpose of the brief, ritualistically couched decree, devoid of the slightest trace of the difficulties and magnitude of the decisions actually taken, was to express that unity between the Jews and the church which Luke so persistently maintains. Here again, then, we have confirmation that Paul's account is to be preferred.

The outcome of the apostolic assembly is important for theology, for the history of the church, and for world history alike. It shows that the church's unity had not fallen in pieces. The danger that the mother church would harden into a sect of Judaism and that Hellenistic Christianity would dissolve into a welter of non-historical mystery cults had been averted.

V

THE FIRST JOURNEY TO CYPRUS

AND ASIA MINOR, AND

THE CONFLICT AT ANTIOCH

Before the meeting in Jerusalem, Paul, along with Barnabas, is said to have gone on a first missionary journey to Cyprus and the south of Asia Minor (Acts 13:14); according to the defective pattern of Luke, who knew nothing of the mission in Arabia, Syria, and Cilicia, this is Paul's very first journey. No trace of it is preserved in the letters; we are thus completely dependent on Acts. There is no real reason for following certain scholars in regarding it as mere invention on Luke's part, a typical Pauline missionary tour, as it were. But, equally, we may not use Luke unexamined to fill in the gap in Paul's life left by the letters. This is true even for the time assigned to the journey. Galatians 1, terse but precise in the matter of dates and places, does not mention it, and leaves no room for it before the apostolic assembly. This means that the author of Acts introduced it at the wrong point in time. In its context there the account forms the effective background to the description of the assembly itself (see Acts 15:4); the speeches of Peter and James, like the "decree," give the Antiochene Gentile mission full legitimation by the original apostles. In actual fact, however, the journey must have followed the assembly. The latter was not, then, the culmination of a great joint missionary enterprise by Paul and Barnabas; instead, it opened the door for their work and gave them, so to speak, free play over against Jerusalem. It is also quite conceivable that they may have paid a visit to Cyprus, Barnabas' native country, and the neighboring districts of south Asia Minor which had a large Jewish population and so held out good prospects of success for their preaching.

As regards details, the particulars given in Acts are of uneven value; we can therefore gain no historically reliable picture. Some of them are brief indications, trustworthy but not very informative, of the various stopping places. They sketch the route taken as follows: from Syrian Antioch via its nearby port, Selucia, to Cyprus (Salamis, Paphos); then to the mainland of Asia Minor (Perga), and northward to Iconium, Lystra, and Derbe; thence, stopping at the same places, back to the sea and direct to the starting point, Antioch. Prominent in the sketch, however, are certain incidents drawn on a broad canvas and obviously legendary, and also some lengthy speeches. Included in the first is the extremely vivid description of the execration of a Jewish sorcerer Bar-Jesus (Elymas), a court magician of the Roman governor in Cyprus, Sergius Paulus. This sorcerer tried to prevent the conversion of Sergius Paulus by Paul, but the net result of his efforts was that the proconsul was so astounded at the judgment which fell on Elymas that he became a believer (Acts 13:8–12). There is also in Acts 14:8–14 an account, just as legendary, of the healing of a cripple at Lystra which so astonished the heathen inhabitants as to make them think that the gods themselves, Zeus and Hermes, were visiting them in human form. This is clearly the old motif of the well-known story of Philemon and Baucis. Only with the utmost effort were the two Christian missionaries able to restrain the crowd's wild excitement; a priest of Zeus was already bringing garlands and oxen and preparing to offer sacrifice. When Paul and Barnabas preached the true God as opposed to the practice of idolatry, this only increased the enthusiasm. Then, all of a sudden, Jews appeared on the scene, making a dead set against the apostles. Eager reception gave way to furious persecution; Paul was stoned and dragged out of the city for dead. Into this narrative, spread over two chapters, are inserted speeches of Paul: the first a long, typical missionary sermon in the synagogue at Pisidian Antioch (13:16–41), the second, equally typical and adapted to the situation, addressed to heathen hearers in Lystra (14:15–17). There are also, on the return journey, words of comfort to the converted Christians in the cities passed through (14:22). In addition, by appointing elders the two missionaries now give the churches visited their form of government. These accounts are important and authoritative sources of information, if not for the life of Paul itself, at least for what was said of him and his work at a later date. They are also supremely valuable as examples of Luke's very artistic way of telling a story and of the ideas held in his own day. Only in a very small degree can we recognize in Acts the Paul of the epistles. Again, the constitution of the church assumed in Acts does not tally with the church order known in the actual Pauline churches of the early days. Thus, the assured historical data for this journey of Paul and Barnabas are very, very meager.

In the Acts account one person deserves particular notice. He appears more than once, casually and not altogether clearly, a certain John Mark, a native of Jerusalem (12:12). He is said to have accompanied the two missionaries as a helper on part of their journey (13:5). Early on, however, for reasons not stated, he left them at Perga and went home (13:13). Because of him, Acts says, Paul and Barnabas quarreled and parted company: when Paul set out on his next great missionary journey to Asia Minor, he refused to take Mark along with him. Thereupon Barnabas took him on his own journey to Cyprus (15:39). This can hardly lack some foundation in fact; however, the setting of the quarrel is far from clear.

It has been conjectured, correctly perhaps, that this very serious quarrel preserves a dim memory of another bitter conflict, of which Luke says nothing, though it is mentioned more precisely by Paul in his description (see above) of his quarrel with Peter at Antioch, when even Barnabas, until then in sympathy with him, deserted him. Galatians 2:11–21 tells how Paul opposed Cephas because in the course of a visit to the mixed church in Galatia, Cephas had originally partaken without scruple of the common meal (at the celebration of the Lord's Supper). But when "certain men came from James" in Jerusalem, he separated himself from fear of the Jews. Not only Peter but the rest of the Jewish Chris-

tians as well, even Barnabas himself, submitted to the Jewish
ritual prescription. This conduct Paul roundly brands as "insin-
cerity" (Gal. 2:13), describing it as "not being straightforward
about the truth of the gospel" (2:14), and reproduces, actually in
the first person, his retort to Peter in the presence of the whole
church (2:14 ff.). The words are not, of course, an exact tran-
script. Imperceptibly, to adapt the incident to the situation then
obtaining in Galatia, Paul goes on to make statements that do not
directly bear on the earlier situation in Antioch. But this lets us
see all the better that, in his view, nothing less was at stake at the
time than the gospel and faith themselves. For Paul the quarrel
was not a matter of a trivial divergence of views on which he
should have been ready to compromise. It was a basic question of
general principle. According to Paul's account, Peter's inconsistency was tantamount to a denial of the truth that men are
justified not by doing what the Law commands, but solely through
faith in Christ, because his second attitude made clear that, for
himself and Jewish Christians, the prescriptions of the Jewish Law
were obligatory, thus forcing Gentile Christians, too, to submit to
Jewish customs. For Paul, any relapse into legality could only
mean that faith based on Christ alone was declared to be sin, and
Christ an agent of sin. In reality, however, sin consisted in harking
back to the Law which Christ's death on the cross had nullified,
and in abandoning the new life which he made possible.

Although Paul was clearly of the opinion that in denying the
gospel Peter and the rest of the Jewish Christians were also denying the agreements reached in Jerusalem, it must in all fairness be
said that, looked at from the others' standpoint, Paul's view of the
matter was unwarranted. For this was the first appearance of the
problem which had not as yet come to the surface at that point,
the question of the unity of Jewish and Gentile Christians in a
mixed church. Thus neither Cephas or James can be accused of
acting in any underhand way. Equally, the blow dealt them by
Barnabas would not have made the Hellenistic Jewish Christians
of Antioch dismiss lock, stock, and barrel their understanding of
the gospel outside the Law. Paul, however, saw deeper. As he was
convinced, the unity of the church, the surmounting of the Law as
the way of salvation, and in consequence the truth of the gospel

were nowhere better manifested than in this very matter of table fellowship between Jews and Gentiles. This is characteristic of Paul. In line with his earlier action at the assembly on the question of the circumcision of Titus, he now highlighted the specific problem in Antioch as one of the issues which touched the very heart of the gospel. As a result, in neither case was he ready to listen to debates based on casuistry, concessions, or compromises. To others it might seem trivial, a thing to be put up with for the very sake of the church's unity: after all, peace with Jerusalem was in jeopardy. But for Paul it became a battlefield for truth and freedom, where he joined the fight even against the allegedly authoritative decisions of a court of the church.

Even if Luke did in fact know of this quarrel at Antioch, these considerations let us see his reason for omitting it in his account of the history of the church and of Paul. Over and over again, church historians have done their utmost either to cover up this embarrassing quarrel between the apostles or to represent it as an episode soon tided over. This attitude continues even today: the final accord between Paul, Barnabas, and the rest of the Jewish Christians is depicted with a sometimes sentimental ingenuity. But there is no idea of this in Galatians; and here for once we are justified in using the generally risky *argumentum e silentio*. For what would it not have meant for Paul if, to parry this Jewish Christian threat to the Galatians, he had been able to produce evidence of a change of opinion on the part of Peter and the rest, and thereby ensure the victory of the gospel over the Law, as previously in the account of the assembly? The fact that he says nothing of this can only mean that not he, but the others who were ready to give in to the strict Jewish Christians, won the day.

Paul's deliberately detailed account of events in Antioch and the fundamental importance he himself attached to them force us to take the conflict very seriously indeed. The problems of Law and gospel, a topic already discussed at the assembly, had come to the surface afresh, though now of course in a different field. What Paul had to undergo was unquestionably a bitter disappointment. No wonder that on his subsequent journeys not Barnabas but others were his fellow workers (cf. the opening words of his letters and Acts 15:39 f.). And from then on, Antioch, too, no longer appears as a kind of mother church for Paul personally and the Gentile Christian churches.

However, there are hints later (1 Cor. 9:6) that the breach with Peter and Barnabas was not full and final, and that Paul reinstated the unity, once more in peril, between the Jerusalem mother church and his churches, and down to the end sought to promote this with all his power. It would also be a mistake to suppose that after the conflict the Hellenistic churches were subjected to a gradual or rapid process of re-Judaizing. Actually, this very district of Syria later became the soil from which sprang a number of very diverse, important expressions of Christian faith and life. The Gospels of Matthew and Luke, perhaps John too, and certainly the theology and church of Ignatius of Antioch (died c. A.D. 110 as a Christian martyr) testify to the amazing range of possible and actual developments of early Christianity in this very area. But initially a heavy price had to be paid—the severing of the tie with Paul and his radical understanding of the gospel.

VI

THE WORLD-WIDE SCOPE

OF THE PAULINE MISSION

Paul is regarded as the apostle to the Gentiles, and rightly so. To the best of our knowledge, no other missionary of primitive Christianity set his sights so high and planned to carry the gospel to the farthest limits of the inhabited world. The Jerusalem church was, as we saw, missionary from the very beginning, but it had never proclaimed the gospel without the Law to the Gentiles. The message of salvation had reached the Greeks through the "Hellenists," and from his call onward, Paul himself had worked as a missionary among the Gentiles. Nevertheless, even his own activities in Arabia, Syria, Cilicia, Antioch, Cyprus, and the south of Asia Minor give no hint at first that his plans embraced the whole world.

At what time did this grandiose idea occur to Paul? We can be tolerably sure of the answer. It was during the course of what Acts' defective enumeration calls the second missionary journey, which, after Antioch (see the preceding section), took Paul and his companions through the middle of Asia Minor to Troas, Macedonia, and Greece, and during the course of which were founded the churches in Galatia (the country around the modern Ankara), Philippi, Thessalonica, and Corinth, all known to us from the letters and from Acts. While Acts gives only a few notes about the journey, they are enough to show that, at the latest in

49

Asia Minor, and perhaps even at the very start of the tour, the missionaries had taken important and far-reaching decisions. As they revisited the churches founded earlier, Paul acquired in Lystra as fellow worker the Timothy who is so often mentioned in his letters. Thereafter, Luke tells us, on their journey through Phrygia and Galatia, the travelers were three times given direct divine direction as to their next objective. First, the Holy Spirit prevented them from going southwest into the Roman province of Asia Minor on the coast, that is to say, the area with the old, famous Greek cities the names of which we find later in the letters to the churches in Revelation (Ephesus, Smyrna, Sardis, Pergamon, etc.). They were also forbidden to go northward to Bithynia, this, too, an area with well-known Greek cities on the Bosphorus and farther to the east on the Black Sea. Even if Luke's account may be stylized—with him the Holy Ghost is frequently the motive force in an action—we have no reason for doubting his information. Both places, Asia Minor and Bithynia, would undoubtedly have opened up to the missionaries a great field, and good roads enabled them to go westward or northward. However, they went diagonally through the central part of Asia Minor to Troas, where, for the third time, they received divine direction. A Macedonian appeared to Paul in a dream and summoned the messengers of the gospel to come over to his country. They at once obeyed. All this is narrated in just a few verses (Acts 16:6–10) probably based on information given in the travel diary (itinerary) of someone who accompanied Paul. Thereupon Acts at once continues with a lengthy account of the origin of the church in Philippi.

Needless to say, the journey was not quite as quick and direct as Acts makes out. For Galatians tells us that on the way through Galatia Paul became ill, and during his probably involuntary stay founded the Galatian church as the result of his preaching (4:13 ff.). Nevertheless, there can be no doubt that after his work there he at once went on toward the northwest. Philippi—to give it its full Latin name, Colonia Augusta Julia Philippensis—was Roman soil in a very special way. To commemorate the defeat of Caesar's murderers by Octavian (later the emperor Augustus) and Antony (42 B.C.), the victor made it into a city in which to settle his veterans and distinguished it by conferring the *Jus Italicum*, the privileges of a Roman city. Here in Philippi grew up the first church on the continent of Europe, one with which afterward the apostle kept closer ties than with any other (Phil. 4:15). Here he suffered his first persecution at the hands of the Roman praetors, and the illegality of his treatment forced him to appeal to his Roman citizenship (Acts 16:19 ff.). But for our present purpose this city is important for a further reason. Philippi was the starting point of the famous road to the west, the Via Egnatia; this line of communication, important for both military and trade reasons, linked the western part of the empire with the eastern. Paul followed it as far as Thessalonica, where a new vigorous church shortly grew up. Then of course he turned off, and instead of going on to Illyria (Dalmatia) on the Adriatic and even farther to Italy and Rome, he went to Greece, via Berea and Athens to Corinth.

We can be perfectly sure that, at the latest, in Asia Minor and on the journey through Macedonia to Thessalonica, Rome was present in Paul's mind as a far-off objective. This is indicated by his own statement later in Romans that he had long planned to come to Rome and preach the gospel there, but had been hindered (1:13; 15:22). On this first journey through Macedonia and Greece Paul as yet probably knew nothing of a Christian church in Rome. At the time he wrote Romans, he had in the interval learned something of this church, the founders of which are unknown. One important source of his information must have been Aquila and Priscilla, a Jewish-Christian married couple in Corinth, who themselves were no doubt members of the church before being expelled from Rome by the emperor Claudius (see below, p. 68). In spite of this Paul did not give up his idea of visiting Rome, although he had really been anticipated. He might easily enough have abandoned it, for it was his principle never to preach where the name of Christ had already been proclaimed (Rom. 15:20; 2 Cor. 10:15 f.). Nonetheless, Rome still remained important to him because of his further mission in the west (Rom. 15:24, 28).

The first obstacle which prevented the apostle when in Thessalonica from going straight on to Rome was persecution by the

pagan civic authorities instigated by the Jews (Acts 17:5 ff.; 1
Thess. 2:14 ff.; 3:1 ff.). This caused the Christians in the city to
send him and his companions under cover of night on to Berea
(Acts 17:10), that is to say, to the southwest into central Greece.
But there, too, after his initial success in the synagogue, persecution broke out, instigated by Jews from Thessalonica who pursued
the apostle thither, and he was sent farther on to Athens. So Acts'
splendid and typical picture of his preaching there on the
Areopagus (Acts 17) must not make us blind to the fact that
Athens was not included in the missionary journey as originally
planned. Paul himself makes only one passing reference to his stay
there; he was anxious about the church in Thessalonica which he
had had so quickly to forsake (1 Thess. 3:1).

At this point there is no need to follow the rest of the journey in
detail—Athens, Corinth, Paul's return to Antioch, and thereafter
his fresh work in Asia Minor, especially in Ephesus (Acts
17–19). Our particular concern at this point is that, at a quite
early date, Paul manifestly wanted to go to Rome, but was forced
by circumstances to abandon this goal: not only because of outward circumstances like the persecution in Thessalonica, but also
because of the opening up of fresh fields of mission from which he
could not hurry away, leaving newborn churches with all their
troubles, practical and spiritual, in the lurch. Yet these exigencies
and obligations which detained him for years never banished from
his mind his far-off objective, Rome and farther west. As we know
from Acts and 1 Clement (A.D. 96), he did in fact come to Rome,
albeit as a prisoner.

Paul's journeys and plans reveal the driving force of his design
to take as his mission field the whole of the inhabited world as far
as Spain (Rom. 15:24, 28), the "pillars of Hercules" as it was
then called, the utmost limits of the world in the west. His whole
strategy is based on this. It is pointless to object that the apostle
must have known of other peoples and lands beyond these frontiers, or to point to the map of the world which a later age was to
draw. Time and again Paul speaks of "all the earth" (Rom.
10:18), "the ends of the world" (10:18), and "all the peoples"
(15:11: as used by the early Christians, the Greek word *ethne*
had two meanings, "nations" and "pagans"). Admittedly, these

terms generally occur in quotations from the Psalms. But as used by Paul they have not only the hymnic liturgical ring of full assurance; they also mean something concrete and down to earth. For this very reason he speaks of himself as "under obligation" to Greeks and barbarians (Rom. 1:14), obliged to bring to them that to which God's grace gives them a title.

When Paul announced that he was going to visit Rome, he summed up all his work to that point in the words, "so that from Jerusalem and as far round as Illyricum I have fully preached the gospel of Christ" (Rom. 15:19). They are characteristic, and have not been given the weight they deserve. In more than one respect Paul's wording has much to tell us. First, it briefly describes the whole of the eastern hemisphere of the Roman empire: here, one might say, Paul speaks as the Hellenistic Roman. Second, he defines his mission as extending from Jerusalem. But this is an odd thing for him to say, for Paul was certainly never a missionary in Jerusalem and Judaea: why then the mention of Jerusalem? The only possible answer is that, in his eyes, Jerusalem was the axial point in God's plan of salvation for mankind and the place from which the gospel went out to the Gentiles. Now the speaker is not the Roman citizen, but the Jew and the Christian. Third, Paul mentions Illyricum, though to judge from all that we are told in Acts and his own letters, he never did missionary work there either. The reason why he mentions this district right on the northwestern limits of Greece is that there, on the coast of modern Dalmatia, ended the great Via Egnatia, to continue from Brindisi on the other side of the Adriatic as the Via Appia leading to Rome. Thus, even the very name of the district again points to Rome and the west. Romans 15:19 has often caused surprise, and rightly so, for it sounds like an extravagant exaggeration. Consider: in a few districts and cities in the eastern half of the Roman empire surrounded by a large heathen population were planted a few small Christian churches which certainly declined in number: yet, Paul speaks of his missionary work in that hemisphere as complete. However, this is an instance of a leading characteristic in Paul's way of thinking. His thought always extends beyond the individual community to countries and districts. Each of the churches founded, but no more than founded, by Paul stands for a

whole district: Philippi for Macedonia (Phil. 4:15), Thessalonica
for Macedonia and Achaia (1 Thess. 1:7 f.), Corinth for Achaia
(1 Cor. 16:15; 2 Cor. 1:1), and Ephesus for Asia (Rom. 16:5; 1
Cor. 16:19; 2 Cor. 1:8). Romans 15:19 is therefore anything but
adventitious and exaggerated. Instead, it expresses the apostle's
amazing confidence that the gospel needed only to be preached for
it to spread automatically: starting from the various cities it would
reach out to the whole of the country round about and pervade it.
"The presumption is that the fire will of itself spread to the right
and the left of where it was kindled" (Harnack). This also sheds
light on the far-off objective on which Paul set his sights in
Romans, Spain. Thus, even Rome is not designed as the end, but
only as a break in his journey. So in this letter the Romans are
prepared in advance for the apostle's missionary service on which
they are to speed him (Rom. 15:24). 1 Clement supposes, quite
wrongly, that Paul was able to accomplish this journey too, and
because of it calls him a "herald" (*keryx*) in the east and the west
who taught the whole world righteousness and came to the
farthest limits of the west (1 Clem. 5:6 f.). Clement is, however,
quite correct in emphasizing the world-wide horizons in which the
apostle did in fact fulfill his mission.

This grandiose plan is also the sole key to the understanding of
Paul's missionary strategy. It is perfectly astonishing to see how
short a time he took in traversing the extensive fields where he
worked, and how quickly he left scarcely founded churches and
traveled farther, instead of taking time to care for them and train
them. Probably only two or three years came between the apostolic assembly (A.D. 48?) and the end of his first stay in Corinth
(autumn of 49 to spring of 51), and the total length of time from
the assembly to the conclusion of his work in the eastern half of
the Roman empire—which includes the numerous events and
journeys of which Acts' picture is incomplete—amounts to
scarcely more than seven years. Paul was most certainly not indifferent to the churches which he left behind. His great sense of
responsibility for them is shown in his letters. And yet he could do
no other than commit the further care of them to his fellow workers and attend to them personally only by means of his letters and

occasional visits. The great goal of carrying the gospel to the ends of the earth kept him always on the move and gave him no rest.

The basis of this tremendous plan of Paul's was faith in Jesus Christ the crucified, whom God exalted as Lord over all, whose lordship endures until the imminent end, when at his coming he is to deliver it to God (1 Cor. 15:24; cf. Rom. 15:16; 2 Cor. 2:14). Whenever Paul speaks of this Lord (Kyrios), he means not only the head of the various churches assembled for worship, but the Lord over the powers of the whole cosmos (Phil. 2:6–11), raised from the dead and exalted, in order to be Lord both of the dead and of the living (Rom. 14:9). It was this Lord who made him apostle to the Gentiles (Rom. 1:5).

What was the significance of Christ's lordship for Paul? In the light of what was previously said about the very material, even geographical and political, understanding of the *orbis terrarum*, it might seem that he understood the *regnum Christi* on the analogy of the Roman empire, perhaps even in a secretly or openly revolutionary sense in antithesis to Kyrios Caesar and his imperium. In that case Paul would have been, so to speak, the proclaimer of a Christ-myth in opposition to the Roman Caesar-myth. If this had been true, the beginnings and presuppositions of the idea of a Christian empire developed in the time of Constantine and afterward would derive from the theology of Paul. But this is a complete misconception of Paul. It is no accident that no emperor's name ever appears in his letters, and that in detail we learn practically nothing about the various political factors of the time—the Roman senate, the provinces of the empire, its constitution and officials, the army, economic and social conditions, political events past or present, etc. Where such matters and questions do crop up marginally, as in the well-known but unique thirteenth chapter of Romans, it is plainly and simply just the actual world in which the apostle delivered his messages and in which his churches lived their lives but which bore no religious significance; naturally it sometimes leaves its mark on the language. Nowhere, of course, does this detached attitude to the world evince either the superiority of the Stoic to the bustle of the world or the educated Greek's loathing and disgust for the grossly materialistic and

power-obsessed behavior of the Romans. Nor can we compare it
with late Jewish apocalyptic's contempt for and enmity toward the
world. The reason why for Paul Christ was Lord is that he died
for the redemption of all men, and his lordship is shown in the
fact that "he bestows his riches upon all who call upon him"
(Rom. 10:12). The gospel of Christ's lordship is thus identical
with the gospel of reconciliation (2 Cor. 5:19 ff.), and of the
righteousness of God based on faith alone (Rom. 1:4). So with
Paul there is no question of a political, imperial understanding of
the inhabited world such as the late Greeks conceived ideally and
the Romans translated into the realm of politics.

Instead, Paul understands the world primarily in terms of man,
man guilty and lost in God's sight, but who out of grace is called
to salvation in Christ. Man, lost and called to salvation, embraces
all men, Jews and Gentiles. All without distinction: this does not
mean that Paul adopted the later classical world's notion of man,
the idea of the essential and natural equality of men. What makes
all men one in Paul's view is not nature, but the fact that God is
one and has now united all by means of Christ's act of redemption
and lordship. This is to be understood in terms of history and its
end in Christ, therefore not on the basis of a general notion of the
world and mankind. Because of this, Paul significantly did not
simply abandon the idea that Israel had a special place in the
saving history. This may be seen in the phrase he uses repeatedly,
"to the Jews first and also to the Greeks." The words do not,
however, imply privileges for the Jews in the sense of a title
granted them which puts the Gentiles in an inferior position. Admittedly, Israel is distinguished because of God's promises. Yet,
these are summed up in the pledge made to Abraham, who was
justified solely on the basis of his faith and made the father of *all*
nations (Rom. 4; Gal. 3). This does not annul, but merely confirms, the fact that salvation is realized in a specific history and is
therefore also destined to lead to a historical objective. It is to this
objective that Paul has committed himself. It is this he strives for
as he goes on his missionary way, resolved to present all the
nations to God as an offering (Rom. 15:16). The apostle did not
need first to establish this *regnum Christi*. It *is* already established
by Christ's exaltation. There the word *is* so near to all that each

can believe it in his heart and confess it with his lips (Rom. 10:8
ff.). His sole task as apostle is to go on to complete God's action
and proclaim it to the ends of the earth. For all the peoples are to
be one in praising God (Rom. 15:9 ff.). He is therefore eager to go
even beyond Rome to Spain, for "they shall see who never have
been told of him, and they shall understand who have never heard
of him" (Rom. 15:21). As was said above, Romans 9–10 and
14–15 give expression to this in words taken from the Psalms and
the prophets. But for Paul these eschatological words of Scripture
had an extremely practical application; they were the source and
origin of his missionary strategy and determined the practical day-
by-day choice of routes and places, regions and peoples. One of
the special features of his theology and missionary work is that he
transposed these religious ideas and eschatological motifs into fac-
tual realization in history, and thus took as it were the word about
Christ and the promises of Scripture at their word. In detail Paul
adopted a variety of ways of doing this, and doing it consistently,
as the whole record of his work shows. Here we shall only give
three illustrations and pointers.

1. His letters reveal an unmistakable tension between the wide
sweep of his missionary plans and care for his churches (see p.
54 f.). For the sake of his great, distant objective he could never
stay long in any particular church, but had to hurry on elsewhere.
On the other hand, his responsibility for his churches more than
once compelled him to change or postpone the great plan. Thus,
his whole activity was determined by two opposed currents, one
driving him onward and another holding him back. This means
that Paul always viewed the particular in the context of the whole,
while at the same time being compelled not to lose sight of the
particular because of the whole. He relates each to the other. This
comes out especially clearly in Romans 14 and 15. Here the apostle has to put an end to a quarrel between two rival groups mutu-
ally opposed or scornful because of each's attitude to certain prescriptions about food, and he summons both parties to unity. His
way of doing so is significant. He does not discuss the subject of
the quarrel casuistically, espouse the one party's cause over the
other's, or even declare the whole thing a trifle. On the contrary,
he shows that their attitude to each other is a matter of funda-

mental importance, though not of course in the way that they imagined it to be. When a man passes this or that judgment on his brother, he arrogates a right which belongs only to God, and causes the ruin of the other for whom Christ died. And Paul goes even further. Such an attitude makes the quarrelers guilty of causing "what is good," God's salvation, to be spoken of in the world as evil (Rom. 14:15 f.). Thus, even in this apparently so trivial matter the Christians in Rome are made answerable for the world and the work of the mission. Their petty quarrel is given a universal setting. The Romans must bear in mind that Christ welcomes all men and that therefore all peoples, Jews and Gentiles, are now to be one in singing his praises (Rom. 15:6–13). If *this* is the context which Paul chooses for speaking of the final objectives of his mission, the choice is quite deliberate.

2. In these same chapters, however, as well as saying that he wishes to bring the Gentiles as an "acceptable offering" (Rom. 15:16), the apostle also speaks about the delivery of the collection to Jerusalem (see p. 41). It has been suggested, very probably correctly, that there is a connection between this and the Old Testament's idea that at the end all the nations are to come to Jerusalem, the city of God, bringing their gifts with them. Applied to the contribution this means that by their gifts for Jerusalem the Gentiles were giving themselves and, as Paul sees it, not as in the Old Testament as a sign of submission to that city, but of obedience in acknowledging the gospel (2 Cor. 9:13) and of giving themselves to the Lord (2 Cor. 8:5). Thus, the Old Testament idea, which knows nothing of a mission to the Gentiles, is given a new interpretation and transposed into a different historical situation.

3. As we learn from many passages in the New Testament and early testimony elsewhere, the subjection and homage of the cosmic powers was part of primitive Christianity's thinking about Christ's exaltation (cf. especially Col.; Eph.; 1 Tim. 3:16; Heb. 1). This derives from and corresponds to the ancient Eastern idea of the enthronement of a world ruler. While Paul, too, undoubtedly felt the concept important, it seldom appears in those letters whose authenticity is not in debate. It does occur in Philippians 2:6–11, but in a hymn not composed by Paul himself but taken

over from the hymnody of the early church. Elsewhere there are
no more than occasional allusions (1 Cor. 15:24–26). For the
main part, Paul transfers the mythological motif of Christ's victory over the cosmic powers into the realm of history. Christ's
lordship is realized in the nations' obedience to the faith. This is
the objective for which the apostle knows himself to have been
commissioned (Rom. 1:5).

VII

THE FIRST CHURCHES IN GREECE:

PHILIPPI, THESSALONICA,

AND ATHENS

The foundation of the church at Philippi introduces a new and very significant chapter in the life of Paul and the story of early Christianity, as Acts clearly shows. Luke hurries on as quickly as he can to describe what happened in Philippi, the first city of Macedonia and a Roman colony; only now does he stop to give another of his pictures on a broad canvas (Acts 16:11–40). Paul, too, attests the significance of this new stage in his work (Phil. 4:15). For knowledge of the foundation of the church we are almost completely dependent on Acts: it does, however, incorporate reliable information derived from one of the apostle's traveling companions. This is at least true of the first part of the story (Acts 16:11–15), the exact information about the route, the city, and the origin of the church. On the Sabbath, Paul and Silas went to a place of prayer outside the city frequented by the tiny Jewish community and there conversed with a few women, one of them a "worshiper of God" (the regular term for Gentile adherents of the Jewish community). She was called Lydia and was a native of Thyatira in Asia Minor and a dealer in purple goods. Lydia accepted the strangers' message, was baptized, and opened not only her heart—the text expresses it better: "the Lord opened her heart"—but her home as well. The members of her household, too, became believers. Events of no apparent moment, and quite unsensational. Yet they formed the beginning of a church which from then on was exceptionally closely attached to the apostle, the beginning, too, of Christianity in Europe. One cannot help remembering the dramatic events in the same district which, barely a century earlier, were the prelude to the founding of Augustus' empire.

Paul himself confirms that his work in Philippi soon led to conflict (1 Thess. 2:2), according to Acts, the first conflict with Roman officials. Luke gives a detailed, artistic, but legendary description of its occasion and course. It begins with a polished, dramatic account of the driving out of an evil spirit. A demon-possessed slave-girl perceives the missionaries to be messengers of the Most High God and runs after them crying aloud. Paul exorcizes the evil spirit in the name of Christ. This ruins the business of the girl's owners. They are up in arms; her soothsaying has been a good source of income. So they lay hold on the strangers and arraign them before the praetors as subverting the Roman section of the population and making unlawful Jewish propaganda. In consequence Paul and Silas are scourged and thrown into prison. This, however, is soon miraculously turned into blessing. In the well-known story in Acts 16:25–40 with its stock motifs, the prisoners are shown to be genuine, divinely commissioned messengers of salvation and proclaimers of a new spirit. Although in fetters, about midnight they sing hymns. These are overheard by the rest of the prisoners. A sudden earthquake bursts the fetters and the prison doors. Wakened, anxious about his prisoners, and already resolved on suicide, the jailor is prevented by Paul's calling to him from his cell. Converted along with his whole household, he tries to make up for the wrong done to the strangers by attending to their needs. The praetors, too, eager to be rid of the whole business, order that the prisoners be quickly set free. Paul, however, demands redress—"We are Roman citizens"—and so forces the magistrates' representatives duly to lead them out.

Lydia and the jailor may well have been actually converted. But did the clash with the Roman magistrates really end up in such a conciliatory way? In the light of 1 Thessalonians 2:2, it seems very doubtful. This speaks only of "suffering and shameful treatment," as the result of which the apostle simply plucked up courage again in Thessalonica. But in that case, it is all the more amazing that following Paul's brief and abruptly terminated stay in Philippi its handful of Christians soon grew into a self-reliant church. For this is what we find in the epistles later addressed to it.

Acts (17:1-10) is again our primary source for the origins of Paul's next church, at Thessalonica (the modern Salonica), some 100 miles west of Philippi. It was the capital city of the Roman province of Macedonia and the seat of a proconsul. In this case there is no trace of an eyewitness account, and again we may not look to the author of Acts for historical accuracy in all the details. Nevertheless, for the most important features the account furnishes a perfectly credible picture. Once more the Jewish synagogue and its numerous Gentile "worshipers of God" are shown as the starting point for the preaching of the gospel. Paul's words gain him adherents especially from among the Greeks, but they also excite jealousy on the part of the Jews, who stir up the rabble and before the city authorities charge the missionaries of "King" Jesus with being rebels against the emperor. Since the accused cannot be seized immediately, proceedings are taken against a certain Jason on the grounds that he has given Paul and his companions lodging, and together with other Christians, he is set free only after giving security. But Paul and Silas go on in haste to Berea.

Here, too, Luke was forced to work with a minimum of facts; his account is stylized and very much shortens the length of Paul's activity in Thessalonica. The apostle's own letters suggest that his work must have lasted for several months, during which he earned his own living, working hard so as not to burden anyone (1 Thess. 2:9). Again, had he not stayed some considerable time, it would be difficult to explain the forceful way in which the church brought spiritual light to all the neighboring districts as mentioned with commendation in 1 Thessalonians 1:7. This letter, written in Corinth after the hurried departure from Thessalonica and the brief stays in Berea and Athens (A.D. 50), is the earliest of Paul's letters that have come down to us and the earliest writing in the New Testament itself. It tells us of what directly preceded it and made Paul write it. From Athens Paul sent Timothy back to Thessalonica to strengthen the church in its afflictions and thereafter to report to him about it. By now Timothy had arrived back in Corinth bringing good news. The church's loyalty remained unshaken, and it stood fast in its faith—a fresh reason for Paul's eagerly looking forward to returning to Thessalonica (3:1-13). But for the time being, the letter was to add strength to the church.

The letter allows us to conclude that the church was composed of Gentile Christians (1 Thess. 1:9 f.) and that its persecutors were Gentiles. This put it in the same position as the churches in Judea persecuted by Jews (2:14-16). Paul also learned of spiritual perplexities among its members. They were perturbed by the delay in Christ's return and concerned about the fate of those who died before it: might they be excluded from the awaited salvation? Paul is at pains to allay this source of anxiety (see below, p. 222) and exhorts them to wait confidently for the Lord's coming, the times and seasons of which have not been revealed, and to lead sober and upright lives as "children of light" who belong to the Lord (4:13 ff., 5:1 ff.).

This brief letter to the Thessalonians has closer connections with the origin of the church than almost any other epistle. This is true in respect not only of time but also of subject matter, its concern being to keep the church, still young and in danger, true to its beginning. This beginning was the breakthrough to faith, the content of which is summed up in words that might almost have come from a catechism: "For they themselves report concerning us what a welcome we had among you, and how you turned to God from idols, to serve a living and true God, and to wait for his Son from heaven, whom he raised from the dead, Jesus who delivers us from the wrath to come" (1:9-10). The letter's dominant themes are thankful remembrance of the church's amazing reception of the apostle's gospel and the influence exercised by its faith now that this had increased and stood the test of persecution. The letter takes the approach of looking to the past in order to confirm the church in its hope for the coming end.

Special attention should also be paid to the fact that into the opening thanksgiving and intercession, which is unusually long, amounting to almost half the letter, Paul inserted a very emphatic apologia for his own apostolic work, a self-defense against possible suspicions that he acted from self-interested motives—making propaganda for his gospel, flattering his hearers, seeking his own glory, and even wanting to enrich himself at their expense (1 Thess. 2:3–6). The detailed way in which he insists on what to our eyes should have gone without saying for an ambassador of Christ may appear strange to the modern reader, or even embarrass him. But we come to judge it all quite differently if we see it against the background of the religious propaganda of the post-classical world. The normal heathen "missionaries," particularly in the large Hellenistic cities, actually behaved in quite a different way from Paul and employed different tactics. They were itinerant apostles and miracle-workers of the most varied persuasions, heralds of heathen gods, and dispensers of salvation, adroit and eloquent, ardent and evoking ardor, but also smart and conceited in extolling the mighty acts of their gods and fooling the masses. These people are known, some even by name, from the pages of Lucian, Philostratus, and other Hellenistic writers. There can be no doubt that they constituted dangerous rivals of the gospel and that general popular opinion expected the Christian missionaries to be able to vie with them. Indeed, the Pauline letters themselves show, as do other early Christian writings, how persuasively this current form of propaganda affected many of the representatives of the Christian mission among the masses, and how closely these preachers often approximated to this contemporary pattern. Here is the starting point if one is fully to understand the attacks on Paul's apostleship and the doubts cast on it as found in the letters to Corinth, Galatia, and Philippi, attacks, be it noted, made by Christians. Of course the situation in 1 Thessalonians is different in that it does not speak of Christian agitators against Paul. But Paul very probably had every reason for contrasting his own work with the dubious activities of the rivals just mentioned. This makes the welcome he received at Thessalonica all the more amazing to him: he came to them as a foreigner ignominiously expelled from Philippi, toiled day and night to procure for himself the necessities of life, and had no impressive proofs of his God's power to offer. Could such a preacher be the bearer of a gospel calling men to turn from idolatry to the true, living God, a gospel in the last analysis deciding the issue between life and death? What manner of God and Lord could he be who left his ambassadors to rush about so miserably without having first equipped them with all possible spectacular signs of his power?

The success of Paul's preaching in Thessalonica was therefore far from being a matter of course. But in his view this was all the greater reason for giving thanks: "That when you received the word of God which you heard from us, you accepted it not as the word of men but as what it really is, the word of God, which is at work in you believers" (1 Thess. 2:13). He was a man, and his preaching was human preaching: these were the very testimonies to the divine origin of the gospel entrusted to him.

According to Paul's own statement (1 Thess. 3:1), Athens represented just a brief stay on the way to Corinth. It was the author of Acts who worked up the memory of it into the well-known magnificent tableau (17:16–34) culminating in Paul's speech on the Areopagus (17:22–31). Brilliant like the city's brilliant name as the incarnation of the spirit of Greece, the tableau was designed to depict the meeting of the Christian gospel with the representatives of classical culture and civilization. In the process Luke also succeeds in introducing the city's *genius loci* and affords the reader a vivid impression of its intellectual and religious climate: its temples and idols as well as its philosophical schools and their audiences, a byword for curiosity, desire for culture, and eagerness to debate, but also for flippancy and self-conceit. Like Socrates, Paul begins his conversations in the agora, and like him is made short work of as wanting to introduce "foreign divinities" and as just a "picker of seeds," a babbler. Thereafter he delivers his great speech on the renowned Areopagus above the market place and facing the Acropolis which rises from it.

The speech itself is again a presentation executed with the touch of a master. Its content is a first-rate witness to post-apostolic preaching and theology, but not up to the historical Paul. Its distinctive feature is that Luke's "Paul," with an inscription on an altar to "the unknown god" as his text, takes up a number of ideas and motifs which have prototypes in post-classical philosophy of religion and criticism of religion, and which Hellenistic-Jewish theology had assimilated before Christian theology and combined with ideas taken from the Old Testament. God has no need of temple and sacrifice and cannot be contained in idols made by man. He has in fact determined the periods and boundaries of the whole cosmos, gives all men life and breath, and has ordained that men, who live and have their being in him, shall seek after him and find him. As we also find with similar Hellenistic-Jewish witnesses and frequently with the second-century Christian apologists, the speech on the Areopagus is expository, not polemical. The specifically Christian content of the speech in Acts 17 is initially kept in the background. Indeed, the idea that men are God's offspring is substantiated by a quotation from a Greek Stoic poet. Not until the very end does Jesus' name appear as the judge of the world, and with it the proclamation of judgment and a resurrection of the dead, which at once moves some to mockery.

While this final result shows us something of how the Christian gospel as understood by the real Paul flies in the face of the natural man's way of thinking, the basic ideas and leading motifs of the Areopagus speech in Acts 17 are more or less the natural knowledge of God according to reason and man's general kinship with God. Of course, the Paul of the letters, too, makes great use of the idea that God has revealed himself to all men in the things that have been made and "is seen by the eye of reason." But the conclusion he draws is that all men are guilty in God's sight (Rom. 1:20 f.). In contrast, the speech on the Areopagus speaks only of the times of ignorance that God overlooked (Acts 17:30). The speaker on the Areopagus is therefore consistent in a further difference from the real Paul that he shows—Acts 17 says nothing about Christ crucified, a stumbling block to Jews and folly to Gentiles (1 Cor. 1:23). Because of this he also speaks about man's natural kinship with God in an entirely different way: nothing, as with Paul, about the miracle of God's acceptance of man and of man's being a child of God in virtue of Christ.

The two pictures cannot be reconciled. Nor is there much to be said for the favorite expedient that in Athens Paul for once experimented with a different style of preaching and did his best to adapt his message to his audience: but it was a failure, and from then on, he all the more resolutely proclaimed the "word of the cross" without recourse to any form of discourse modeled on Greek wisdom (1 Cor. 1:18 ff.). This presumes that as preacher Paul had various possibilities open to him, and this in respect of the matter which, on his own statements, was of the very essence of his message and which, while presented in different ways in the letters, is their one and only subject, from first to last. Accordingly, today the historian or theologian is obliged to put a question mark against what is in its own way a magnificent traditional picture. If Paul actually did preach in Athens—while there is no mention of this in his letters, it is nevertheless very probable and may form the historical core of Luke's picture—we may certainly suppose that he failed there; Luke says nothing of a foundation of a church. But the reason for the failure was hardly an attempt to adapt his messages to Greek culture and philosophy. It was owing to the self-same gospel which he proclaimed alike in Athens as everywhere—the gospel of guilt and grace, God's wrath and salvation through the cross of Christ. Perhaps 1 Corinthians, written some time after his visit to Athens, preserves memories of the straits to which he was reduced there: "When I came to you, brethren, I did not come proclaiming to you the testimony of God in lofty words or wisdom. For I decided to know nothing among you except Jesus Christ and him crucified. And I was with you in weakness and in much fear and trembling; and my speech and my message were not in plausible words of wisdom, but in demonstration of the Spirit and power" (1 Cor. 2:1-4).

VIII

CORINTH

Only when we come to Corinth do we find ourselves once more on the firm ground of history. The account in Acts furnishes reliable, detailed information about which there is no dispute (18:1–17). Of course, here, too, Paul's own letters are of incomparably greater value, but they begin only from the standpoint of several years later, and then reflect an exciting, sometimes stormy, history of the apostle's experience with this church down to the end of his missionary work. On all this the Lucan account is silent. But it does give important information about the beginnings of the church there.

Corinth was a city of an entirely different character from Athens, which though long insignificant politically, was still world-famed as a center of culture. Completely destroyed in the third Punic war but rebuilt by Caesar in the first century B.C., since 27 B.C. Corinth had been the capital of the Roman province of Achaia (i.e., the central and southern parts of Greece) and the seat of the proconsul. In Paul's day it was a wealthy modern commercial city, a center of trade, favored by its situation on the narrow isthmus over which goods brought by sea were transported. It had two harbors, one on the west giving access to the Adriatic, the other on the east opening onto the Aegean. Among the motley pagan inhabitants was a considerable body of Jews.

The quite large amount of information contained in early and later classical writers—Aristotle, Strabo, Pausanias, Horace, Apuleius, etc.—as well as recent excavations afford a vivid picture of the hustle and bustle in the huge market place, the temples, theaters, and baths. But they also reveal the city's proverbial immorality. The Isthmian games held outside the gates attracted many visitors (cf. Schiller's *Kraniche des Ibicus*). This background helps us to understand both the many religious, social, and moral problems treated at length in the Corinthian letters and also what these say about the extremely proletarian character of the church (1 Cor. 1:26 ff.).

In Corinth Paul worked in a tentmaking establishment belonging to a Jew, Aquila, himself a tentmaker, and lodged in his house. Aquila and his wife Priscilla must have been Christians before being forced to leave Rome owing to the decree of Claudius (Acts 18:2). The reason for their expulsion may have been disturbances among the Jews because of the gospel: an obscure note in Suetonius' *Lives of the Caesars* (Life of Claudius 25.4) could be taken in this sense. Romans 16:4 and 1 Corinthians 16:19 show how much this couple's faith, care for the church, and spirit of self-sacrifice meant for Paul and the church not only in Corinth but also in Ephesus, to which place they soon moved. Thanks to money brought by Silas and Timothy from the churches in Macedonia, Paul was soon able to devote himself entirely to preaching and missionary work (Acts 18:5). But in Corinth, too, this led to conflicts with the Jews, forcing the apostle to transfer his work from the public synagogue to the private house of Titius Justus, a "worshiper of God." A church quickly arose, the membership being partly Jewish but largely Gentile. Paul was able to work for a year and a half here in Corinth. Then, however, the Jews made an uproar and before Gallio, the new proconsul, accused him of treasonable conduct. Gallio rejected their charges as no concern of his, a matter for the Jews themselves to settle. As a result, the excitement of the mob assembled in the market place before the proconsul's *bema* (judgment seat)—still to be seen today—turned against the Jews themselves. One of their leading officials was beaten up, and Paul and the Christians were left unmolested. After the uproar he stayed some time longer in the city, and then went on with Aquila and Priscilla to Ephesus. From there he traveled without them to Palestine and Antioch and then back to Ephesus. At this point Acts' account is brief in the extreme. It mentions only the stopping places on the journey and the districts which Paul once again passed through, the churches in Galatia and Phrygia where he had already worked. Only when Paul is back in Ephesus, where he stayed for some time, does the author of Acts again give a more detailed description.

We shall first trace the development of the church at Corinth from the time when Paul bade farewell to it (A.D. 51) down to the beginning of his extensive correspondence with it. How had it fared? 1 Corinthians, written in Ephesus (1 Cor. 16:8) probably in the spring of 54, and a short previous letter to which Paul expressly refers (5:9), give so many details about the church's past and present life that one is almost bewildered. The apostle is replying to a large number of questions put to him or commenting on news brought to him partly by word of mouth and partly by letter. This means that with the Corinthian epistles more than any others we must always bear in mind the situations and problems with which they deal. At the same time, of course, this helps us to appreciate the difficulties facing the present-day commentator: often he can only guess, infer the questions from the answers, and reconstruct the people concerned and the matters under discussion from allusion and passing mention.

Acts tells us that in the interval between Paul's departure from Corinth and the writing of 1 Corinthians, another convert had been sent from Ephesus to look after the Corinthian church. He was Apollos, a Jew from Alexandria, fervent in spirit and eloquent (Acts 18:24 ff.; 19:1). Paul, too, mentions him more than once in 1 Corinthians (1:12; 3:4 ff., 22; 4:6; 16:12) and always with commendation, though, as we are bound to presume, his birthplace and the fact that he was not a convert of Paul's own made him in many respects different from the apostle and won for him like-minded adherents who swore by him (1 Cor. 1:12). But there is not the slightest reason for saddling Apollos and his teaching with the responsibility for the cleavage in the church which soon ensued. When Paul wrote 1 Corinthians, Apollos was with him in Ephesus, and Paul himself begged him, though initially without success, to go back to Corinth along with others to help the church in its difficulties (16:12).

After Paul's departure the church in Corinth had increased amazingly and been very active, and had by no means relapsed into spiritual poverty or barrenness (1:4–9). Nevertheless, it presents a confused picture. Its wealth exposed it to great dangers, and while advising it, the apostle was also forced sharply to criticize it. The very first question, treated at length (chaps. 1–4), shows that the church had seriously departed from the foundation that Paul himself had laid. It had split up into rival groups, thus imperiling the unity of the body of Christ, the church. The slogans of these groups—"I belong to Paul, I to Apollos, I to Cephas, I to Christ" (1:12)—do not let us see the differences in detail. Significantly, however, Paul never thought of entering into discussion of their various ideas and inclinations, and of favoring one side to the exclusion of the rest. All parties, his own adherents included, showed that they had forsaken the gospel of Christ crucified and replaced it with a puffed-up, supposedly "spiritual" wisdom which was in fact very human. In the excess of spiritual experience and knowledge, the Corinthians had lost sight of Christ as the basis and foundation of their freedom and thus prostituted themselves to human "authorities" (3:21 ff.).

Whatever the composition and rival standpoints of the parties, the really dangerous thing which Paul had to tackle in 1 Corinthians was the sudden appearance in the life of the church of people filled with the spirit ("enthusiasts"). These fanatics boasted that they, and they alone, had already reached the state of "perfection" and were in possession of "spirit" and "knowledge" (2:6; 3:1 ff.; 8:1). The latter does not mean intellectual knowledge, but knowledge derived from revelation, which, as in the mystery religions and gnosticism, allowed them already to share in the powers of the divine world and liberated them from the lower world's domination, the powers of fate and death.

The emergence of this movement in the church at Corinth was anything but marginal and insignificant. Not only the movement itself, but the claims made by the "people filled with the spirit" and their behavior, had brought to a violent head a series of problems affecting the whole church and conjured up a very dan-

gerous crisis. They show to what an extent even the details of the
daily life of the young Hellenistic church were still bound up with
its pagan past and its environment, and how it was not yet in a
position to organize its life on assured valid standards derived
from the power of faith.

According to our ideas, the questions on which Paul had to
pronounce in his letter range from the utterly secular—say, menus
and shopping for food—through the way to treat company, the
permissibility of settling lawsuits in heathen courts, the regulation
of the social distinctions in the church, the correct mode of living
in view of the morals and conventions of paganism, down to the
real problems of the Christian community, its worship, faith, and
hope.

The present-day reader may be surprised to find that in Corinth
the dominant question as to the Christian's proper conduct in his
own sphere of life, his freedom and its limits, what he might do
without scruple and what was forbidden him as a Christian, often
arose in areas where one would not have expected it. A chief
reason for this is that in the post-classical world in which Christianity grew up, the spheres of the cultic and the secular in paganism ran into one another in quite a different way from what they
do today. This explains, for example, why, in 1 Corinthians 8–10
Paul was obliged to discuss at such length what was for the Corinthians anything but a captious question, whether a Christian might
buy meat offered for sale in the market place which might have
been left over from the sacrifices in one of the nearby temples and
found its way to the stalls. Or the question of whether a Christian
might have an easy mind in joining heathen friends and relatives
at a meal following a sacrifice.

To these and other everyday questions the "spirit-filled" people
had given a considered answer applicable in every case: "All
things are lawful" (1 Cor. 6:12; 10:23). They paraded their
freedom to the point of licentiousness, in contrast to the rest,
whose scruples made them uneasy about any defilement and, to
preserve their faith, forced them into a strict asceticism. The
"spirituals" indeed went further: they even used their watchword
"freedom" to justify intercourse with prostitutes, which in the
common pagan view was quite unexceptionable and permissible.

Why should the Christian have inhibitions in this matter? This sort of thing was just natural, the result of being in the world, and without effects on the "spirit-filled" person's "real self" (6:12 ff.).

Paul does not deal with the questions by way of casuistry and law. He allows freedom where it is compatible with faith. But he also says "No, and no again" where there is notorious playing fast and loose with the Christian faith, where outrage is done to moral principles accepted on all hands—even by the heathen (5:1 ff.)— and where it involves betrayal of the new life available in Christ to believers (6:1 ff., etc.).

1 Corinthians 8–10 in particular is significant in that Paul resolutely brushes aside all the "enthusiasts" ' pseudo-theological arguments to justify themselves by taking the theme of responsibility for the others before God and the world as his line of approach to the questions. This is also very apparent in the detailed treatment of the serious abuses in the Corinthians' worship. When they celebrated the Lord's Supper, they were sincerely convinced that in the sacrament they participated in the redemption wrought by Christ. Yet, at the common meal accompanying it, those better off did not bother about the poorer who came later and had nothing with them. In Paul's view this was profanation of the "body" of Christ, the church (1 Cor. 10 and 11; see below, p. 193). He takes the same means of checking the tumultuous contests of the "spirituals" who broke out into ecstatic utterance during worship, and insists on the intelligible clear word of preaching which might convince outsiders and unbelievers and win them over.

The mark of the "enthusiasts" was that they disavowed responsible obligation toward the rest and thus sought to transcend the limits of time and history imposed on the Christian life. This is the reason why the great chapter in 1 Corinthians, chapter 15, insists, against those who believe themselves to be already partaking in the life of heaven, that the resurrection of the dead lies still in the future. Bewildering as are the manifestations of extravagant enthusiasm in the Corinthian church both in number and oddness, and various as are the apostle's counterarguments and directions, the key motif, which runs through the whole letter, is perfectly obvious here. Paul erects even the supposedly trivial and isolated into a matter of principle and judges it in the light of the gospel of salvation viewed in its entirety. As guiding lines he takes the saving word concerning the Crucified One, regarded as "the foolishness of God" which negates the validity of human wisdom; the true freedom which alone opens a man's eyes to see his neighbor in love (cf. 1 Cor. 13); the voice of reason as opposed to all fanaticism; the emphatic reminder that living in time imposes limitations; and, finally, the gospel concerning the future when, and only when, the whole man will be renewed.

Paul took two ways of flinging himself into this chaos and reducing it to order. First, he sent 1 Corinthians, it being in fact, as shown by 1 Corinthians 5:9, at least his second letter to this church. Second, he sent his true helper Timothy to Corinth (4:17; 16:5 ff.). Initially both seem to have had some effect. Nevertheless, as 2 Corinthians shows, this was not lasting, and Paul had soon to pass through a renewed and much more acute phase in the struggle with opponents who led the church astray and stirred it to rebellion against the apostle himself.

We can at least sketch the causes and course of these dramatic events—that is, assuming, as we do, that the writing designated in the New Testament canon as 2 Corinthians is not a unity but a collection of several Pauline letters written to Corinth at various times and in different situations, and put together by someone later who wanted to transmit them to other churches. (For the reasons for assuming this and the literary analysis of "second" Corinthians, see Appendix II.)

The cause of this fresh struggle was that after Paul wrote 1 Corinthians, itinerant "Christian" preachers appeared on the scene. Some of the things Paul says of them (2 Cor. 3:1; 10:12 ff.; 11:4, 22 ff.) lead us to suppose that their arrival was fairly recent, and that they were outsiders who had forced their way in; they were furnished with letters of recommendation from other churches and were also vigorous in commending themselves. They, too, called themselves "apostles" and "servants of Christ" (2 Cor. 11:5, 23; 12:11) and could even make the same claim as Paul himself, which he could not dispute, to be members of the chosen people (2 Cor. 11:22). This shows that in primitive Christianity the term "apostle" was not confined to the twelve disciples; never do the Pauline letters use it in this narrower sense. The restricted usage appears first in a single passage in Matthew's Gospel (10:2); thereafter it becomes frequent particularly in Luke's writings, and since then has made history by forming part of the church's tradition. But both in Paul's view and in that of other early Christians, even opponents of his, an apostle is the missionary sent forth by the risen and exalted Christ. Only on the basis of this common ground could it and must it have led to the passionately debated question, seen in Paul's letters to Corinth and other churches, as to the legitimation of the true apostle and the distinguishing marks of the false.

We have already seen in 1 Thessalonians how urgent a question this was in the post-classical world and its religious propaganda. In Thessalonica it was of course against the miracle-workers of paganism that Paul had to defend the legitimacy of his apostleship. In Corinth there was a difference; here Christian missionaries were behaving exactly like their heathen rivals, and as a result despised Paul and his gospel and openly opposed him. In their view, he lacked all the marks of the true apostle authorized by Christ. These marks, which they claimed for themselves, did not fail to make an impression on the churches. What miraculous heavenly revelations, miracles, and convincing manifestations of the "Spirit" could he produce (2 Cor. 12:1 ff.), he weak and in appearance insignificant, dumb when it came to speaking in the Spirit and bold only when writing from a distance (2 Cor. 10:1; 11:6)?

Although, as we can see from Paul's numerous allusions and quotations, his opponents' charges did not stop short of the basest of calumniations, they are not to be brushed aside as mere caricatures. After all, these men impressed the Corinthian church as being "angels of light" and "servants of righteousness," and in Paul's own words, even if he understood them in exactly the opposite sense, they had not been without "demonstration of the Spirit and power" (1 Cor. 2:4). Accordingly, even if perforce and against his will, Paul had to compare himself with them and like a "fool" boast that he, too, if he wished, could come forward with the same excellencies as his opponents. But this he refuses to do, for his boast is precisely the weakness for which they mock him; the power of Christ is made perfect in it (2 Cor. 12:9).

He also designates as his "boast" the church moved to faith by his preaching, the hardship of his daily work, and the whole series of his sufferings and persecutions during the course of his service. For him, these were the true signs of the apostle. In contrast to his opponents' falsification of the gospel and their self-seeking exploitation of it, he claims of himself: "For we are not, like so many, peddlers of God's word; but as men of sincerity, as commissioned by God, in the sight of God we speak in Christ" (2 Cor. 2:17). He then unmasks the pretended apostles of Christ and exposes them for false apostles and servants of Satan (11:13 ff.). This all goes to show that in the battle forced upon him for the recognition of his apostolate more was at stake than his own personal honor. Elsewhere he asserts with a lofty freedom that personal friendship and enmity are matters of indifference to him: "What then? Only that in every way, whether in pretense or in truth, Christ is proclaimed" (Phil. 1:18), and rejects any overvaluing of his own person: "What is Apollos? What is Paul? Servants through whom you believed" (1 Cor. 3:5). Here, however, because of the disturbance caused by these new opponents in Corinth, in preparing the way for which the earlier "enthusiasts" had of course played no small part, as Paul defended his apostolic office he had simultaneously to fight for his gospel and his understanding of what constituted a Christian.

The series of fragments preserved in 2 Corinthians makes fairly clear the various aspects and stages of this struggle the apostle had forced upon him. He obviously heard of his opponents and their agitation right at the very start of the business, when as yet there was no danger of the church's lapsing as a body. It was most probably then that he wrote 2 Corinthians 2:14–7:4. Though he defends his apostolic office and engages in vigorous polemic against the false apostles, he still has the situation in hand and is confident of bringing the church to reason and not losing it (2 Cor. 6:11 f.; 7:4). However, his letter did not have the desired effect, and his opponents so exacerbated the situation that, contrary to his previous plans, he had to resolve to pay a brief visit to Corinth. But this proved a tremendous shock to him. He found the church in open rebellion against him, and an agitator from their midst so wronged him (2 Cor. 2:5; 7:12)—certainly not in the sense of a personal insult, but of detraction from his apostolic work in general—that he could stay no longer. With nothing achieved he returned to Ephesus, from where, in great agitation, "out of much affliction and anguish of heart and with many tears" (2 Cor. 2:4), he sent a further letter to Corinth, the most important fragments of which, it has long been assumed, are preserved in 2 Corinthians 10–13. Here Paul fights in sheer despair, and not only with the misguided leaders but with the church which because of their agitation had almost given up hope (2 Cor. 11:20 f.). Along with this distressed and moving letter Paul sent Titus to the rebel church, charging him with the heavy task of putting it to rights. He himself cut short his stay in Asia Minor and in great anxiety went the length of Macedonia to meet Titus, from whom he received news of the success of his mission. The two things— the apostle's letter, terribly sharp yet written from the bottom of his heart, and the sending of his fellow worker—had most certainly not been without effect. The church came to see reason and repented, and now wanted to prove this to its apostle in every possible way. On his side Paul was now able to write an enthusiastic letter of reconciliation to the Corinthians and urged them to forgive, as he himself had done long ago, even the member at whose hands he had suffered intolerable mortification. Large parts of this letter are contained in 2 Corinthians 1:1–2:14 and 7:5–16, and they give us a review of the events here described. Following the prospect held out in 2 Corinthians 13:1 and 9:3 f., Paul traveled from Macedonia to Corinth for the third and last time and found the church at peace. At least in Romans, written during this visit, there is no idea of battles and storms.

IX

EPHESUS

The exciting story of Paul's dealings with Corinth is merely one episode in his several years' work in Ephesus. Acts—and this we may accept—reckons his stay there as lasting two to three years (19:8–10; 20:31). However, it yields no connected and historically reliable accounts. Apart from some pieces of serviceable local information, the author obviously had at his disposal only a small amount of material of very uneven quality, one or two episodes and anecdotes with the stamp of legend on them, and perhaps here and there some hazy recollections. Artist as Luke was, he was able to make this the basis of a fairly concise and impressive picture of the renowned metropolis of Asia Minor and, as with Athens, capture something of the *genius loci* (Acts 19). The point of it all is to glorify the great missionary who with his gospel reaches *all* the inhabitants of Asia, Jews and Greeks. His capacity for working miracles is so immense that handkerchiefs and aprons which he handled are laid on the sick, who are healed forthwith and delivered from evil spirits. Jewish exorcists attempt the same things in the name of Jesus, but fail miserably. Paul has such enormous success that a number of people renounce magic arts, make a public profession of error, and publicly burn their magical books—well known in the ancient world—to the enormous value of 50,000 silver denarii. Paul even overcomes the sect of John the Baptist and wins disciples of his for the true faith. Indeed, his preaching shatters the worship of Artemis, whose shrine at Ephesus was reckoned to be one of the seven wonders of the world. This ruins the business of a pagan named Demetrius, a manufacturer of objects of religious devotion and souvenirs. He incites his employees, and these, shouting "Great is Artemis of the Ephesians," set the people in an uproar. There is a gathering in the theater, and a Jew tries in vain to deal with the shouting mob until, finally, it is quietened by a representative of the magistrates. Paul and those with him, he says, are neither sacrilegious nor blasphemers of the gods. If Demetrius and his colleagues have any cause for complaint, it should be duly decided in court, but the people should not run the risk of incurring the charge of rioting before the proconsul. Paul himself is not involved in all the commotion and is able to go forth from the city victorious, paganism shattered and Jewry powerless.

For historical purposes, not very much can be done with this description of Paul's work in Ephesus. Some of the information here may be useful, and the author must have had good reason for treating Ephesus as a highlight in the apostle's missionary work. Nevertheless, reliable sources are hard to discover in Acts 19, and the descriptions of the various scenes down to the triumphal picture of the riot are so typical of Luke's narrative skill and of his view of history that we need to be very cautious indeed in using them.

This is reinforced by the fact that the apostle's own letters written during his stay in Ephesus, and sometimes bearing directly or indirectly on that city, give a very different picture, of which Acts has preserved practically nothing. Scattered data not in each case absolutely verifiable, and therefore to be carefully scrutinized, are most questionable. In general they are not connected accounts, but rather as it were various incidents, people, and situations flashed on the screen. Nevertheless, in many cases their clarity makes up for their lack of exact contexts. In addition to the apostle's correspondence with Corinth (see above), Galatians, Philippians, and Philemon were almost certainly written at Corinth, and in addition an unexpected piece of evidence, the long, very detailed list of greetings at the end of Romans (chap.

16). This, it is generally agreed, is not its correct place; it must have been written at or about the same time as Romans, that is, shortly after Paul left Ephesus, and originally formed part of a letter to the church there now lost (see Appendixes I and II).

Review of Romans reveals not only how intensively Paul must have applied himself to his work in Ephesus, but also how greatly the church increased. We also learn of the active help he received from many of its members. The list contains no fewer than twenty-six names, and as has often been said, this is rather odd to come upon in Romans, for Paul had no firsthand knowledge of the church there. But it fits in all the better with Ephesus, particularly as the list is headed by the names of Aquila and Priscilla, who are to be looked for there (see above, p. 68), and of one Epaenetus, designated as the "first-fruits of Asia," the first convert to Christianity in the province. The often very individualized descriptions added to various names reveal Paul's exact remembrance of the people he mentions and their relatives, houses, churches, and servants, tell of close personal relationships with them, or expressly speak in high terms of his own and the whole church's debt to them as witnesses approved by trial, and of their courage and readiness to sacrifice and suffer—men and women, Jewish and Gentile Christians, bond and free alike.

The letter to Philippi, written while Paul was imprisoned in Ephesus, is a further witness to this growth in the church at Ephesus and its activity: his arrest did not reduce it to a timid silence. On the contrary, it became all the bolder and more imperturbable in its witness. There had not been sincerity in every case, as Philippians 1:14–17 says expressly. He can probably vouch for it, Paul says, with the majority of the church members attached to their apostle: they were well aware of what was required of them at just this very moment because of his imprisonment and the gospel for which he suffered. So, he goes on, they leaped into the breach, and just at the time when he personally was condemned to be silent, the gospel has been unexpectedly advanced (Phil. 1:12 ff.). All the same, he also makes no secret that there were some of this majority who, through hatred, envy, and evil disposition toward himself, thought that the stage was now set for them and did all they could in a shady way to depress the prisoner: they tried to let him see that things were getting along quite nicely without him. The nature of this vexatious course of action is no longer known. There is no reason for imagining false teachers; they were most probably personal opponents and rivals. Otherwise, Paul could hardly have brushed aside as of so little consequence the question whether their motives were good or questionable with the words: "What then? Only that in every way, whether in pretense or in truth, Christ is proclaimed; and in that I rejoice" (Phil. 1:18).

As Luke says, in Ephesus, as elsewhere, Paul certainly began by preaching in the synagogue. But after a few months, opposition from the Jews forced him to move, like the itinerant preachers of his day, to the lecture room of a certain Tyrannus (Acts 19:8–10). We may suppose that in the course of the preceding conflicts he had as a heretic more than once suffered the synagogue's punishment of thirty-nine lashes mentioned in 2 Corinthians 11:24. In the "painful letter" written in Ephesus he lists this among many other sufferings and adversities endured during the course of his apostolic work—be it noted, in a bitter, ironic answer to the vaunted mighty acts of the "spirituals" in Corinth—which constitute the "achievements" that he reckons as his glory. Of all these vicissitudes, Acts only mentions the imprisonment in Philippi and says nothing at all of troubles in Ephesus. While we cannot know for certain how many of the sufferings and perils enumerated in 2 Corinthians 11, some of them almost fatal, fell within the period of his several years' stay in that city, it must have been the scene of a considerable part of them. There were also clashes with the Roman authorities, of which the brief reference in 1 Corinthians 15:32 to "fighting with wild beasts at Ephesus," metaphorical and not to be taken literally, is irrefutable evidence. Elsewhere, too—in the appalling catalogue of sufferings in 2 Corinthians 11:22–33—we read of a host of terrible afflictions and hardships which he had to endure at the hands of Jews and Gentiles: beatings, stonings, and imprisonment. We are also told of hardships and dangers in journeys by land and sea, many of which again certainly fell within his time in Ephesus: dangers in the city and in the wilderness, dangers in crossing rivers, threats and attacks by robbers, dangers by shipwreck when

he was a day and a night adrift on the sea; hunger and thirst, cold
and lack of clothing. In addition, wherever he was staying, daily
pressure on him and the cares of all his churches: "Who is weak,
and I am not weak? Who is made to fall, and I am not indignant?
If I must boast, I will boast of the things that show my weakness.
The God and Father of the Lord Jesus, he who is blessed for ever,
knows that I do not lie" (2 Cor. 11:29–31).

From all this we can infer not only the immense amount of
work with which Paul had to cope in the growing church in
Ephesus, but also the scale of missionary and pastoral activity in
the surrounding country and in his churches elsewhere, and this is
confirmed by the letters he wrote from Ephesus, in which he came
to grips with their questions and disorders, strengthening, encour-
aging, and teaching them but also giving warnings and contending
with them.

As well as the Corinthian letters, Galatians deserves particular
consideration here. (For its occasion and content see above, p.
32). As can readily be seen, the seductive teaching of the
"Judaizing" intruders brought the Gentile communities to the
verge of defection because the Judaizers not only operated with
genuinely Jewish conceptions (circumcision, Law, tradition, etc.),
but also combined these with ideas about cosmic powers derived
from astral worship, to which, they said, even the true Christian
should pay due respect. In consequence, their interest was focused
not so much on the moral Law of the Old Testament and Judaism
as on magical-ritual ways of behavior and the observance of holy
seasons and days (Gal. 4:10), which allowed the devotees to
participate in "redemption." Accordingly, Galatians flatly asserts,
against Paul's opponents and those who so promptly espoused
their cause in the confidence of being members of the chosen
people Israel, that any man who received circumcision was under
obligation to keep the whole Law (Gal. 5:3). Hence in this very
context of opposition to those who regarded themselves as "filled
with the Spirit" (Gal. 6:1, 3 f., 7), with a view to putting them to
shame, Paul contrasts their mutual "biting" and devouring with
the Law, which can be fulfilled only in the command to "love your
neighbor as yourself" (Gal. 5:13 ff.). He contrasts the "works of

the flesh" and "the fruits of the Spirit" (Gal. 5:19 ff.) and gives the admonition: "If we live by the Spirit, let us also walk by the Spirit" (Gal. 5:25). At the same time he also raises the urgent question of how those "who formerly did not know God but were in bondage to other gods that are no gods, can, now that they have come to know God, or rather to be known of [elected by] him, 'turn back' again to the weak and beggarly elemental spirits" (Gal. 4:8 f.; note the irony).

Galatians, which in attacking "Judaistic" legalism proclaims the true freedom based on Christ, consequently contains more exhortation, admonition, and summons to obey the "law of Christ" (Gal. 6:2) than any other letter, and to quite a remarkable degree —a third of the whole letter.

Paul regarded the Galatian heresy as a deadly peril to his own gospel of justification by faith alone and not by doing the works of the Law. Accordingly, justification forms the central topic, being given an exhaustive treatment unparalleled except in Romans. It is proclaimed on every page with an anger inflamed by the defection of his churches, yet still seeking to win them back.

The letter to the Philippians—or, to be more accurate, this little collection, like 2 Corinthians, of several successive letters composed to meet various different situations—must have been written shortly after Galatians. We have no idea of the reason for Paul's imprisonment: Acts never even mentions it. There may possibly have been public conflicts with the imperial authorities, a memory of which, though turned to very different account, is preserved in Acts 19 in the Demetrius incident. However that may be, when Paul wrote Philippians he was in the custody of the praetorian guard stationed in the palace of the Roman governor (Phil. 1:13), due to make his defense and have sentence passed upon him. He is obviously in no very strict custody. He is not completely cut off from the outside world, is able to have some intercourse with his guards—they have even become aware of the special situation of this prisoner for Christ's sake—gets regular news of the church at Philippi, and is able to receive visitors and gifts, to send fellow workers, and to write letters (Phil. 1:12 ff.; 2:19 ff.). This is also confirmed by the only private letter of his which we have, the note to Philemon written during the same imprisonment. It was sent to a well-to-do Christian in Colossae, a city in the upper valley of the Lycus, to which the gospel was carried by Christians from Ephesus. The recipient and the church which met in his house were personally known to the apostle, and Paul numbers Philemon as one of his fellow workers. The occasion of the letter was as follows. A slave called Onesimus ran away from Philemon and took refuge with Paul in prison. There he became a Christian. Paul therefore writes to Philemon and requests that the fugitive, who before his flight had obviously been stealing from his master, be taken back again; not, however, as a "good for nothing" ("useless," R.S.V.) (a pun on the name Onesimus), but as someone who will be "useful," and not as a slave, but as a beloved brother, as a son and substitute for Paul himself. The letter shows the apostle dealing with the social question of slavery, not programmatically and on principle, but "in Christ," with whom the distinctions between master and servant, bond and free, no longer exist (Gal. 3:28; 1 Cor. 7:22 f.); to these the church is indifferent. In addition, the letter's ingenuousness affords a unique glimpse into Paul's warmth of heart, his ability to identify himself to the full with others, his skill as a pastor, yes, and his sense of humor, which did not desert him even in prison.

The numerous means of communication still open to Paul make clear that, at the time of writing his letters to Philippi and Philemon, his lot was still tolerable. This should not, however, blind us to the fact that his imprisonment lasted several weeks and months (cf. Phil. 2:25–30) and that, in particular, he was in grave danger. For as he himself says (Phil. 1:20 ff.), there was absolutely no certainty as to the result of his arrest and his impending trial—he might be acquitted, but equally he might be sentenced to death. His remarks in 2 Corinthians 1:8 ff. show that he did in fact again escape death and continue to serve his churches. But it was a very near thing. He had despaired of life and had only God to thank for his deliverance. He apparently left Ephesus soon after his imprisonment, in a very different fashion, of course, from what Acts would have us believe.

Fragmentary though it is, all the information scattered throughout the letters combines to produce a very clear picture of the apostle's activities in Ephesus. It confirms that the city and its church became a center for the mission in Asia Minor: here, too, Paul did not spare himself in caring for the churches he had previously founded.

There is, however, one further respect in which Ephesus was of great importance in the life of Paul. As we have already seen, it was either during his stay there or in the months immediately following it that he wrote all the letters which may be described as the classics of his gospel and theology—his correspondence with Corinth, Galatians, and Philippians, and, last but not least, Romans, written shortly after his departure from the church at Ephesus (cf. chap. 10). This most certainly does not imply that the Pauline theology really took shape only in these years. The great theme of his preaching, salvation in Christ for all, Jews and Greeks alike, and in consequence the end of the Law as the means of salvation, was given him at the moment of his conversion, and it remained unchanged until his death. But his great letters show his amazing skill in setting out the various aspects of his gospel in sharp outline and in all their nuances. No small part of this was due to his conflicts with the Jews and, in particular, with the "Christian" false teachers and evil influences in his churches—at Corinth, Galatia, and Philippi (cf. Phil. 3). Yet, important as these were for the final expression of the central ideas in his theology, we must never be misled into thinking that the basic features in his theology were simply a counterblast to one or another of the false teachers. This would be giving heresy more than its due. Nothing then could be more perverse than any attempt to track down opponents' provocations and slogans on every page, and so to underestimate the powers inherent in the gospel itself, as well as men's very diverse experiences of faith and the situations in which faith held fast—these, from first to last, are the formative factors in the Pauline theology. At the same time, the conflicts and troubles which it had to overcome, heresies outside and birth pangs within, form an element which cannot be ignored.

But it was not a lone battle that Paul fought. These same letters, either written in Ephesus or containing references to his stay there, show that he had the support of a number of fellow workers, named or unknown, who were loyal members of the church there, or on whom in certain cases he could rely even for difficult tasks in churches outside Ephesus. Over and over again he testifies to their zeal in service as missionaries, their readiness to help, and the effectiveness of their work; not only Timothy and Titus, but Aquila and Priscilla, Apollos, Epaphras, Epaphroditus, and many others. This would be inconceivable had not Paul been, with some of them at least, in constant communication on matters of theology, in which he was the pupil as well as the teacher. While the sources do not go into this, it is a necessary inference supported by analogy from the practice of contemporary pagan itinerant teachers in their teaching and schools, and certainly also from that of the Hellenistic synagogue.

In addition, the post-Pauline age furnishes us with authoritative evidence for the formation of a kind of Pauline school and a tradition of his teaching preserved by his disciples, though in many respects they developed it. These are responsible especially for the letters to the Colossians and Ephesians. Though themselves post-Pauline, these letters are nevertheless well acquainted with Paul's thought, were even given out in his name, and clearly indicate that their place of composition was Ephesus. The three letters to Timothy and Titus likewise purport to be Pauline: they, too, are keenly interested in preserving his teaching. Their place of origin cannot be exactly determined. But, wherever it was, they imply both the authority of the apostle himself and the work and standing of his closest disciples in Asia Minor.

This is not to suggest, however, that for a considerable period Paul, his fellow workers, and his disciples had an undisputed sway in Asia Minor and other districts. The heresy that Paul himself combated in more places than one doubtless very soon became a serious danger in Ephesus as well. It is no accident that the list of greetings in Romans 16, in all probability destined for Ephesus, as well as Philippians 3 and other letters, contains urgent admonitions to be on guard against the seductions of the false teachers (Rom. 16:17–20). Elsewhere, too, the sources show that the influence of the Pauline gospel lasted only a short time as the determinative factor in Asia Minor. The Book of Revelation, conceived in the last decade of the first century in a very different spirit, has not a word to say about Paul.

X

ROMANS AS

PAUL'S TESTAMENT

It may be thought odd that at this point in the story of Paul's life we should insert a section on the greatest of his main letters. Its expressly theological and didactic character suggests that the appropriate place to discuss it is the connected presentation of Pauline theology to be given in the third part of this book. Its basic ideas will in fact be fully reviewed there. Here our prime concern with Romans is for the historical and biographical evidence it contains. In the process, of course, the indissoluble connection between the apostle's experience and his theology may again come to view.

At first sight it would seem that this letter had the least to offer for purposes of biography. There is a surprising absence of what is elsewhere characteristic of Paul's correspondence and lends it the charm of historical realism, direct references to an actual historical situation, either that of the church addressed or Paul's own. A very little, though it has much to tell us, is found more or less tucked away toward the end of the letter. But by and large, Romans does not follow the pattern of the rest of Paul's letters.

As has often been emphasized, no small part of the peculiarity of Romans is a result of its being written to a church founded not by Paul himself but by persons unknown: neither party therefore knew the other. The oldest witness to the existence of this church, destined to play such a role in church history, is Romans itself, and this makes the letter particularly important. Yet it has practically nothing to tell about the church's beginnings and earliest history. The one thing we can see for certain is that at the time when the letter was written the majority, if not all, of the members were Gentile Christians (Rom. 1:5 f., 13; 11:13; 15:15 ff.). The extent of Paul's knowledge of the church at Rome when he wrote to it is hard to say. He had certainly learned something about it from his intimate friends Aquila and Priscilla, who must have been members before their departure from Italy. His information about its existing state seems to have been meager. Nothing is said of news brought to him and its bearers, whom it is his habit to mention by name. Similarly, there is nothing about fellow workers of his own or opponents in Rome (Rom. 16), and almost nothing about events, questions, and emergencies in the community. Chapters 14 and 15 are the one exception. Here the apostle strives to settle a dispute between "weak" members who observed certain ritual regulations in the matter of food and the "strong" who on that account despised them but themselves were unfavorably judged by the other party. Otherwise, the letter is composed of lengthy informative expositions of leading themes in the Pauline gospel without a firm reference to the Roman church itself. It was therefore long regarded as a kind of *Summa* of the Pauline theology.

Rightly recognizing that none of the other letters is a theological treatise, a kind of "dogmatics," recent expositions have gone to all possible lengths to try to relate Romans, too, to a specific situation. The reason, it is said, for the element of teaching in the letter is that the apostle intended to introduce himself and his gospel to this church which he did not know personally, and to gain its support for his planned further missionary work in the west. This need not be rejected out of hand, though nothing is expressly said of such an intention. Yet, as an explanation of the occasion, character, and purpose of the letter, it is not adequate. Again, an attempt has been made to show that Romans does in fact reveal a fairly exact knowledge of the state of the Roman church. It, too, it is alleged, was under threats from Judaizing and "spiritual" false teachers. It was to counter the former that the letter says so much about Paul's teaching on justification by faith, while the emphatic ethical admonitions were drawn up with the libertarian fanatics in view. It is further maintained that what characterized the situation in Rome was the mutual rivalry between Jewish and Gentile Christians, as corroborated by chapters 14 and 15. Those who explain the letter as directed toward an existent situation rely in particular on the not inconsiderable amount of dialogue and polemic in Romans. But we should be cautious in what we infer from it. As no other, this letter shows a plethora of examples taken from the vivid teaching form called the "diatribe" (see above). This was cultivated in Hellenistic Judaism, and Paul used it frequently. The diatribe gave no ordered development of particular topics. Instead, there are questions and counterquestions, captious objections to, or even angry rebuttals of, what has just been said. Then, by means of answers, further questions, and insistence on first principles, appeal is made to the objector's own reason. Thus, we see attempts at assertion on the part of the sophistic unprincipled intellect which, instead of admitting defeat by the apostle's arguments, tries to make capital for itself: the Jew who with his casuistry makes a play of being logically consistent in order to show Paul's teaching on Law and justification to be absurd or blasphemous (e.g., Rom. 3:1–9), or who, mistakenly taking predestination as determinism, infers that in God's eyes he is without guilt (Rom. 9:19 ff.). But Paul also uses the same method with the Gentile Christian who conceitedly exalts himself above the unbelieving, rejected Jewish nation (Rom. 11:19 ff.). In each case, however, the objections arise out of the subject matter, or rather out of a misunderstanding of it, and not an actual historical situation. To take such passages as indications of distinct groups or individuals is therefore not to the point. Unlike other letters, Romans has nothing to say about Judaizers or representatives of "enthusiasm," that is to say, Christian false teachers.

On the other hand, from Romans 15:14–33, we can be absolutely sure that Paul's purpose in writing his letter to Rome was to announce the long-planned visit he had always had to put off, and to prepare for his further work in the west. At the time of writing he had already left Ephesus and was looking on his work in the

eastern half of the empire as terminated (Rom. 15:19). He would
have liked to start right away on the journey to Rome and to
Spain beyond (15:24, 28), but he had first to bring to Jerusalem
the collection taken in his churches in Asia Minor, Macedonia,
and Greece. Only when this was successfully accomplished would
he be free for his further work (15:25 ff.). This information
enables us to date Romans exactly: during Paul's final three
months' stay in Greece, probably in Corinth, mentioned in Acts
20:2 f. (winter 55/56? See chronological table).

The concluding words of Paul's news of himself in Romans 15
tell us that he viewed the journey to Jerusalem with some anxiety.
He was afraid of persecution from the Jews, and was even more
anxious as to whether the mother church would receive him and
the collection at all. He therefore asks the Christians in Rome to
strive together with him in prayer that he may be delivered from
the dangers to which he is exposed and not be rejected by the
"saints" in Jerusalem (15:30–32).

The reason for his apprehensions about the Jews is easy to see.
He had not been unknown to them, either. He was known as a
former Pharisee and a fanatical persecutor of the church in its
early days, and since then, plenty had been heard of his proclamation of Christ without the Law to the Gentile. Accordingly, the
Jews certainly, and the strictly orthodox Jewish-Christians too,
regarded him as a renegade, a destroyer of the Law, and God's
enemy. As we learn from Acts 20:3, danger was already ahead at
the time of his departure from Corinth. Jews, possibly pilgrims for
Passover, who also wanted to make the journey and take the same
ship, contrived a plot against him. In consequence, with a few
companions he went by land through Macedonia. He stayed a
short time in Philippi and Troas, and only then, in Asia Minor,
took ship (Acts 20:14).

This raises the question as to why Paul actually undertook this
journey. After all, it once more held him back from setting out for
Rome and the west as he was so eager to do. His resolve is far
from self-evident. Even in 1 Corinthians he was of the mind to tell
the church's delegates to go without him: he would lead them only
if there were special need of this (1 Cor. 16:3 f.). Why then this
present resolve to join in the journey, when the very fact of his

presence could spell danger not only for all but also for the collection itself? There cannot be the faintest doubt that the churches' representatives were men who could be trusted—Acts actually names them, even if it does not connect them with the collection (20:4)—and as Gentile Christians they were unknown to the Jews and therefore not in danger of arousing the Jews' hatred to the same extent as Paul.

However, we must also consider the question from the angle of the mother church in Jerusalem. How could the collection possibly have been a bone of contention between Paul and this church? The matter had been resolved at the apostolic assembly (Gal. 2:10). Paul, before starting on the journey, had been tremendously active in gathering the money (cf. especially 2 Cor. 8 and 9) and had met with success, the number of the delegates showing that a goodly sum had been collected. There is only one possible answer. As was pointed out in the discussion of the apostolic assembly, Paul and his churches never viewed the collection as merely a means of relieving distress. Nor is it to be taken as evidence that Gentile Christians had to acquiesce in the "governmental" claim to leadership made by the Jerusalem mother church. It was intended to demonstrate the unity of the church— Jews and Gentiles were one. But would the Jerusalem church, led by the orthodox Jewish-Christian James, the brother of the Lord, be ready to accept a demonstration of this kind and join in it? This was very problematical.

This is where we have to seek the reasons for Paul's resolve to go in person. The purpose of the collection and its ultimate fortune were intimately connected with a question already hotly debated at the apostolic assembly—was the gospel without the Law proclaimed by Paul among the Gentiles a true gospel? But this involved a further question—were Gentiles, too, members of full and unconditional standing in the body of Christ? This is what now made Paul feel compelled once more to appear in Jerusalem in what was an extremely critical situation. His resolve shows the extent to which the unity of the church (which hardly anyone had done more to jeopardize) had continued as the unwavering objective of his endeavors, not simply as a dogma demanded by theology, but as something to be striven for and realized here and now.

It was worth risking everything for, the gospel itself excepted. Quite obviously Paul's purpose in seeking to meet the people in Jerusalem and in interesting the Romans, whom he did not know, in his labors was that he might enter the new stage of his mission in the west not, as it were, as a buccaneer, but with the full agreement of the mother church. At the time of the apostolic assembly the reasons for Paul's going to Jerusalem were the truth of his gospel, his freedom to proclaim it, and the unity of the church. Now, and for the last time, they bring him there once more.

Only with this view of the situation can we fully understand both the theme and the character of Romans. What it in fact turns on are the questions connected with the apostle's theology and its aims, which he was shortly to have to justify and stand up for in Jerusalem, and which were also to continue as the basis of his coming mission to the Gentiles: justification by faith alone, for Gentiles as well as Jews (chaps. 1–4), deliverance through Christ and his Spirit from the destructive powers of sin, death, and the Law (chaps. 5–8), the destiny of Israel, God's chosen people, the hardening of its heart and eventual salvation (chaps. 9–11), and, finally, the apostle's further mission to the ends of the earth and the praise of God on the lips of all the nations (chap. 15).

As we have already seen, the idea that the theme of Romans and Paul's reflections on it were dictated by conditions obtaining in the church at Rome gets us nowhere. However, this may suggest a more important consideration. A surprisingly large number of the topics listed in Romans appear in the letters written three or four years before it, Galatians, Philippians, and Corinthians. Many of the ideas and motifs and, often, even the actual way of putting them are here taken up again. The following list, which could easily be extended, gives some particularly striking examples:

justification not by works of the Law, but by faith alone (Gal. 3–4; Phil. 3; cf. in particular Rom. 1–4; 9:30–10:4);
Abraham justified on the basis of his faith, and the father of many nations (Gal. 3; Rom. 4);

Adam, head and embodiment of the lost, and Christ, head of a
new humanity (1 Cor. 15:22 ff., 45 ff.; Rom. 5:12 ff.);
the wretchedness of the carnal man subject to Law, sin, and
death (Rom. 7:7-25—briefly already in 1 Cor. 15:56 f.);
the sending of the Son of God in the flesh for our redemption
and the testimony of the Spirit in the believers' hearts that
they are children of God (Gal. 4:4 ff.; Rom. 8);
the church as the body of Christ, though its members are
diverse (the gifts of the Spirit; cf. 1 Cor. 12 and Rom.
12:4 ff.);
also, the way of treating the issue in Romans 14 and 15 is
obviously the same as the leitmotiv in 1 Corinthians 8–10 (the
question of food offered to idols): Paul does not side with
either of the parties, but makes the whole thing turn on
consideration for the other man's conscience and on faith and
responsibility for him.

Such a recapitulation is without parallel in the whole of the
Pauline corpus. It is in no sense a matter of mere repetition or
even quotation. Though the subjects are the same, there is a
marked difference in treatment between Romans and the earlier
letters. In the latter, the topics occur almost without exception in
the context of discussion of positions and attitudes taken up by
opponents and imperiling the church, in particular those represented by Judaizers or gnostic "enthusiasts." Romans, on the
other hand, bears no trace of these earlier contestants. Nor is
there any sense of urgency. In concreteness, even, Romans 14 and
15 fall far short of 1 Corinthians 8–10. For example, not a word
is said about the consequences of the party strife in Rome, although it must have broken out in connection with the meals in
common and called in question table fellowship at the Lord's
Supper.

Though in Romans, too, Paul opposes others, these are not
sections and opponents in a particular church. Instead, his exposition of salvation as he understands it and his justification of his
gospel for the Gentiles is made through a contrast with the Jews'
understanding of it and their claim to possess it exclusively. Now,
in Romans, the ideas and motifs enumerated are not found, as in

the earlier letters, in disconnection and as bearing on this or that actual situation. They are reasoned out, substantiated more fully and in detail, and given universal application. It is no accident that the words "all," "each," or negatively "no one," are more frequent in Romans than in any other letter. What Paul had previously said is now not only set down systematically, but also oriented to the world-wide horizons of his gospel and mission, and gives, for the first time, his mature and considered thought.

In the list of the passages in Romans with parallels in the earlier letters we omitted Romans 9–11, the dilemma raised for the gospel by Israel, her election, her hardening of her heart, and her salvation. This has in fact no parallel in the Pauline letters, and constitutes a unique subject of Romans. But even the reason for this is easy to see: Paul was on the point of discussions with the Jerusalem church. His approach to this extremely difficult question is just what we should expect of him. In chapters 1–8 he expounds his teaching on justification. Now (chaps. 9–11) he relates it to Israel's history and at the same time tries to explain the paradox of his gospel—first to the Gentiles and then back again to the people originally chosen. Thus, these chapters, too, bear on the crucial question to be thrashed out in Jerusalem.

This helps us to understand why, in its own way, Romans, too, is throughout polemical. However, in it Paul's opponent is not this or that section in a particular church, but the Jews and their understanding of salvation, which was still extremely influential in the early Jewish-Christian church, particularly in Jerusalem. Paul's polemic is therefore not mere shadow-boxing. In a way the Jew symbolizes man in his highest potentialities; he represents the "religious man" whom the Law tells what God requires of him, who appeals to the special statute granted him in the plan of salvation, and who refuses to admit that he has failed to measure up to God's claim on him and is in consequence abandoned to sin and death. As contrasted with this man who prides himself on being religious, Paul expounds his message, for Jew and Gentile alike, about the Law, and about grace proffered to all who believe in Christ. Paul's man, however, is not somewhere outside among the unbelievers; he is, in disguise, a Jewish Christian too, of Jerusalem and elsewhere, and equally, as Romans 11 shows, a Gentile Chris-

tian who now boasts to the Jews that he is saved, and not they.
Thus the apostle can never speak of the gospel without at the
same time speaking of this man who is lost, but who through
Christ has now a new life opened up for him.

This all shows that Romans, too, is not a general theological
treatise. Like all the rest of Paul's letters, it bears on actual events.
But the form which it takes and its exceptional character are not
due to the specific situation obtaining in the church at Rome, with
which Paul will *soon* have to deal and to which he now speaks,
but arises from his own *past* experiences with his churches. At the
same time, however, he has in mind the impending important
meeting with the mother church in Jerusalem and the rounding off
of his work as apostle.

This is the reason why in this, the greatest of his letters, Paul
says so much about himself, about his conversion and call, his life
and work, the gospel which he proclaimed and the battles he had
had to fight, and also about his theology. Romans not only tells us
the questions and experiences which made Paul a Christian, the
servant of Christ, and the apostle to the Gentiles. It also shows
how he worked at his ideas and their effects upon himself.

Historically, Romans may be described as Paul's testament. But
that does not mean that he composed it deliberately as a last
declaration of his will before his death. Actually, he was still
hoping to be able to start on his great missionary work in the west,
though he could not gloss over his anxiety that the conflicts to be
expected in Jerusalem might frustrate his plans. In actual fact, if
not literally, the letter is his last will and testament. Paul's anxieties were all too well grounded.

XI

PAUL'S FINAL JOURNEY

TO JERUSALEM, IMPRISONMENT,

AND DEATH

Romans tells us of the storms brewing at the time of Paul's departure for Jerusalem. This, as it turned out, was the beginning of the end. From this point on, we are dependent on Acts. Yet here, too, statements in the letters help us to be critical of Luke's picture and to supplement it. For his account of the journey to Jerusalem at least, Luke had a reliable source at his disposal, a brief list of stopping places. But, as so often happens in Acts, other passages are in sharp contrast—elaborate tableaux and speeches obviously of the author's own invention based on the general picture of Paul which he has inserted into the itinerary. As was said above, no suspicion attaches to the statements regarding the ominous circumstances at the start which made Paul and some of his companions take the land route via Macedonia to Asia Minor. This is also true of the list of his fellow travelers with their names and home churches (Acts 20:3 ff.). It is, of course, surprising that Luke does not mention, either, what we know from Paul himself, the purpose of the journey, the bringing of the collection to Jerusalem, or the fact that his companions were official delegates of the churches in the Pauline mission sphere in the eastern part of the empire, Asia Minor, Macedonia, and Greece. Acts' remarkable silence here has to be kept in mind for the rest of Luke's story as well, a gap in his picture which we can with confidence fill in from the letters.

The itinerary of the journey by land and the sea voyage essentially gave details only of the route, the islands along the coast by which they passed, and the places where they landed. Luke supplements it by means of several typical tableaux on a broad canvas, the narrative style of which itself sets them in relief to their bare context. One of them, obviously reminiscent of stories about Elijah and Elisha (1 Kings 17; 2 Kings 4), is a dramatic legend of Paul's bringing back to life a young man who, overcome by sleep during the apostle's sermon at Troas, fell down through a window (Acts 20:7-12). But in particular, the author of Acts makes a very significant tableau out of Paul's stay in Miletus, about 30 miles south of Ephesus. The apostle obviously had to avoid Ephesus because of the danger threatening him there (cf. 2 Cor. 1:8 f.), so Paul has the "elders" of Ephesus come to him at Miletus. After prophesying the martyrdom awaiting him, he takes moving farewell of them in a great speech (Acts 20:17-38). While a masterpiece, this speech, too, is of no direct service for the life of Paul. The constitution of the churches assumed here— government by elders—is historically suspect: Paul's own letters say nothing of this. In particular, however, the style and content of the speech are characteristic of a later day. It looks back over the whole of the apostle's work and forward to his death, and also announces the advent of the false teachers who after his departure are to ravage the church like ravening wolves. For a protection Paul gives the elders the legacy of his pure doctrine and constitutes them "overseers" (episcopi) of the flock of Christ appointed by the Holy Spirit. This is not the later Catholic "succession." At the same time, the idea set out here of an authoritative tradition in conjunction with the ecclesiastical office, whose holders are as such also bearers of the Spirit, is typical of the views later developed in the church, especially in the battle against heresy. Much the same views are also found in the Deutero-Pauline Pastorals, in the form of an exemplar for elders and bishops.

The account of the further route of the journey initially bears the marks of a worked-up itinerary. Via Cos and Rhodes the company sailed along the coast of Asia Minor to Patara. There they changed ship and voyaged in the open sea via Crete to Syria, where they stayed a week with Christians while the ship unloaded. Then, via Ptolemais (the modern Haifa) they went on to Caesarea. Here they were guests of the missionary Philip, known to us also from Acts 6 and 8, whence they went upcountry to Jerusalem. A further reason makes this information of value—it tells us of otherwise unknown early Christian churches in Palestine on the Mediterranean. There can be no doubt that it is based on sound tradition in spite of having been artistically shaped by Luke in order to throw Paul's imminent end into even bolder relief and to delineate him as the man of God, deaf to all warnings and ready to suffer and die. There is no presumption in Acts, as had been Paul's own hope (Rom. 15:30 ff.), that his fortunes in Jerusalem might still take a turn for the better.

The account of the events in Jerusalem up to the time of Paul's arrest evidence old and trustworthy tradition. Of course they become clear only when connected with the matter of which we know from Paul but on which Acts is completely silent, the bringing of the collection, which was the purpose of the whole journey. Luke mentions the collection only once and incidentally, later on in a speech of Paul's to the governor after his arrest (Acts 24:17), but he understands it as an alms to demonstrate Paul's loyalty to the Jewish nation; he had therefore no knowledge of its true purpose.

According to the account given in Acts, which is perfectly trustworthy, James at once advised Paul to counter the Jewish-Christian church's lack of confidence in him as destroyer of the Law by undertaking a ritual act in the temple. He was to take part in a ceremony of discharging the vows of four "Nazirites" without means to bear the expense of the requisite sacrifices. What is in question is a Jewish custom based on the Old Testament, in terms of which religious men devoted themselves to the service of Yahweh, originally (it would seem) for life, but later also for a stated period: they put themselves under strict obligation to drink no wine, to not cut their hair, and to avoid all manner of ritual defilement (e.g., contact with a dead body). At the end of the time a sacrifice took place in the temple in the presence of a priest. In later Judaism, bearing the cost of this for others was regarded as a particularly meritorious good work.

It has been surmised—rightly—that the reason for James' suggestion was the difficulties felt by the Jerusalem church about acceptance of the collection. The plan was intended to reduce its lack of confidence in Paul and at the same time make clear to non-Christian Jews that the mother church did not welcome an enemy of the Law and of God with open arms for the sake of money. This lets us understand the motive actuating James. But it also explains why Paul agreed with the proposed compromise. By taking part in this private ceremony involving only himself personally, he in no way prejudiced himself, nor did he call in question his teaching that the Law was no longer a way of salvation. The fact that for him obedience to the Jewish ritual law was no longer obligatory did not in the least imply his prohibition of any observance of the Law among Jews. Thus, in actual fact, by being ready to act as he did, Paul was only exercising the freedom which, as he himself said, laid down his lines of conduct as a missionary in other respects as well: "To the Jews I became as a Jew, in order to win Jews; to those under the law I became as one under the law—though not being myself under the law—that I might win those under the law. To those outside the law I became as one outside the law—not being without law toward God but [bound] under the law of Christ—that I might win those outside the law. . . . I have become all things to all men, that I might by all means save some" (1 Cor. 9:20–22). There are therefore no reasons for suspecting Paul's conduct here described in Acts as part of Luke's effort to portray him as the exemplary Jew.

This meant, of course, failure to demonstrate the unity of Jewish and Gentile members in the church, the unity which Paul wanted to effect so as to make it easier for the collection to be received in the Jerusalem church. We do not know what was the fate of the collection, taken by the Gentile Christians for the mother church and organized so energetically on both the practical and the theological level. As we have already seen, Luke takes no notice of it. But he is probably to be believed when he says that Paul's participation in the cultic ceremony involving him in more

45046

than a week's purifications in the temple, since he came from
heathen soil, turned out disastrously for him. Diaspora Jews who
knew him encountered him there, falsely accused him of bringing
into the temple a non-Jew among his companions, Trophimus
from Ephesus. Because of this alleged sacrilege, which even the
Romans noted, the Jews imposed the death penalty for it, stirring
up such a commotion against him that the Roman guard inter-
vened and, to save him from being lynched by the Jewish rabble,
took him into protective custody (Acts 21:27-36). After that
Paul was a prisoner of the Romans; and very soon it ceased to be
protective custody: he was a prisoner on trial.

We can reconstruct the course of events up to the time of Paul's
arrest with some measure of probability, especially if we take
account of the background as seen in the letters. For what follows,
the length of time he was prisoner in Jerusalem and Caesarea, his
conveyance to Rome, and his death, we have only scraps of information, and these uncertain. We must not be led astray by
Acts, which for this final period, too, offers a long series of detailed, dramatic descriptions, both tableaux and, in particular,
several great speeches. They are the work of the author. Luke
certainly had no official record or other reliable traditions at his
disposal. But this made him all the more eager to paint imposing
pictures, using the great prisoner's bearing to show his contempo-
raries the relationship between Judaism and Christianity, and at
the same time to defend Christianity at the bar of pagan Roman
law courts against the charge of being a danger to the state. Luke
shows a fair knowledge of the Judaism of the time, the unrest of
the land, the Roman army of occupation, and the procurators in
office. Nevertheless, this does not amount to proof of the historicity of the proceedings in detail. Rather, he only does his best
to fill in the vacuum, the interval during which Paul had to wait
for final sentence to be passed upon him. Luke does what he can
to sketch and impress on the reader the principal figures and
groups concerned. Once this is recognized as the leading motif in
his representation, all idea can be abandoned of scrutinizing the
record in detail with a view to determining what is possible and
conceivable, and what improbable and impossible.

One of Luke's tableaux is the speech to the people which the

Roman officer allows Paul, just saved from the infuriated crowd, to make standing on the temple steps, another great description of his conversion on the way to Damascus (Acts 22:1–21), later to be repeated for a third time before King Agrippa (26:1–32), and also a defense of the mission to the Gentiles as willed by God. The examination, too, before the council (22:30–23:11), which shows Paul standing before the same court as his master Christ once did, is designed to show only one thing, that the prisoner is a believing Pharisee, whose innocence even the orthodox Jews must acknowledge in spite of themselves in contrast to the Sadducees, who will have nothing to do with a resurrection of the dead. From scene to scene the picture of the Jews as Paul's mortal enemies becomes more and more pronounced and furious. In contrast, the representatives of the Roman government play the part of protectors: the officer of the guard, the commander of the garrison in Jerusalem who had Paul taken with a strong escort of cavalry and infantry to the procurator's residence at Caesarea to save him from the Jews, and finally the procurator Felix himself and his successor Porcius Festus. These two last are not simply set in crude contrast to the Jews as white against black. The first expresses interest in Paul's teaching about Christ, though of course he grows uneasy when the prisoner's words about justice and self-control and the future judgment come home to him; he puts Paul off to a more convenient time in the hope of a bribe (24:24 ff.). The other, Festus, is constrained to attest Paul's innocence to King Agrippa (25:25 ff.). At the crucial moment, however, he dismisses Paul's words as madness, and ventures on no decision, not wanting to incur the displeasure of the Jews. Agrippa, too, confesses that he is near to becoming a believer on the strength of Paul's account of his conversion (26:28). Meanwhile, however, Paul himself has blocked the way to acquittal and release. For when Festus proposes that he should be tried in Jerusalem, he appeals to the emperor's tribunal in Rome (25:9–11).

Even if these accounts, as a whole and in many of their details, do not withstand the test of historical criticism, they nevertheless undoubtedly rest upon at least some important historical facts. Among them are certainly these: Paul's being taken to Caesarea after his arrest by the Romans; the two years' postponement of his trial (Acts 24:27; the figure must have a foundation in fact), from the governorship of Felix into the time of his successor Festus; and finally, though lack of proper sources means uncertainty as to the processes at law, the prisoner's appeal to the emperor's court at Rome. In consequence of this, Paul's case was not decided within the judicature of the Roman governor of Palestine, but he was sent along with others to the capital as a prisoner awaiting trial: at all events, however, this did not mean as a political rebel found guilty of high treason.

This eventful voyage in a party commanded by a Roman centurion, Julius, from Caesarea is given a detailed and highly dramatic description (Acts 27:1–44). It starts on a merchant ship sailing to Asia Minor along the coast as far as Myra in Lycia. There the travelers take another ship, one from Alexandria bound for Italy. Contrary winds make the going slow as far as Crete, and from then on, things become more and more dangerous, because it is now the time of the autumn and winter gales. In the Adriatic, between Crete and Malta, the ship runs into a violent storm. With great difficulty they try to save their lives by throwing the cargo overboard, drift helplessly for fourteen days, and finally suffer shipwreck off Malta; all escape to land, but with the utmost difficulty, either swimming or on planks. Acts describes the whole thing with tremendous realism and actually shows an amazing command of specialized knowledge of seamanship. But what the narrator really wanted to effect was to show Paul, amid the hurry-scurry of sailors and soldiers, the owner, the captain, and the centurion, as the man of God unique in wisdom and confidence, even in skill in seamanship, and, in particular, in strength of faith and power to work miracles, the man to whom in the end they all owe their lives.

This magnificent description was long reckoned as a particularly reliable historical account that could have come only from an eyewitness: that is to say, it was supposed that Luke himself took part in the voyage, especially since, like one or two earlier passages, the whole section is drafted in the first person plural. Recent research, however, has shaken this confidence. Even the word "we" is in no sense certain evidence of an eyewitness account. In actual fact it is frequently found as an effective trick of style, this, too, in other accounts in ancient literature of perils at sea. Moreover, in the long twenty-seventh chapter of Acts Paul appears in just a few incidents, miracles, and speeches—when he is the typically Lucan Paul—as the ever undaunted deliverer to whom God gives counsel. All of these can quite easily be detached from the rest of the narrative, especially since they are clearly different in character and often manifestly out of keeping with it.

We can be pretty certain, then, that for his dramatic account of the voyage from Palestine to Italy, the author of Acts drew on a piece of writing already in existence and originally having nothing to do with Paul, and filled it out after the fashion employed elsewhere in secular Hellenistic travels and short stories. Voyages and their perils are part of such stock in trade.

Surprisingly enough, during the last stage of the journey, from Malta onward, Paul no longer seems to be a prisoner; in Puteoli (on the gulf of Naples) he stays a week as the guest of Christian brethren: just outside Rome, at the Forum of Appius and Three Taverns on the Via Appia, Christians from Rome receive him with all ceremony: and in the capital he is allowed to stay in quarters of his own choosing, though he does have a soldier to guard him. With practically no mention now of his being a prisoner, he quite openly and unhindered receives visits from the leading Jews and preaches to them the gospel of the kingdom of God and of Jesus attested by the Law and the prophets. Some are convinced; others persist in unbelief. "And he lived there two whole years at his own expense, and welcomed all who came to him, preaching the kingdom of God and teaching about the Lord Jesus Christ quite openly and unhindered" (Acts 28:30 f.). So ends the account, and the whole book itself.

Historically speaking, such an untroubled end is perfectly inconceivable, and in any case it is odd that although Luke knew how Paul's case continued and of his death by violence (Acts 20:22 ff.; 21:10 ff.), he gives not even a hint about them. All the same, we can see why Acts ends as it does if we remember what it promised at its start, to describe how the gospel spread from Jerusalem and Judea via Samaria to the ends of the earth (1:8). The author may therefore take farewell of the great missionary to the Gentiles as the latter now rounds off his work in Rome. This also makes the silence about Paul's martyrdom perfectly understandable. Acts was written not only to edify the faithful, but to give a defense of Christianity to the pagan empire. The picture of Paul was intended to let the empire have an impression of the greatness of the Christian religion and its peaceable inclinations, and to make Rome resolve on the same prudent and fair attitude toward the church as had already been shown by many representatives of its government in the course of their dealings with Paul.

Paul's actual end will have been quite different. In Rome, too, he would in fact have been detained for some time under not too strict conditions—the two years mentioned in Acts 28:30 are perfectly possible—but he could scarcely have preached in the unhindered way in which Luke pictures him doing. Therefore, his protracted case will at last have been taken up again, and he himself probably suffered martyrdom at the hands of Nero, likely in the beginning of the sixties. As we saw, this was assumed in Acts itself (cf. also 2 Tim. 4:6 ff.). Leaving aside later legendary descriptions of his end in the Acts of Paul (end of second century), the earliest testimony to his martyrdom, a reliable one, is to be found in 1 Clement, written in Rome in the nineties of the first century: "Let us set before our eyes the good apostles. Peter, who because of unrighteous jealousy suffered not one nor two but many trials, and having given his testimony went to the glorious place which was his due. Because of jealousy and strife Paul showed the way to win the prize of endurance. Seven times he was in bonds, he was driven away as an exile, he was a herald both in East and West, he won the noble glory of his faith. He taught righteousness to all the world, and when he had reached the limit of the West he gave his testimony before rulers, and thus passed from the world and was taken up into the Holy Place, the greatest example of endurance" (1 Clem. 5:4–7).

Here, too, the picture of the two martyr apostles and their death is a vague one. It dissolves into rhetorical panegyric modeled on the classical motif of the truly wise man battling in the arena of the spirit. It contains very little about Paul himself and gives no details of his death. But this throws no doubt on the fact that his death was a violent one. The only question is whether, as 1 Clement assumes, he was able to realize his plan of evangelizing in the farthest west, that is, in Spain. Combining Clement with Acts, this would involve his release from a first imprisonment in Rome, and the suffering of a second some time after. But this is quite unlikely, nor can it be proved, as is often attempted, from the Pastorals. In reality, the information in 1 Clement may be a deduction from Romans 15:24 f., 28, Clement believing that Paul's hope was in fact realized.

Thus, Paul's fortunes in his last years are obscure. This is all the more reason, now that we have given the story of his life, for going back to the firm historical foundation of his own letters and inquiring into what was more important in Paul's eyes than his own life and death.

PART
TWO
GOSPEL
AND
THEOLOGY

I

PAUL AND THE GOSPEL

OF THE PRIMITIVE CHURCH

Anyone who endeavors to understand Paul, whether he believes himself to be familiar with the Christian faith or is antagonistic to it, must accept that he will find no gradual approaches or easy ways. Nowhere in the apostle's letters are there passages of apologetic or preliminary instruction which, as it were, take the reader by the hand; everywhere Paul plunges at once *in medias res*. There is something to be said for the charge often explicitly or at least implicitly brought against him, that his theology makes unreasonable demands. It would seem quite impossible to make oneself at home in Paul's alien world of thought or feel oneself addressed personally. As a result, some people turn their back on him and leave him alone, others he challenges and profoundly disturbs.

Paul's theology is not a repetition of Jesus' preaching of the coming of God's kingdom. Jesus Christ himself and the salvation based on and made available through his death on the cross, his resurrection, and his exaltation as Lord form the subject of Paul's proclamation. This means that a complete shift came about which the modern mind finds hard to understand and often deplores. It has exposed the apostle to the reproach of having falsified Christianity and thus of having rather shadily become its real "founder." Paul, it is alleged, turned Jesus' good tidings into a gospel of redemption replete with Jewish ideas and Hellenistic mythologies.

It is true that between the preaching of the historical Jesus and the gospel not only of Paul but of the post-Easter church in general there is a fundamental difference: only the unthinking can miss it. It can also be detected in the strange diversity of the writings in the New Testament. Oversimplifying and schematizing, the Gospels tell of Jesus' preaching and work on earth up to the time of his death and resurrection. But with the post-Easter witnesses and the apostolic preaching (Epistles, Acts, Revelation), the death and resurrection are the basis and starting point. The proclaimer has become the subject of proclamation, his life has assumed dimensions that it did not have on earth, and for Jesus' own words are substituted the word about Jesus Christ, his death, resurrection, and second coming at the end of the world. Even if it is improper to make Paul the first to have been responsible for this process, his letters do confront us very sharply with this astonishing shift. Never does he make the slightest effort to expound the teaching of the historical Jesus. Nowhere does he speak of the rabbi from Nazareth, the prophet and miracle-worker who ate with tax collectors and sinners, or of his Sermon on the Mount, his parables of the kingdom of God, and his encounters with Pharisees and scribes. His letters do not even mention the Lord's Prayer. When he quotes the Lord's words (1 Cor. 7:10 f.; 9:14; 11:23; 1 Thess. 4:15), they are taken from very diverse areas and are not really representative. Certainly, some of his advice to his churches is obviously dictated by memory of words of Jesus, which shows that either because of his encounters with Christians or after his conversion he must have acquired a certain amount of knowledge of the tradition about Jesus. But this, slight as it is and mentioned in passing, does not alter the total picture. The Jesus of history is apparently dismissed. Paul himself never met him. And, as he himself asserts in debates with opponents who obviously based their case on the fact that they had known Jesus, even if Paul did know Christ from a human point of view, he regarded him thus no longer (2 Cor. 5:16). This whole body of facts is not to be minimized. There is therefore no point in trying, from apologetic motives, somehow to get around an impossibility. Down to this very day the critics have always had a keener eye for this basic problem not only in the theology of Paul but also in primitive Christianity's faith and thinking *in toto* than have had the larger body of scholars who aim too soon at building bridges, even if these critics have generally felt the shift to be odd and a distortion.

Comparative religion shows that no small part of the shift was due to apocalyptic thought current in later Judaism and to mythological concepts in the post-classical world which surrounded Judaism. Nonetheless, there is no sound basis for the common idea that this led to the replacing of the historical Jesus by a mythical divine being, and that this world was written off as hopeless. For it fails to see that this very shift proclaims a very definite understanding of the facts concerning Jesus, one radically different, of course, from that current in the modern world. In our categories, this state of affairs can be conveyed only by means of a number of negations. For the historian the frontier separating yesterday from today and tomorrow is in principle closed. Significantly, he speaks of "what has passed," defines its place, and sets it in an already existent body of coordinates of time and space, though he does take into consideration the influence of past on present and future. And if he transmutes the abiding part of past history and its great figures into conceptual, moral, and religious truths divorced from time and history, this is no accident.

Primitive Christianity's understanding of the facts connected with Christ cannot be comprised within the limits of such a mode of thought. It is based on Jesus' resurrection. However much and in however many and varied ways the witnesses of the post-Easter church understand and convey this as an event in space and time, in reality it signifies more: the resurrection is God's mighty and sovereign penetration of the man-made fabric of earthly history, the breaking in of the eschaton, God's epiphany, and, in consequence, the establishment of the facts concerning Christ as saving events. Thus, for primitive Christian faith Jesus is no longer a figure who appeared in the course of past history, a man like other men, belonging to his own time and a victim of circumstances, impressive or even exemplary in the way he endured his fate even in failure. Instead, his person, significance, and bearing on present and future are set within the horizons of those dealings of God with the world and man which made all the difference for time and eternity. This significance of Jesus for salvation finds expression in the numerous honorific titles applied to him by the primitive Christian witnesses and confessions, titles deriving from the Old Testament and Judaism or from Hellenistic Greek: Messiah, Christ, Kyrios, Son of Man, Son of God, and so on. Quite obviously, none of them is intended to oust the historical Jesus. There is no abandoning of him. Nor has his name, Jesus, become something fortuitous, devoid of significance, or even replaceable. Instead, all these honorific titles say that he, and he alone, is and brings God's salvation to the world. Thus, what initially looked like an abandonment of history in fact expresses in an all-embracing way the understanding of the events connected uniquely with him as saving event, in which those addressed in the word of preaching and who respond in faith form part and into which they are incorporated.

This does not do away with the difference between Jesus' own preaching and the gospel of the post-Easter church. Rather, the facts of the case demand and promote the difference. This difference consists in the fact that while Jesus in his own words and actions proclaimed the dawning of the kingdom of God, for the post-Easter gospel—without prejudice to all the changing and even opposed concepts of it—through Jesus' death, resurrection, and exaltation, the turning point of the ages, the establishment of salvation, and God's advent and lordship have become actual fact. This is the reason why Jesus' disciples could not simply cherish his heritage and the teaching he bequeathed to them, as did the pupils of the rabbis and philosophers, and hand on his words. The gospel of the primitive church (the kerygma) was bound to change and make Jesus himself its subject matter, because faith had to be kept with God's word, act, and dealings with men in him.

In the oldest churches and especially in the early Hellenistic ones this kerygma already found various expressions which, while often not expressly marked, are generally fairly easy to recognize because of form and content, in formulas of belief, confessions, hymns, liturgical turns of phrase, and prayers used in worship, as well as in scribal reflections, i.e., reflections based on exegesis of the Old Testament; thus from an early date the kerygma took firm shape in fixed and well-defined traditions.

This process, initially oral, in the history of primitive Christian faith and thought has left a great variety of expressions in the New Testament and extracanonical writings. We have already spoken of the large element of struggle right from the very start for the correct understanding of what came about in Christ. Paul's conversion and call were preceded by the irruption of the "Hellenists" into the Jerusalem mother church, the first persecutions, the beginnings of the Christian mission, and the spread of the faith among Greek-speaking Gentiles. But the deep-seated differences in the understanding of Judaism and the Law, Christ, and salvation raised the question of the right understanding of the Old Testament and of God's dealings with his chosen people and the world there recorded and now fulfilled in Christ. Nevertheless, in spite of all advance and development, and of the difference in the world to which the gospel had now to be preached in a different language, however much the earliest church's well-defined traditions were combined with other ways of expressing the faith, they were never simply jettisoned.

To this Paul's letters are a living testimony. It is not simply that he, too, regularly bases his arguments on the Old Testament Scriptures. Quite as often he uses the kerygmatic traditions of the church before him and of his own day. He expressly reminds the Corinthians of what he himself received and handed down, of what became the bedrock of their faith (1 Cor. 15:3 ff.; cf. also 11:23 ff.). The form and wording of other passages either show us or at least allow us to presume such traditional formulas. They occur especially in terse, summary statements of a confessional nature about Christ's death and rising again, in the context of teaching on baptism and the Lord's Supper, in directions concerning proper conduct and worship, in interpretations of the Old Testament, and also in turns of phrase in prayers and blessings. In his own view, Paul was one in a succession and accordingly—especially in the matter of his Christology, although it does have its own special features—we should not raise the question of any particular "originality" he may possess. This shows that the nature of the apostle's theology is completely misconceived when he himself is viewed as a "religious genius" and his theology regarded simply as the direct result of his own personal and individual experiences.

Therefore, while not minimizing what is unique in his faith and thought, we have at the same time to keep asking ourselves what he owes to the tradition of Judaism in which he grew up, to that of the primitive church, as well as to his disciples and fellow workers, and even his opponents.

In this sense Paul's gospel and theology are exposition and development of the primitive Christian kerygma. Still, for all the high value he puts on the tradition, sometimes impressing its actual wording on the church (1 Cor. 15:2), he never treats it as an authoritatively established sacred text. Its authority is not formal—that is to say, it does not depend on the mere fact of its having been transmitted—but rests on its subject matter as proclaimed in the *Evangelium*.

Paul considered himself set apart, called and sent forth in order to preach (Rom. 1:1; Gal. 1:15). For him performance of this apostolic service meant as little telling the story of Jesus as it did giving teaching about God and the things of God or imparting religious truths and experiences. Instead, it meant announcing and bringing home to people what God did for the world in Christ to deliver and save it, and proclaiming who were called to lay hold on faith. The term "preaching," hackneyed and to a large extent devoid of meaning, makes it difficult to see the original reference to the work done by a herald (keryx, kerygma, keryssein). It is God himself who speaks and acts through his ambassadors (2 Cor. 5:20). Thus, using a metaphor familiar to the ancient world for the epiphany of a divine being, Paul can say of his service in the gospel, "to one a fragrance from death to death, to the other a fragrance from life to life" (2 Cor. 2:16).

As to what comes about in the gospel, Paul sounds the note of apocalyptic: "in it the righteousness of God is revealed [*apocalyptetai*]" (Rom. 1:17)—events with tremendous dimensions, having the force of finality, the end of the present world and the beginning of a new era. It is as if the dazzling light of the last day flashes forth in this message. But this does not mean, as one might expect, that Paul is announcing an event still lying in the future and, as in the Jewish apocalypses, painting imaginative pictures of the destruction of the world and the splendors of the new aeon. He speaks of a present event, an event already here in the gospel itself. The gospel, then, does not simply inform about future salvation and destruction: God's saving advent has already been given effect in it. The gospel itself *is* "the power of God for salvation to everyone who has faith" (Rom. 1:16). This does not fit into any apocalyptic pattern. What Jewish and primitive Christian apocalyptic looked for in the near or remote future is already present reality in the gospel!

These words from the beginning of Romans are a signpost pointing to the unmistakably personal and peculiar factor in Paul's understanding of the primitive kerygma. This consists above all else in the fact that Paul expounds and develops the *Christian gospel as the gospel of justification by faith alone*. So far from this doctrine's being common property in the primitive church, it is a specifically Pauline creation. Nowhere else is faith in Christ, which links Paul with the rest of early Christianity, advanced, considered, and worked out along this line and expressed by these means. It not only made deadly enemies of the Jews: it also brought Paul into discredit with the Christians of his day and made him an outsider. And yet, just because of it, he became the apostle to the Gentiles, and not only caused the severance of Christianity from Judaism but also gave the unity of the church composed of Jews and Gentiles its first real theological basis.

To our present-day way of looking at things, of course, Paul's doctrine of justification seems at first to be a barrier against the wide spread of his gospel. For its dominant place in his theology manifestly reflects, first, that at his initial encounter with the gospel he was an orthodox Jew, and second, that, as was to be expected, as the world of the former Pharisee's experience and thought, the Law remained a determining factor in his understanding of salvation even when he became a Christian and an apostle. His way of thinking in the categories of Law, righteousness, and justification does indeed mark Paul out as a former practicing Jew, and from the Jewish standpoint a renegade one. It is therefore easy to see in this very doctrine no more than the quite specific time and situation which brought the Pauline theology to birth and so enforced limitations upon it.

In addition, modern research has sometimes questioned the dictum that justification forms the heart of Paul's theology, and

has advanced the view that it is no more than a special and
unimportant "anti-Jewish" polemic which is never—as happened
with the sixteenth-century reformers—to be overestimated and
made into the keystone (W. Wrede). Similarly, Albert Schweitzer
called it "a side crater within the main crater" of Paul's mysticism
of redemption.

This thesis can find support in the fact that the doctrine is set
forth expressly and in detail only in Galatians, Romans, and
Philippians, and that other important subjects and ideas in the
Pauline theology are not directly derivable from it. In the Corinthian epistles it is entirely in the background. Yet it is not absent,
and these are the very epistles which show that when Paul set out
his gospel in Corinth, where he had to adapt his language to
Gentile Christians, he did so in just the same way as to churches
who were better acquainted with Jewish tradition. Above all else,
however, his last great letter, Romans, shows how much the basic
theme in his theology with which he began remained the same to
the end.

Thus, it would be wrong to assign to the Pauline doctrine of
justification only a limited importance within the context of a
polemic directed by circumstances. In reality it was in the matter
of, and by means of, this very doctrine that the apostle broke root
and branch with the traditions of Judaism and Jewish Christianity,
and at the same time made the "Law" as well as what is called
"God's righteousness" valid for all. Thus, the thesis should be put
the other way around: his whole preaching, even when it says
nothing expressly about justification, can be properly understood
only when taken in closest connection with that doctrine and related to it.

That Paul's doctrine of justification is to be regarded not as
theological theorizing on the primitive gospel, but as its proper
development and exposition, is shown by Romans, where, within a
few verses of each other, he gives two very different comprehensive summaries of the subject matter of the gospel. First, in a
credo that he inherited, he confesses Christ as "descended from
David according to the flesh and designated Son of God in power
according to the Spirit of holiness by his resurrection from the
dead" (Rom. 1:3 f.). The second is undoubtedly Paul's own

composition: "For I am not ashamed of the gospel: it is the power of God for salvation to every one who has faith, to the Jew first and also to the Greek. For in it the righteousness of God is revealed through faith for faith; as it is written, 'He who through faith is righteous shall live'" (Rom. 1:16–17). At first sight it would appear that the two had scarcely anything in common. In actual fact, the old creed was never drawn up with justification by faith alone in view, nor did it occur to anyone before or after Paul to give it such a frame of reference. Yet there can be no doubt that Paul thought of both alike as giving a full statement of the content of the gospel. Thus, in no sense is the first, the inherited one (Rom. 1:3 f.), to be regarded as a mark of reverence to the tradition and evidence of his own orthodoxy before he goes on to announce his own, the proper, gospel, which Romans expounds throughout. Rather, to show that Christological statements cannot be separated from soteriological ones or, better expressed, to set out the gospel concerning Christ *as* a gospel of justification, and vice versa, is a decisive concern of his whole theology. The ways taken by his faith and thought, and his ponderings and revolutionary insights into the tradition he took over and kept, causing his own theology to forge ahead into entirely new fields of thought— of this there is certainly little in the opening chapter of Romans (cf. Appendix III). However, the chapter does announce the questions which the book is to go on to consider at greater length.

First, however, let us refer to an important characteristic of Paul's theology which is generally too little attended to. Paul's theology resists all efforts to reproduce it as a rounded-off system carefully arranged under headings, as it were, a *Summa theologiae*. Much erudite exposition proceeds as if there were no such difficulty and diligently arranges into groups the apostle's various statements about God, Christ, man, redemption, the sacraments, the church, last things, and so on. Indeed, the more it succeeds in turning the scattered data into an aggregate classified under heads, the more respect it is accorded. But that is quite wrong, even if the requisite reference is given for each proposition. The plain fact is that Paul's statements are just not found thus arranged as fundamental doctrines of dogmatics: practically always they are in fragmentation and invariably woven in with others. Admittedly, no exposition, the present one included, can avoid ordering Paul's trains of thought under leading topics and problems. Yet this is makeshift; in actual fact, everything is intertwined.

This is anything but a matter of course. Hellenistic Jewish theology and to no less a degree that of early Christianity—especially the so-called apologists of the second century onward—most certainly developed a form of systematics and a well-defined range of stock themes of religious teaching, e.g., the doctrine of the one true God as opposed to the many gods of the heathen; God's power as creator and his goodness; his dealings with Israel; mankind's great errors and infatuations; the fulfillment in Christ of the Old Testament prophecies of salvation; the call to repentance, and, finally, the divine judgment of the righteous and the wicked.

Although references for many of these themes can also be found in Paul and show these traditions as their background, still, it is quite significant that he hardly ever deals with them in this order, and that all attempts to systematize them fail. The real reason for this is not fortuitous, the changing situation from letter to letter (though this certainly often does play a part). Nor, we may be certain, was it due to the apostle's versatile and assuredly ardent temperament. Absolutely nothing can be said for the antithesis that Paul was "practical" and not a "theorizer," let alone the blunt verdict that the gift of systematic thought was withheld from him. His letters are evidence of the very reverse: no other of early Christianity's apostles or writers had this capacity to the same degree; he displayed it in amazing measure even when he was battling at his hardest. The real reason why his mode of thought is cast in a different mold is the peculiar nature and subject matter of his theology. The latter is so much dominated by the *encounter between God, man, and the world* that, strictly speaking, no room is left for these "stock themes." Everything is entwined in the general theme of judgment and grace. This encounter is the thing to which Paul holds fast in all his thinking. But this means that every statement about God, Christ, Spirit, Law, judgment, and salvation is at the same time one about man in his world, the old lost man and the new one set free by God.

To lead man as confronted by God to self-understanding and thus to reflection on his situation and life in the world: this is the steadfast aim of the apostle's preaching and theology, even when these processes reveal to man unredeemed the enigma and contradiction of his being (Rom. 7:7 ff.), and to the believer that we know only in part (1 Cor. 13:12 ff.). Thus, contrary to a common assertion, reason and faith are certainly not in fundamental and hopeless opposition. Instead, whether he speaks of unredeemed man or of redeemed, Paul makes vigorous use of reason, understanding, and conscience, and argues with the aim of persuading and convincing. It follows, therefore, that he renounces a form of discourse cultivated in the world around him and employed by numerous Christian preachers of his day, apodictic revelation. To be sure, with Paul the "word of the cross" is sharply opposed to the "wisdom of this world" (1 Cor. 1:18 ff.; 2:6 ff.). But the latter stands for a particular mode of human thinking and understanding with a special subject matter, which was shipwrecked on the wisdom of God and cast man down into his lost state. This however confirms rather than alters the fact that this same man to whom liberating grace is available must also understand the paradox of God's act in the cross of Christ. It is in this sense that Paul calls his gospel a weapon "to destroy strongholds as we destroy arguments and every proud obstacle to the knowledge of God" (2 Cor. 10:3 ff.).

II

LOST: MAN AND THE WORLD

THE LAW

What does the gospel mean by the revelation of "the righteousness of God from faith to faith" (Rom. 1:17)? Paul can give an answer only by way of introducing and expounding the subject of mankind's and the world's lost state in the sight of God. According to Romans, this is manifested in the fact that all whom God summons to life, that is, all who are subject to God's law, are "without excuse" and objects of his wrath (1:18–21). For Paul this drastic verdict is no general, timeless truth wrested from the Law itself as he reflected upon it and pondered over it in despair. Instead, it was possible and attainable only on the basis of the Christian salvation. When the gospel light shines forth, man's existence under the Law is shown as lostness before God. Using a metaphor from the Old Testament, Paul says that through Christ the veil of the Law is removed (2 Cor. 3:14).

This in itself reveals a significant characteristic of Paul's concept of the Law, one which differentiates him from other representatives of primitive Christianity. To say what is perfectly correct historically, that the meaning of Christ's coming was deducible from the Law, was, in his view, not enough. Put in such general terms, the statement was true for all the first Christian converts from Judaism. For Paul, however—and for him alone —it also held true when put the other way around: only in the light of Christ could one deduce the status of the Law. The Law was the basis of, and the limitation put upon, the unredeemed existence of all men, both Jew and Gentile.

Wherever Paul discusses the problem of Law, it is always in this perspective of gospel. The priority is important to keep in mind. It is to be seen right at the beginning of Romans: the long passage dealing with the revelation of God's wrath is preceded by 1:17, the keynote of the epistle, with its reference to the gospel. The tidings of salvation proclaim the eschatological world-transforming "Now" (Rom. 3:21, etc.) toward which God has been moving and which signifies the standpoint that alone gives meaning to all the apostle's statements about Law. Never are Law and man's, particularly the devout man's, experience themselves made the source of his knowledge of that lost state from which the Law is powerless to deliver him.

Paul's thoughts and preaching do not therefore follow the logic of the preaching and practice of repentance as seen especially in pietism. There, in disregard of the gospel, men are shown the depth of their sin, and every effort is made to bring them to despair of themselves; or to put it in present-day terms: the pietist does not begin his theology with a chapter of existentialist philosophy and then go on to speak of gospel and faith. With him there is no proclamation of the gospel until a person realizes that his own resources are at an end and that the Law is of no avail to set him free. When Paul expounds the saving good news, it is generally in statements summarily characterizing man's state as lost; and this is *not* an evolutionary stage now left behind, on which he can look back with a sigh of relief (cf. Rom. 3:23; 6:15 ff.; 7:7 ff.; 8:5 ff.; 2 Cor. 3:7 ff., etc.).

Paul was at one with all the devout of the Old Testament in believing that, in its original intention, the Law was God's call to and sign of salvation and life (Rom. 2:6 ff.; 7:10): it was there to be obeyed. Applying to all, not just to Jews, it was summarized in the Decalogue and the command to love one's neighbor as oneself (Rom. 7:7; 13:9; Gal. 5:14). While Paul never abandoned this basic conviction, he was led to see what became all-important to himself personally, what he expressed in a more profound and radical way than did any Jew or Greek before him, and what no other theologian of primitive Christianity repeated after him, namely, that this same holy, righteous, and good Law (Rom. 7:12, 16) was in fact powerless to give salvation and life. This brought him to an entirely new understanding of the *Law's universality*. By this term he meant more than—as was meant, for example, in Hellenistic Judaism long before his own day—the applicability of the Law to all; he meant its all-embracing effects: it declared that all men, Jew and Gentile alike, are guilty in God's sight. This inextricable solidarity of all men under the Law as lost is the truly revolutionary aspect of his gospel.

In what does the plight of the human race consist? The answer is given in Romans 1:18–3:20, where the keyword is the "revelation of God's wrath." The trouble with man is not that he has no knowledge of God, but that he does not admit God's truth, and "in wickedness suppresses it" (Rom. 1:18). "For what can be known about God is plain to them [men], because God has shown it to them. Ever since the creation of the world his invisible nature, namely, his eternal power and deity, has been clearly perceived in the things that have been made" (Rom. 1:19 f.). This is the language of Jewish wisdom teaching as influenced by Greece. But unlike this, Paul does not speak, for purposes of apologetic or teaching, of a conclusion based on his own reflections to which he had to open men's minds; it is dictated by the facts of the case: these at once turn against man, accusing him: "So they are without excuse; for although they knew God they did not honor him as God or give thanks to him, but they became futile in their thinking and their senseless minds were darkened" (Rom. 1:20–21). The created world reveals God. But man, also God's creation and summoned to life, has become guilty in his sight and been "given up" (Rom. 1:24, 26, 28) to a life of sinister perversion. The creator and the creature have exchanged roles, and this in the very matter of what men call "religion." The shipwreck that man has made of his life, exchanging natural relations for unnatural and so involving himself in guilt and doom, is a manifestation of God's wrath.

In these lengthy expositions in Romans 1 this was all said in respect of the Gentiles, and as far as these were concerned, the wholehearted assent of devout Jews could be counted on. But it at once boomerangs and hits the Jew himself: he, the proper subject of the section, has a still clearer charge brought against him in connection with the trust committed to him, the word of Scripture and the Mosaic Law (Rom. 2 and 3). Thus Paul rules out all possibility of separating Jews from Gentiles in the way the Pharisees did. All, not just the Jews, were given God's law, though in different ways—the one on the tables of stone at Sinai, the other by having it written on their hearts—and all, not just the Gentiles, will come into judgment. All are guilty and prisoners: "all men are under the power of sin" (Rom. 3:9; cf. 3:10–20). Paul means something more than, and different from, the bare truism that morally speaking all men are sinners and fail to measure up to ethical requirements. He does not absolutely deny in the case of either Gentiles or Jews that to some extent at any rate they do what the Law commands (Rom. 2:14; Phil. 3:6). Nevertheless, such zealous action fails to undo man's bondage to sin and sin's enthralling power; it does not make him "righteous." The way to God still remains closed, and man is thrown upon himself. Indeed, Paul's example of the prisoner of sin is this very Jew zealous for the Law. Under the illusion that he is devout, in his quest of righteousness he fancies that the hopelessly barred access to God is open, or imagines that he can open it by his works. But he is lost. This, and nothing else, is what the Law reveals to man. The only knowledge imparted by the Law is knowledge of sin (Rom. 3:20). Fairly and squarely then, Paul disputes the Law's function of still being able to lead men to salvation. Down to this very day, this crowning point in Paul's idea of the Law exasperates Jews. It was also unheard of in primitive Christianity.

Paul gives the reasons for his apparently pretentious conclusion later in Romans, in a great passage in which he considers the whole history of mankind (5:12–21). Adam and Christ, each standing at the beginning and as the head, the former representing mankind fallen victim to death, the latter representing mankind as set free for righteousness and life—the two are contrasted in the all-embracing influence they exert and related as type and antitype.

Paul was not the first to conceive an idea of this kind. Before his day the visions and contemplations of Jewish apocalyptic had

contrasted the present aeon, evil and passing away, with the coming aeon of salvation. But, and this is the most important thing,
Hellenistic Judaism as influenced by the Gnostics acquaints us not
only with metaphysical speculations about man's divine origin and
destiny, but also about his fall and the tragedy of his ensnarement
in the inferior world dominated by hostile powers opposed to God.
While there can be no doubt that Romans 5 makes use of such a
scheme of ideas and concepts, it did not adopt them just as they
were. They were reshaped and understood in a new way. The
tension between the tradition which Paul took up and his own
reinterpretation of it can be seen in the very syntax: the first
sentence is not carried through to its end, but is more than once
interrupted by explanations and amendments. The scheme as such
implies the idea of a fateful destiny lowering over the whole of
mankind. And in actual fact, Romans 5 thus interpreted has had a
lasting influence on the doctrine of "original sin," or at least on it
as commonly understood, and has largely contributed to a dubious
deprecation of sex in the general Christian consciousness. But
such thinking has more affinities with the pre-Pauline tradition
than with Paul himself. We have therefore to notice carefully
where and how he breaks up the traditional scheme and readjusts
it. Paul's very field of thought is different. He never goes beyond
the realm of history, nor does he speculate on man's origins or on
the mythic-cosmic reasons for his fallen state, be they the devil or
fate. Instead, at the very beginning of his discussion, he keeps to
Adam's sin, the characteristic sin of all men, that is to say, man's
desire to assert his own will against God, the desire that brought
Adam under the curse of death. Thus, man's will, and not sin
itself conceived as an objective reality, is the cause of sin. The
very way in which the passage begins, " . . . *because* they all
sinned," rules out any idea of fate. In Paul's view sin is most
certainly not merely the moral failure on the part of the individual, but an act and an enslaving power in one. In the same way,
death is not something appointed and natural, but the power
which makes its victim prisoner and sets the seal on his lost
state.

If Paul entertains no idea of a tragic fate in connection with
man as represented by Adam, he has as little idea that the new

man is "by nature legitimated" to Christ: because the gift of grace and its power are to be appropriated in faith (Rom. 5:15 ff.).

The tradition had to be radically altered in this way, stripped of its metaphysical character, and related to history, before Paul could utilize it and its correspondences and say: as the one, so the many; as Adam, so also Christ. But this means that the field to which Adam brought condemnation and that in which Christ effected salvation are one and the same. Because of this, at the end of the passage, in place of the simple correspondence (as-so) we find: "Where sin increased, grace abounded all the more" (Rom. 5:20). In consequence Paul assigns to the Law given by Moses, for which the speculative tradition had no room, a historical position between Adam and Christ, and therefore an all-important role: it makes man's guilt an offense and heightens his "transgression" (Rom. 5:13; cf. 4:15). The Law alone reveals sin and man's lost state in their true colors.

These ideas concerning the Law are again taken up in a well-known passage (Rom. 7:7–25) and considered with a profundity unmatched by any Jew or Greek. Here, too, the subject is a history that shapes human nature. In Romans 7, however, the broad vistas of the Adam-Christ idea are apparently abandoned and narrowed down to the experiences of an "I." To this very day the passage is often taken as biographical, the confession of Paul the former Pharisee who failed to measure up to the Law. But this is quite wrong. The Law never brought Paul into despair, and elsewhere, as he looks back on his past, he is emphatic in declaring that as to righteousness according to the Law he was blameless (Phil. 3:4 ff.; Gal. 1:13 f.; see above, p. 11). In reality, the "I" in Romans 7 represents man without Christ, subject to the Law, sin, and death, in an extremity which of course can be measured only in the light of the gospel. That Paul now suddenly speaks in the first person and not abstractly and generally in the third person about man or even Adam is, of course, significant. The reason is that what a man really is is revealed to him only when he understands himself not merely as a member of a society (mankind), but in his own personal existence, and therefore affected in his own person. This comes about, Paul says, in encounter with the Law, God's summons to life, summarized in the Tenth Com-

mandment ("Thou shalt not covet"). Thus, even if Romans 7:
7–25 far transcends himself and applies to all men, Paul can
speak of this matter only in the first person singular.

What comes about when man encounters the Law? The traditional Jewish answer was that the Law restrained sin, saved a man
from it, and indicated the way to what was good. Paul's, however,
is astonishingly different. No, he says: the Law revealed and
stirred up my covetousness. Only through the Law did I come to
know sin; hitherto slumbering, the "dead" thing now for the first
time "revived"; for when a man encounters the Law, his own
covetousness enters in as a factor. Because of my origin and
nature, when I encountered the Law it was as one for long completely self-centered. Indeed, sin managed to turn the divine commandment against itself and into an instrument for my own self-
assertion. And therefore the paradox: because I coveted so
fiercely, the commandment given me that I might live drove me
along the road to death (Rom. 7:10). This took place "when the
commandment came." I died, deceived by sin and killed by means
of this weapon in its hand (7:9 ff.). In terms that might almost
have been taken from myth, Paul here speaks of a duel in which
only the one party can come out alive. But the idea of sin as a
demonic power is misleading; for just as certainly as sin is not
simply moral failure, as the force robbing a man of his power and
destroying him it always remains man's own culpable act. Thus,
each time I encounter the Law and the commandment, I enter the
lists as sin's prisoner born for death.

This is the background of Paul's understanding of the human
situation, the hopeless perversion of his being. It comes to expression, in a way which he himself cannot follow, in a contradiction
that tears him apart, the desperate opposition between the
"fleshly" man (i.e., man fallen victim to himself) and the "spiritual" God-given Law (Rom. 7:19). But there is more to it. To
this opposition man might resign himself; he might come to terms
with it. But the perversion is expressed in a contradiction in man
himself: will and its accomplishment part company ("I will what
is good and do what is evil," Rom. 7:15). Will does not issue in
action, and action is involuntary. And finally, and worst of all: I
am no more my own master ("it is not I who do it, but sin which

dwells within me," Rom. 7:17 f., 20), in spite of the fact that, with my "mind," my "inmost self," and my will directed toward what is "good," life, I assent to the Law and even delight in it. Paul does not mean this as the Gnostics did: they spoke of the divine "spark of life" in man (as we speak of the "basic goodness" of man). Instead, it all just sets sign and seal on man's being lost, a state which is terrible in the truest sense of the word. Man's discord is part of his human nature. He himself *is* the contradiction. This is the "I" of the cry "Wretched man that I am! Who will deliver me from this body of death?" (Rom. 7:24).

In Romans 7:7–25, as in Romans 5, Paul does not stop to consider man's divine origin and that for which he was destined ideally. Instead, he keeps to man as he is and his "history," making no distinction between the devout Jew who would wrest his own righteousness from the Law and the transgressor in rebellion against God's will. In spite of all the features special to each passage, they are very closely related. Romans 7 prevents Adam-Christ from being misunderstood as mere speculation belonging to the realms of mythology or of a theology of history, while Romans 5 guards Romans 7 against being misunderstood as a mere analysis of the inner life and of human existence.

The process described in Romans 7 might suggest that in the encounter with sin the Law itself became a power operated by the devil or death. But this deduction, as blasphemous to Paul's mind as to ours, he repudiates impassionately. Though fallen into the hands of sin and to all appearance fallen away from its divinely destined purpose, the Law was still held firmly in God's hands. But it was given another function: not to diminish sin, but to "increase" it (Rom. 5:20), and to show sin in the plenitude of its power to destroy (7:13). Even if indirectly and in a paradoxical way, by the very denying of life instead of opening up accounts to it, the Nomos remained in the service of the divine will to save. This is what Paul means when he says that the Law was "custodian till Christ came" (Gal. 3:24 f.). He is comparing it with the slave to whom in the ancient world children under age were subject until they attained their majority, when they were free and entered upon their inheritance. Or, using another metaphor which, like the first, is not to be taken as referring to the individual, but to an

aeon, all the ages before Christ: the Law is the prison to which all
are consigned and where they are kept under restraint until the
day of their release (Gal. 3:22 ff.; 4:1 ff.; Rom. 11:32).

Right down to the present time all representatives of the Jewish
faith have been moved to anger by the tremendous paradoxes in
Paul's doctrine of the Law and found them intolerable, while
Christian theology has scarcely apprehended them for what they
really are. Schoeps recently reproached Paul with having, in dependence on a contemporary perverted understanding of the Law,
abridged its true significance for the Old Testament and Judaism
and caricatured it. Paul did not, Schoeps says, give due place to its
character as covenant-law and gift of grace; hence the ostensibly
harsh and distorted antitheses in his theology: old and new covenant, Law and Christ, works and faith. Buber has called Paul a
Gnostic who, like John and unlike Christ, peopled the world with
demons. However, these reproaches fail to grasp Paul's real position, though there is no denying that many of his ideas and concepts are tied to his own age. It is wrong to pass judgment on him
as an exegete whose task was to expound Scripture from the
standpoint of the Old Testament. As we have seen, he actually
does not, like the Old Testament, describe the Law's nature in
respect of its origin: he considers the situation of man for whom,
because of his sin, the revelation once given opens up no way to
God, with the additional result that the holiness, righteousness,
and goodness of the Law that makes demands on him are of no
avail.

In his realization that no one, neither strict observer of the Law
nor transgressor, Jew or Gentile, was in a position to find the way
to God, Paul's feet remained planted on the bedrock of the faith
of the Old Testament and Judaism; there, all along, *the* most
important existential question in respect of salvation or perdition
was that of man's relationship to God and vice versa. Nevertheless, he broke up the bedrock of Jewish thought by putting all men
under obligation to obey the Law: their lost state, from which
grace alone could deliver them, made all alike. By allowing that
the Law was the one thing aimed at making man responsible in his
actual existence, Paul, to use modern terms, happily made it impossible to turn the real question, about God, into a general ques-

tion about *Weltanschauung*. This world view vainly puts the question of a God "forthcoming" in the world or the supra-world, the result being the ousting of the truth that in reality one can speak of God only as the one who "comes to" us in word and action. In this consists the importance of Paul's understanding of the Law and, supremely, of what is meant by salvation in his preaching and theology.

MAN IN THE WORLD

The sum total of mankind as represented in Romans 5 by Adam clearly narrows down in Romans 7 to man as "I." This means that in principle it is not proper to speak of man and his concerns abstractly, in collective and general terms, but only of him as an individual. This does not, however, call in question that what Paul says of him is of universal application, but rather acknowledges it. Man and the world are always firmly coordinated, but at the same time, because of the power of sin, both of them, the created world and the creature man, are prisoners, lost in the sight of God and standing in need of redemption. The world may be the horizon of human life, yet man puts his stamp upon it and determines it. It, too, lies in the dark shadows cast by guilty man. Because of this, the whole creation has been subjected to "futility," the wastage of coming into being and perishing, and to "bondage to decay," and therefore waits with eager longing for the revelation of the glorious liberty of the children of God (Rom. 8:19–21).

Paul's use of the word "world" is in line with this. Very often he means humanity in general (Rom. 3:19; 11:12; 2 Cor. 5:19, etc.). But "world" also has the sense of the world in which man lives his life, the embodiment of his concerns (1 Cor. 7:31 ff.), that upon which he rests his confidence and glory, and from which he seeks to derive his standards and wisdom (1 Cor. 1:18 ff.; 2:6 ff.). Transient (2 Cor. 4:18), man's overlord, and blinding him, it is the realm of Satan, the god of this aeon (2 Cor. 4:4).

The steadfast relationship between man and the world also comes out in the terms Paul uses *in connection with man*. Though we already met with quite a considerable number of them when we looked at his doctrine of the Law, we may gather together the most important again here, by way of supplementation and explanation. Nowhere—in contrast, say, to Philo—does Paul consider them philosophically. Just as he never embarks upon abstract discussion of the being of God or the term "God" or makes creation an "article of doctrine," so, too, he makes no theoretical pronouncements about man. Nonetheless, certain of his terms and turns of phrase clearly reveal his picture of man. All of them designate not just one part of man, but the whole man in different aspects. We may omit stock terms which are simply paraphrases for man or mankind (e.g., the Old Testament's "all flesh," "flesh and blood," etc.), and look at some which are particularly characteristic of Paul. The most comprehensive, and theologically important, is "body" (*sōma*). Admittedly, this is not obvious everywhere. Quite often "body" has its normal meaning: bodily presence (1 Cor. 5:3; 2 Cor. 10:10), bodily suffering and pain (Gal. 6:17; 1 Cor. 9:27; 2 Cor. 4:10); or it may refer to sexual intercourse (1 Cor. 6:15 f.; 7:4); or to the weakening and decay of physical force (Rom. 4:19). Paul also knew the common classical metaphor of the one body and its many members (Rom. 12:4 ff.; 1 Cor. 12:12 ff.). But the most important thing is that he never regards the body and corporeality as just one part of man, as is done, for example, in the classical (Orphic) formula of the body as a tomb (*sōma/sēma*), the prison of the soul, or as did the "enthusiasts" at Corinth, who made a distinction between the body as the inferior, earthly part and the higher "pneumatic self" (1 Cor. 6:12 ff.). As used by Paul, "body" is man as he actually is. Man does not *have* a body, he *is* a body (Bultmann). "Your bodies [or even: your members] belong to Christ" (1 Cor. 6:15) therefore means the same as "you are the body of Christ" (1 Cor. 12:17). "Present your bodies as a living sacrifice" (Rom. 12:1) is equivalent to "yourselves." In "my body" means in "me," etc. "Body" expresses particularly the fact that man is a living being, never merely existing as a thing does, but experiencing, conducting himself in such and such a way, controlling himself or even throwing away and losing himself—man in all his potentialities. But this is the very reverse of being dependent on himself. Instead, "body" designates man as the one who never belongs to himself, but always has a master set over him, sin, death, or the Lord. Because of this, man in his corporeality is always asked: To whom do you belong? (1 Cor. 6:13, 15 ff.). As concerns man's actual existence in this world, this means that his potentialities are forfeited and lost, and that all he can look for is release. In this connection, when considering the existence of believers, Paul sometimes speaks "dualistically" of being present in the body. This is, of course, no metaphysical dualism depreciating corporeality as such. It is meant to characterize man's involvement in time and history, a limitation from which he can be delivered only by death (2 Cor. 5:1–10). As created by the Lord and owned by him, the Christian together with his body and its members is released to serve the ends of righteousness and appointed to life (Rom. 6:12–23). This he may do now: effect has been given it through the power of the divine spirit (Rom. 8:10–13). But it reaches its consummation only at God's hands in the new creation. This embraces the whole man, body and soul. That is why Paul so strongly opposed the fanatics at Corinth and their teaching about the bodily (and not fleshly) resurrection of the dead (1 Cor. 1:15).

Unlike Greek thought, Paul gives no leading role to the term "soul" (*psyche*). With him, "soul" is not the higher, divine, immortal personality, but, as in the Old Testament, man in his manner of life, sentiments, and disposition (Phil. 1:27; 2:2, 19; 1 Thess. 2:8). Similarly, Paul sometimes speaks of the (human) "spirit" (*pneuma*)—to be carefully distinguished from God's spirit; here he means man as regards his consciousness, intelligence, and understanding. The spirit knows a man's thoughts (1 Cor. 2:11) and perceives the witness of the divine spirit (Rom. 8:16). Another term he often uses originates not in Greece, but in the Old Testament and Judaism, the term "heart": it means man in respect of his desiring and wishing (Rom. 10:1; 1:24; 1 Cor. 4:5), or his sorrows and his love (e.g., Rom. 9:2; 2 Cor. 2:4; 7:3, etc.). On the other hand, terms like "conscience" and "reason" do derive from Greece—to the Old Testament and Judaism they are unknown. For the former the most important reference is Romans 2:15. Conscience (*syneidesis*) is man's knowledge of himself accompanying his action, whether that be things already done or an obligation to be fulfilled (1 Cor. 4:4; Rom. 9:1;

13:5). As Paul sees it, conscience is not a supreme court deciding between good and evil, but rather an unerring witness to truth, never to be ignored or done violence to, because it tells a man what he really is and not what he appears to do or wants to be (1 Cor. 8:7 ff.). Paul took over this term, probably via Hellenistic Judaism, from Stoic popular philosophy, in which, as in Romans 2, it is used in the context of the metaphor of a court of law (accuser, witness, judge). With Paul, however, the verdict of conscience and God's judgment are not identical: conscience only establishes that God's will is not concealed from anyone, and points a man away from now accusing, now defending himself, to God's future crystal-clear verdict on mankind. Borrowing a term from Greek philosophy of religion and Jewish wisdom teaching, Paul can say that with the eye of "reason" (*nous*) a man may perceive God's invisible nature in the works of creation; through it he hears his summons (Rom. 1:20). Reason leads even the un-redeemed man to assent to God's law (Rom. 7:22). Its functions are those of understanding, testing, deciding, and judging (2 Cor. 4:4; 10:5; Rom. 12:2; 1 Thess. 5:21; Rom. 3:28; 1 Cor. 4:1). Reason thus designates man in respect of his having enlightenment as to his world. But as before: reason is not a better "self" in man. Paul never designates or understands it, as did the Stoics, as the Logos in virtue of which man shares in the divine reason. Nor does he think of it, as in gnosticism, as the supernatural spirit which made a man the member of a world of light. Even the man who by use of his reason wills what is good for himself, i.e., life, and by means of it assents to God's law is lost (Rom. 7:14 ff.). Nonetheless, Paul does not declare reason as such to be useless. Even when he sharply contrasts the "foolishness of the gospel" with the "wisdom of this world," he appeals to understanding (1 Cor. 1:18 ff.), just as he evaluates all communication in worship by the standard of what can be understood and convince others (1 Cor. 14). Without this it would never get the better of the thinking of the man who asserts himself against God and lead him captive to obey Christ (2 Cor. 10:3 ff.). Further, the believer is not deprived of reason. Rather, his reason is "renewed" by grace (Rom. 12:1).

The natural man is "sold under *sin*" (*hamartia*) (Rom. 7:14).

Significantly, sin practically always occurs in the singular, and is spoken of as a power embodied in a person. Coming into the world because of Adam's disobedience (Rom. 5:12), it achieved dominion over all (Rom. 5:21). It is armed like a leader of mercenary troops and pays off its subordinates with death ("for the wages of sin is death," Rom. 6:23). In itself, this way of speaking of sin shows that "sin" is more than just a collective term for various sinful acts, however much it may manifest itself in moral lapses (Rom. 1:26 ff.; 2:21 ff.; 3:10 f., etc.). Essentially, sin is hostility to God (Rom. 5:6 ff.; 8:7), to whom it refuses honor and thanksgiving. It always has man in its power; neither the good works of the Gentiles (Rom. 2:14) nor those of the devout Jew directed toward his "own righteousness" avail to annul its jurisdiction. The clearest characterization of this disposition on man's part lies in the term "flesh" (*sarx*). Very often, it is true, Paul uses it, as does the Old Testament, to denote man the creature *in differentiation to God*. Flesh is man in his transience (Gal. 4:13; 2 Cor. 12:7; 4:11; Phil. 1:22, 24, etc.), in respect of his descent, kinship, or position in society (Rom. 1:3; 4:1; 9:3, 8; 1 Cor. 10:18; 1:26). Earthly material benefits that perish, such as food and gold, are "fleshly" (Rom. 15:27; 1 Cor. 9:11). Nonetheless, in many instances in Paul "flesh" has a fuller meaning not found in the Old Testament. Then it designates man's being and attitude *as opposed to and in contradiction to God and God's Spirit*. Here, generally with a verb along with it, "flesh" means the basis on which and the end in view of which man understands himself and lives his life (e.g., Rom. 8:4; 2 Cor. 10:2; 11:18); it even means the powers to which he has fallen victim in his heady urge to assert himself, including both gross sensual desire (Gal. 5:13 f., 24) and the religious privileges on which the Jew or the "enthusiasts" base their confidence (2 Cor. 11:18; Gal. 6:12 f.; Phil. 3:3 f.). Men think that by adopting such an attitude they stand on their own feet, and they may seem to do so. But in reality they subject themselves. Like sin, flesh is a power that enslaves (Rom. 7:14, 18; 8:6 f., 12 f.; Gal. 5:16, 24).

Man's falling victim to himself and to the powers that destroy ends up in *death*. His urge to assert himself and his concerns produces a harvest which death, so to speak, gathers into its barn (Rom. 7:5). Sowing in the flesh is sowing destruction (Gal. 6:8; cf. Rom. 6:23; 8:13; 2 Cor. 7:10). Very often this process is described in various metaphors, some of them no more than allusive. They show that, for Paul, "death" designates more than dying and nothingness beyond the grave. Death and its annihilating power advance against the unredeemed man even while he is still alive, causing him to live in fear (Rom. 8:15) or grief (2 Cor. 7:10), or with the mind that seeks to meet death with the devil-may-care slogan "Let us eat and drink, for tomorrow we die" (1 Cor. 15:32). Thus flesh and sin of themselves lead to death (Rom. 6:16). Sin is the goad in death's hand (1 Cor. 15:56). Together with sin, death has dominion over unredeemed humanity (Rom. 5:12–21), and until the end of the world it remains Christ's last enemy (1 Cor. 15:26).

To cancel the power of evil and death the Law has no avail (Rom. 8:3). Actually, it only sets its seal on it and establishes it. As a means of salvation it has been abolished; Christ is the end of the Law (Rom. 10:4).

III

THE SAVING EVENT

For Paul, as for the Reformers after him, the gospel of justification by faith alone was the article by which the church stood or fell. But this must not blind us to the difficulties this doctrine makes for the modern mind. These result partly from the expression of the doctrine in the language and thought forms of Paul's own day. But a contributory factor is the ecclesiastical tradition inaugurated by the apostle himself. This, largely fossilized, has lost its power. Just as, in days gone by, Christian churches were built on the foundations of former heathen basilicas, but in such a way that hardly a trace of the latter could still be recognized, so too Paul's doctrine of justification is often merely a ghost eking out a sham existence in formulas protected by piety. Not that—in the reformed tradition, in all events—it is disputed and unknown. Rather, it is so very widely accepted and well known as now to be taken as a matter of course. We treat it as we might an invention or discovery which eluded earlier generations but is now taken for granted by their descendants. Thus, the more or less common words of Christian discourse no longer represent the power, but the weakness, of something once said in a former day. The fact that the doctrine is taken for granted conceals and often simply betrays the extent to which it is itself incomprehensible. It is no longer what it once was. A doctrine of justification that has become a matter of course and been banished into a catechism as a proposition or into a treatise on dogmatics as a paragraph is most certainly not the doctrine as Paul knew it. The results are plain to see: in what was for Paul the very heart of the gospel, where his word encountered man in his situation with a force that convulsed him and set him free, the church's proclamation now speaks only to an illusion. And where preaching and theology have not long since moved over to fields supposedly more relevant to the times, one quite often searches for traces of an effort, sincere but futile, to break up boulders with a wretched plow and convert a tract of land into small, tidy gardens.

This shows what an effort is required to reintroduce Paul's doctrine and rekindle the fire with which it once burned. Our task today, then, is what it was in the past: to open our minds to his teaching, spell it out again, and do all we can to understand it afresh.

"Again to spell out" Paul's doctrine of justification can never mean an academic resolution of it into its various conceptual component parts and then a further addition of these into an orderly system. The primary thing is what is done in Christ and made effective in the gospel, and it immediately manifests itself in the close frame of reference into which the various terms used in Paul's message are put. Each one of them points to the rest, and none is sufficient in itself. Each needs to be examined for the contribution it makes toward the understanding of what is proclaimed in the gospel.

THE RIGHTEOUSNESS OF GOD

What Paul teaches is not the general theological proposition that God is righteous. The distinctive feature in his gospel is that God's righteousness is conveyed to believers. But what does this signify? And what meanings are to be attached to righteousness, making righteous, becoming righteous, and justification?

None of the modern languages of the Western world has a term which fully renders all that the root "righteous" meant for Paul and the Bible. At the same time, it would not be advisable to reject the old translation "righteousness." If we did so, we should also soon lose sight of what Paul had in mind. But what was this? Astonishing as it may seem, in Romans 1:17 Paul speaks, *in one and the same sentence*, of the righteousness of God and that of the believer: nor are these two things, but one, God's righteousness. As a result, Paul can also say, "righteousness from God that depends on faith," "righteousness through faith" (cf. Phil. 3:9; Rom. 9:30; 10:4, 6; Gal. 2:16, etc.). In Paul's view, this and this alone delivers man from death and opens up the way to eternal life (Rom. 1:17; Phil. 3:9 ff.). He is brusquely opposing and ruling out the "righteousness" which the devout man wants to wrest for himself on the basis of the works of the Law, for, Paul says, all that his zeal achieves is his "own" righteousness (Rom. 10:3) and never God's (cf. Rom. 9:30–10:4; 3:21, 31).

Used in this way with reference to God and man alike, "righteousness" and "righteous" of themselves show that righteousness is not to be regarded as a quality, as in Greek (and Latin). This mistaken way of conceiving it as equivalent to the Greek cardinal virtue and the Roman ideal of justice for long led theology astray. For Luther, it initially made God's righteousness an object of terror, because as a matter of course he understood it in terms of the judical norm whose requirements sinful man never satisfies. How could a righteousness like this ever form the subject of the *gospel?* Only after long anguish and struggle did he suddenly reach a new, liberating understanding of the term—in its significance for the Bible and for Paul. Conceived as a property, an ethical attribute attaching to God the judge and to man, it makes absolutely no sense. Properties cannot be conveyed. What they do is characterize people's distinctive qualities, and they can link only things in the same category, e.g., righteous and unrighteous. Paul's meaning, however, is in fact a link between entirely different categories, God and man, God and his enemies (Rom. 5:10), indeed—the paradox at its greatest—God and the ungodly (Rom. 4:5; cf. 5:6). God attributes his righteousness to man who is a sinner and not righteous in himself. God is righteous and proves his righteousness by justifying the person who has faith (Rom. 3:26). Righteousness can now in actual fact be predicated of both while still remaining God's righteousness. There is, however, a difference, strictly maintained, between the two. In the case of God, the

138   PAUL

active voice is used: to pronounce righteous and thereby to make
righteous (cf. Rom. 3:26; 4:5; 8:30, 33; Gal. 3:8, etc.); with
man, on the other hand, it is the passive: pronounced righteous,
made righteous (cf. Rom. 2:13; 3:20, 28, etc.). Grammatically,
then, the genitive in "God's righteousness" is not subjective (if so,
the transcendent God would be made utterly remote and inacces-
sible to man), but a genitive of origin. That is to say: God creates
his righteousness for man, puts him in the right—man who apart
from this verdict and act is lost, but now may have life in his
sight.

In all these turns of phrase God is and remains the judge, and
man's relationship to him is conceived as a legal one. God's verdict alone decides whether a man is to be or not to be, live or die.
Because for Paul the word never lost its juridical meaning, he
could demand righteousness from Greeks as well as from Jews.
But the new and surprising element in his gospel is that God the
judge is not himself subject to an unchangeable norm greater than
himself and inevitably determining his verdict. He alone determines what righteousness and being righteous are. Only because
of this can Paul say that righteousness has been manifested *"apart
from law"* (Rom. 3:21)—for man an impossible statement. If
man in his presumption puts himself outside the Law and over-
steps its limits, the result is lawlessness, and he must be brought to
know that in reality he cannot thus escape from it; more than ever
he needs to be made to feel its force. God, however, is not the
slave of his Law: the Law serves as his servant. God does not
require to point out his righteousness in the sight of the Law; the
Law is there to point to God's righteousness; it points beyond
itself (Rom. 3:21b). In making known to us that we are not
righteous in God's sight, it bears witness to him who alone is
righteous and makes righteous and acquits through grace. God
does not leave men to themselves. He accepts the godless. Thus,
he does not seclude himself in his righteousness, but includes the
sinner in it and brings him from afar near to himself. God both
pronounces and performs this justification of the sinner. His word
accomplishes his pronouncement. There is no place here for a
legal fiction, an "as if."

Paul's thinking on this subject is based not on Greek thought, but on the Old Testament and Judaism, though his utterances go far beyond the latter. Righteousness, being righteous, and verbal forms such as declare righteous, acquit, create right, etc., are basic Old Testament terms connected with Yahweh's covenant with his chosen people. Predicated of God, they designate his faithfulness to the covenant and the fact that of his goodness and grace he constantly reaffirms it. Correspondingly, the righteousness of the devout in the Old Testament also consists in conduct in keeping with the covenant, that is to say, in obedience to Yahweh's call and to the directions which maintain his people in this relationship. The fact that man fails to satisfy God and "that no man living is righteous before God" (Ps. 143:2; Job 4:17) is, to be sure, often expressed in moving terms in the psalms and prayers of the Old Testament and Judaism; there is also ample evidence in the recently discovered Qumran texts. All the more does the devout place his confidence in God's faithfulness and mercy. Thus in Judaism itself there are sayings that sound completely "Pauline": "For herein is thy righteousness and goodness manifested, Lord, that thou hast mercy on those who have no treasury of good works" (2 Esd. 8:36). Or in the Qumran Manual of Discipline: "Though I stumble by reason of the wickedness of my flesh, through God's righteousness my justification remains for ever" (1QS XI, 12). Nevertheless, the similarities between such statements and Paul's must not blind us to the great differences. The Jewish ones are always in the context of God's unique relationship to his chosen people and never imply questioning of the law as the means of salvation. For Judaism Paul's characteristic addition to his quotation from the Psalms (143:2: "For no human being will be justified in his sight") of "by works of the law" (Rom. 3:20; Gal. 2:16) would have been absolutely inconceivable. For this reason the Jew also finds Paul's opposition of works and faith absurd.

GRACE

Through Christ—through faith alone! In proclaiming this gospel Paul did more than merely add fresh themes to the idea in the tradition of the Old Testament and Judaism that only God justifies and that the devout are dependent on his grace. He gave to *solo deo* (by God alone) and *sola gratia* (by grace alone) a fundamentally new and all-comprehensive meaning. God's righteousness for faith is now based on and manifested apart from Law in the "expiation" made by Christ (Rom. 3:21 f.). The idea of Christ's expiation is not a creation of Paul's own. It derives from the early Jewish Christian theology which saw in Christ's death a proof of God's faithfulness to the covenant, and still wholly related it to the restoration of the Sinai covenant broken by Israel's sin. There are in fact echoes of this in Romans 3:25. But in Paul's own interpretation it at once falls into the background; with him expiation stands for God's world-wide and world-transforming act of salvation in the present, available to all who accept it by faith in Christ (Rom. 3:26). In the process the sacrificial idea is not conceived as an act of self-affirmation on God's part and certainly not as sinful mankind's expiation of itself. Paul never raises the question discussed in later theology as to the conditions which God in his saving work had to satisfy so as to avoid damage to himself. What Paul's idea conveys is the grace of God who has made his righteousness available to all in Christ and gives believers part in it in order to rescue them from the damage which they suffered while apart from Christ. Paul gives no thoughts on what lies behind this grace.Without comment he expresses the idea of the *new* covenant, which is fundamentally opposed to the old Sinai covenant, restricted as this was to Israel (cf. 2 Cor. 3:6 ff.; Gal. 4:24; Rom. 11:27).

Paul concludes his great exposition of justification in Romans 3:21 ff. with a shout of victory: "Then what becomes of our boasting? It is excluded. On what principle? On the principle of works? No, but on the principle of faith. For we hold that a man is justified by faith apart from works of law" (3:27–28). It is like the other in 1 Corinthians 15:55: "O death, where is thy victory? O death, where is thy sting?" Men did not wrest this victory, but God: all men have part in it, as surely as God is the God not only of the Jews, but also of the Gentiles (Rom. 3:29).

Whenever the apostle speaks of God's *grace* (Rom. 3:24; 5:2, 15; 2 Cor. 8:9; Gal. 1:6; 5:4, etc.) and also of his *love* (Rom. 5:8; 8:35, 39; 2 Cor. 5:14; Gal. 2:20), he does not just think of a general disposition on God's part, but means God's act which came to pass in the death of Christ. This love meets with nothing worthy of itself, but only weakness, the ungodly, sinners, and enemies (Rom. 5:6-8). Its paradox, for human reason an absurdity (5:7), shows its divine sublimity. As was well said by G. Radbruch, "Grace is most closely related to miracle. As miracle breaks the laws of nature, grace breaks the laws of law, and both alike result in conferring great and unmerited good fortune on all who are able to lay claim to them." Grace does not jeopardize the order imposed by law, nor does it cancel out the distinction between good and evil and lead to anarchy. It establishes a new order, the new covenant.

For "justification" Paul also uses, with the same meaning, the word *"reconciliation"* (Rom. 5:10 f.; 2 Cor. 5:18 f.). Reconciliation is like justification in being the work of God alone in the self-surrender of Christ. Paul never says that Christ's sacrifice *reconciles* God. "God reconciled the world to himself" (2 Cor. 5:19). In keeping with this, his summons runs, "be reconciled to God" (an imperative passive!). This also makes clear that God's saving act in the death of Christ embraces the whole world. This is particularly the subject of the post-Pauline letters to the Colossians and the Ephesians (Col. 1:20 ff.; Eph. 2:16). God's act of deliverance establishes a state of salvation, "a grace in which we *stand"* (Rom. 5:1 f.).

FAITH

In Paul's gospel even faith is not found as a topic apart. It is never spoken of as a religious disposition and a devout bearing. It is significant that, at one with the rest of the New Testament (apart from Heb. 11:1), Paul never defines faith. The nature of faith is given in the object to which faith is directed, the divine grace. Never is it found apart from that in which it has faith; never is it itself a subject of consideration. Faith always means faith in . . . (Gal. 2:16; Rom. 10:14; Phil. 1:29, etc.) or faith that . . . (1 Thess. 4:14; Rom. 6:8; often along with an objective genitive). It signifies acceptance, in obedient trust and trustful obedience, of God's saving act as proclaimed in the gospel (Rom.

1:5, 6:16; 2 Cor. 10:5, etc.). As such it is a condition for salvation, but not in the sense that men must have succeeded in their resolve to attain it before being allowed to participate in salvation. Condition does not mean precondition or achievement. If it did, faith itself would indeed be just another "work," like the works of the Law, which the Jew strives to produce as the basis of his being recognized by God and declared righteous. Whether this is conceived as the highest degree of devotion to God or as a state of the soul (Philo), or as a kind of substitute which might compensate for man's incapacity to please God and induce him to take the will to be good for the deed, which is always evil, is of no consequence. Any of these would invalidate the hard-and-fast contrast between works and faith and mean abandoning justification of the godless.

Even before Paul's day Judaism saw Abraham as *the* prototype of the true believer, not as a moral paragon, but as the father of Israel. He it was whom God called forth from among the nations (Gen. 12). With Abraham God made his covenant, attaching circumcision as its sign for all his descendants (Gen. 15; 17). Abraham was the founder of Israel as God's chosen people. This tradition was continued in primitive Christianity, as evidenced by the many references in the Gospels and Acts. The earliest Christians, too, claimed to be Abraham's sons and heirs of the promise made to him. The God whom they confessed was the "God of Abraham, of Isaac, and of Jacob" (Mark 12:26 and parallels), just as Jesus, as Messiah, was called Abraham's son (Matt. 1:1 f.; Gal. 3:16). Abraham's behavior showed Jew and Christian alike what was meant by faith. The classic Old Testament passages appealed to were Genesis 12 (Abraham's obedience to God's call), Genesis 22 (his readiness at God's command to offer up even his son), and Genesis 15 (his unrestricted trust in God's promise of a great posterity). This faith God counted to him as righteousness. This is the precise sense—as previously in Judaism —in which Hebrews 11 names him as one of the "cloud of witnesses," thinking of his going out in obedience without knowledge of destination, but simply on the strength of God's word to him (Heb. 11:8), thinking, too, for the second time, of the offering up of Isaac (11:17 ff.). The Epistle of James also expressly adduces this same practical testing of Abraham's faith (2:20 ff.) and along with this passage of Scripture quotes the classic Genesis 15:6, to make it clear that not faith alone but faith and works together are justified in God's sight.

Paul, too, takes the instance of Abraham to illustrate what it means to have faith. But he makes no use of Genesis 12 and 22, confining himself to Genesis 15:6: "Abraham believed God: and he reckoned it to him as righteousness" (Rom. 4:3; Gal. 3:6). The lengthy statements about Abraham's faith and God's blessing which made him the "father of many nations" (Rom. 4; Gal. 3) are a kind of midrash, a Jewish form of the application of Scripture to explain a proposition of faith. They are, of course, fundamentally different in content from traditional Jewish ideas, and what at first sight seems to be odd scribal reflection is in reality a life-and-death struggle about the bases and principles of Jewish and Christian faith. As Jews, and also the Epistle of James, are convinced, God's justification of Abraham was the well-merited reward for his supreme proof of devotion. Paul, however, understands it not as a "gift due," but as a "gift of grace" (Rom. 4:4 f.). The insight which he derives from Abraham's story, positively blasphemous even for non-Jewish ears, is that "God justifies the ungodly" (Rom. 4:5). The expression is forceful, and not to be watered down. It hardly needs saying, of course, that the subject under discussion is not moral defects on Abraham's part, as if Paul were wanting to pick holes in him or demote him from the honor in which he was held by Jews. At the same time he is here cast as the prototype of men—of all men who on the basis of nature are without access to God, sinners and his enemies (cf. Rom. 5:6 ff.). This man, Abraham, was loved by God, who pronounced him righteous on the basis of his faith.

Paul's doctrine also directs a deadly blow at the long-cherished Jewish idea of the covenant, symbolized in the sign of circumcision. In the manner of a scribe, but entirely un-Jewish in what he says, Paul concludes that since Genesis 17 (the gift of circumcision) comes after Genesis 15 (Abraham's justification by faith and not works), circumcision was meant only to set a seal on and endorse the righteousness conferred on him by his faith while he was still a Gentile (Rom. 4:11). Abraham thus became the "fa-

ther of many nations," that is, of the Gentiles as well as the Jews.
In other words, salvation is not tied to the promise made exclusively to Israel on earth and to be found in the sphere of the Law,
but is also to be found where the only things that matter are the
grace of God and faith (Rom. 4:16; cf. Gal. 3:6–18). This is the
way by which to "follow in Abraham's footsteps" and regard him
as leader (Rom. 4:12), a way diametrically opposed to that of the
Jews, who pursue a chimera.

This faith, in contrast to faith in doing what the Law commands, is firmly based on God's promise to Abraham: it is not
merely general trust in God. By human standards it is like the
Creator himself confronting nothingness, but holding fast to the
word of him "who gives life to the dead and calls into existence
the things that do not exist" (Rom. 4:17). It is thus faith based
on hope where in men's sight there is nothing to hope for ("hope
against hope," Rom. 4:18), just as Abraham saw nothing of the
"many nations" whose father he was yet to become. God's promise is his sole guarantee. This does not mean that he was blind to
reality and took refuge in illusions: "He did not weaken in faith
when he considered his own body, which was as good as dead
because he was about a hundred years old, or when he considered
the barrenness of Sarah's womb. No distrust made him waver
concerning the promise of God, but he grew strong in his faith as
he gave glory to God, fully convinced that God was able to do
what he had promised" (Rom. 4:19 ff.). This faith God reckons
as righteousness, the faith with which Abraham waited for the
promise to be, and the faith on whose fulfillment in the death and
resurrection of Christ believers now base their lives (Rom. 4:23
ff.).

In this way, then, step by step, Romans 4 fights the battle with
the Jews concerning Abraham, the true meaning of the chosen
people, the "saving history" and eternal salvation; and all that the
Jew claims for himself in distinction from the Gentile is made over
to those who have faith, Jew and Gentile alike.

The term "faith" as used in primitive Christianity and by Paul
has much in common with "faith" as found in the Old Testament
and Judaism. In the Old Testament it means reliance upon what is
valid, assured, and reliable—the covenant, the Law, God's prom-

ises. Here the Hebrew verb *he'emin* (from the same root as our
"Amen") makes contact with the Greek words *pistis*, faithfulness
(between man and man), *pisteudein*, to have and place confidence
in, and *pistos*, true or trustworthy and something that can be
relied upon. Although originally this Greek word group had no
kind of religious significance, it lay at hand for Hellenistic Judaism and Christianity, when for the first time the words became key
terms of religion and designated "faith." Faith includes patient
waiting and imperturbable hope, and has nothing in common with
vague conjectures and hopes which men "make," or with general
opinions and convictions, as the word is degraded to on our
lips.

But however many elements were simply taken over by the
Christian faith, they do not exhaust the term's full significance. It
stands in particular for acceptance of the gospel. Here God's saving act in Christ is itself faith's subject matter. Admittedly, in the
Old Testament and Judaism, too, faith is based on acts of God for
Israel (e.g., the deliverance from Egypt, Yahweh's wondrous
works in the wilderness, the overthrowing of Israel's foes, her
entry into the promised land). But these themselves are not the
subject matter of faith; rather, they are events which can be
pointed to and told of in the history of Israel and the world. The
case is altogether different with primitive Christianity and Paul.
Here the saving events proclaimed in the gospel, Christ's death,
resurrection, and exaltation, are themselves accepted and appropriated in faith. Therefore, "faith comes from what is heard [in
preaching], and what is heard comes by the preaching of Christ"
(Rom. 10:17). In this direct coordination of word and faith
God's righteousness becomes the righteousness of faith. Thus faith
is the same as receiving and obeying; and, conversely, Paul frequently makes synonyms of lack of faith and disobedience (Rom.
1:8 and 16:19; 1 Thess. 1:8 and Rom. 15:18; Rom. 10:3 and
10:16; 2 Cor. 10:5 f.; Rom. 10:21; 11:30 ff.; 15:31, etc.).

The heart of the matter is that here governing and mediating
third parties between God and the believer no longer exist. Since
the Law no longer stands between God and man, man has the
wrong track taken away from him and is prevented from setting
up between himself and God the phantom of his own works and

wisdom. Grace is absolutely unconditional (Rom. 3:24; Gal. 2:21), and so too is faith. It brings nothing accomplished beforehand with it, but is renunciation of human accomplishment and never a reason for "boasting," i.e., self-assertion in God's presence.

As a result, abandonment of self is a prescriptive element in surrender to God in faith—abandonment of an understanding of oneself which runs, presumptuous and despairing alike, in the blood of the old man, and acceptance of a new one made available through the grace of God (Rom. 5:3; 14:14; 1 Cor. 15:10; Gal. 2:20; Phil. 1:19). Thus faith is at one and the same time the end of the old existence and the beginning of a new one in which the believer has now to "stand" and prove himself (1 Cor. 16:13; Gal. 5:1; Phil. 1:27; 4:1; 1 Thess. 3:8). He sets out on the road but is not at the goal: "Not that I have already obtained this or am already perfect; but I press on to make it my own, because Christ Jesus has made me his own" (Phil. 3:12).

Such faith affects each and every part of an individual's life. In this sense, accordingly, there is also increase in faith (2 Cor. 10:15) and weakening and lack of it (Rom. 14:1; 1 Thess. 3:10), and for each man a different "measure" of it (Rom. 12:3).

SAVING EVENT AND SAVING HISTORY

In our treatment of the saving event, we have so far spoken of it as if it concerned only the individual. This was deliberate. Where the subject is faith, one has no alternative but to speak of the individual, his lost condition, and his deliverance. Faith is never the matter of a body of people, but of the individual, to whose "conscience" therefore Paul wishes to be made known along with the truth of his gospel (2 Cor. 4:2; 5:11). This has nothing to do with modern subjectivism, individualism, and existentialism, and in no way restricts the outward reach of the Pauline doctrine of justification: it is for all the world and all time. On the contrary, making faith an individual matter allows salvation to be universal and gives it its basis.

The individualistic interpretation of Paul's gospel which the

Reformation in particular is alleged to have inaugurated has been strongly challenged in recent Pauline research. This is not any denial of the fundamental importance of the doctrine of God's righteousness. What critics maintain is that the world-wide and future dimension in God's righteousness as proclaimed by Paul has been lost sight of and that because its apocalyptic horizons have been misconstrued, it has been narrowed down to relate only to the individual. This is seen, it is said, in the fact that, pre-eminently if not indeed exclusively, God's righteousness is conceived as *gift* to mankind. In reality Paul meant by the term "God's lordship over the world eschatologically revealed in Christ." "The right in virtue of which God effects his purpose in a world which, though fallen away from him, as creature still belongs to him absolutely" (Käsemann). Primarily God's righteousness is to be conceived as *power*, and only inasmuch as it is imparted to the whole of creation and includes all—Gentiles as well as the people of the covenant—as objects of salvation is it to be further described as *gift*. Because Paul, the new interpretation says, sets his sights not on the individual but on a new human race and a new creation, he and above all his gospel of justification never left the realm of apocalyptic.

However, these propositions really put the emphasis on the wrong places. For surprisingly little is said here of the coordination of God's righteousness and faith, a special and decisive feature for Paul. It is this that lacks precedent in the Old Testament and apocalyptic and is a genuine creation of Paul's own. In spite of his undoubted dependence on Jewish tradition, it makes his thought totally opposed to that of apocalyptic. The latter is primarily and essentially oriented on the cosmos and therefore fixes its gaze on the course of world history, the individual being only a particle in a concatenation of fate or salvation. From such a view Paul delivers a man by addressing him as a sinner with responsibility and as God's creature whom he treats with mercy. In the process he also delivers faith and theology from the appalling errors in the treatment of the problem of theodicy in which Jewish apocalyptic, as seen particularly in 2 Esdras, had inevitably to end and founder, a problem always a menace to faith.

We must not let ourselves be deceived by the fact that,

etymologically, theodicy means just the same as Paul's term
"God's righteousness." Nevertheless, the two modes of thought
and the questions put are totally different. Theodicy wants to
fathom God's righteousness in the events of the world and the life
of the individual and seeks to give man ground to stand on which
he never gets. Paul's doctrine of justification, on the other hand,
lays hold on man in his actual situation, and says that God has
sought and found him there.

Earlier, in the context of Paul's teaching on the Law, we re-
marked on the great contrast between it and all modes of thought
which take a general view of God and the world (p. 128). The
same is also true of his conception of salvation and in particular
of his doctrine of justification. It focuses man's gaze on God's
righteousness revealed for faith in the gospel, saying that this
encounter with God, and it alone, bestows salvation.

This does not mean that Paul "made a private thing" of God's
relationship to man and vice versa and played down the dimensions of world and history. In his doctrine of justification Paul in
no sense abandoned the idea of God's dealings with his "chosen
people" rather than with individuals, from of old the great theme
of the faith of the Old Testament and Judaism. But in what way
did he conceive of the saving history? The answer is already given
in the section dealing with Abraham considered above (Rom. 4).
Paul's numerous citations of Scripture are not just quotations
from a book of maxims or oracles with no relation to a specific
time. Similarly, Abraham's faith is not a universal example of the
religious attitude unrelated as before. In Romans Paul calls him
"our forefather" (4:1), and even to the Corinthians—Gentile
Christians—he speaks of the Israel which went out into the desert
at God's command as "our fathers" (1 Cor. 10:1). In both cases,
then, believers are brought into historical connection with Israel.
Admittedly, this "saving history" is an extremely paradoxical kind
of history. What elsewhere is called history, and what the religious
Jew in particular understood as such, is determined by a natural
continuity of fathers and sons on this earth and a demonstrable
succession of generations. History thus conceived sets frontiers
and distinctions between men and nations, and to this day constitutes for the Jew the basis of his inalienable pre-eminence over the

non-Jew. In history in Paul's sense of the term the only continuity is God himself, his promise and the faith that trusts his word. All other forms of continuity are shattered, because Paul's God is not the guarantor of a history that can be seen, but the one "who gives life to the dead and calls into existence the things that do not exist" (Rom. 4:17). Nonetheless, Paul means history, real history. For between Abraham of old and believers today there is as it were a solid bridge, whose first pillar is the grace vouchsafed to Abraham and whose last is God's grace now available in faith *for all men*.

What made the problem of history and saving history so particularly urgent for Paul was Israel's relationship to the Gentiles. This is the subject of the detailed arguments about Israel's election, the hardening of her heart, and her final salvation (Rom. 9–11). The arguments have even been regarded as the key to the whole letter and to Paul's doctrine of God's righteousness. Nevertheless, it is not fortuitous that the apostle did not put them at the beginning of the letter, but prefaced them with the exposition of justification in chapters 1–8 with its antitheses of Law and Christ, works and faith—and hence without appeal to Israel's peculiar destiny and a historical event still lying in the future. Admittedly, the theme in chapters 9–11 is already raised in the question in Romans 3:1 as to Israel's precedence in the matter of saving history: "Then what advantage has the Jew? Or what is the value of circumcision?" as it also is in the reiterated "to the Jew first and also to the Greek" (Rom. 1:16, etc.). But continuous and detailed discussion of the questions has to wait for Romans 9–11. The train of thought and the expressions used show that the apostle was here trying to apply the fundamental ideas in the preceding chapters to the special problem of Israel. Chapters 9–11 are thus meant to elucidate what preceded them and to draw the logical conclusions of this for the chosen people's present and future. We must not shut our eyes to the unresolved tensions and doubts and objections in these expositions. They result because on the one hand Paul is speaking of the historical and empirical Israel as the chosen people and acknowledging the promises made to her in history (Rom. 9:4 ff.; 11:28 f.; cf. earlier, 3:1), but on the other hand he shatters in pieces the traditional Jewish concept of the chosen people. For what constitutes the true Israel is not natural continuity here on earth, but solely God's free grace (cf. earlier, Rom. 2:28 f.). What then follows for historical Israel? The only possible answer is a paradox. Right from the very beginning the unique nature and destiny of the empirical-historical Israel lay in the fact that she was to live her life not on the basis of demonstrable historical events, for failure to measure up to which God might, as it were, proceed against her, but on that of the divine word over which she had no command—in other words, on the basis of the free sovereign power of election. This election which initiated her history does not come at the beginning of that history, as Romans 9:7 ff. shows by the instance of Isaac, thereafter to become a single event in history here on earth. Rather, it *continues* to manifest itself as the basic law of Israel's life (for what followed this is elucidated by means of God's free election of Jacob in preference to Esau, Rom. 9:11 ff.).

The main idea in Romans 9–11 is that God's word to Israel has not "failed" (Rom. 9:6)—Paul means the word of free grace and mercy, which in reverse is seen as hardening of the heart and rejection (Pharaoh, Rom. 9). As a result, it depends not upon man's "will or exertion," but solely upon God's mercy (Rom. 9:16). This blunt idea of *predestination* is not to be taken as implying determinism of the kind that makes man merely a puppet in the hands of a blind Destiny. Indeed, it exactly defines what pure grace is and refers man to his due place, where seeking rights with his creator becomes presumption. Nor does the idea of predestination hark back to an eternity before the world began when the die was cast determining men's lots; it holds fast to the word of grace (Rom. 9:22). Of this it may be said that it is so "near" to you that you can believe and confess it, and so be made righteous and saved (Rom. 10:8 ff.). God left nothing undone. He sent his preachers; they proclaimed the word, and men heard it. Nevertheless, in spite of all God's unremitting urgent efforts for his people, Israel did not believe but, disobedient and contrary, denied him who held out his hands to her all day long (Rom. 10:14–21).

Has Israel in so doing forfeited her election forever? Paul denies this most emphatically (Rom. 11:29). In his view, precisely because of her blindness and her refusal of the gospel Israel typifies the lost condition of all men and their being referred to God's mercy. Even in her present hardening she is still the recipient of the promise and will still be vouchsafed salvation, even if in a way she never expected. Because of her rejection of the gospel and her own rejection, Paul incites her by reversing his own order "to the Jew first and then to the Greek," and now apportions salvation first to the Gentile, in order to make Israel "jealous" (Rom. 10:19; 11:11) and thus carry her back to her beginnings and to her final salvation. This corresponds to the apostle's own way of missioning. He obviously expects and proclaims this consummation as due to fall within the short time leading up to the imminent Parousia (Rom. 11:26 f.) and the coming "life from the dead" (Rom. 11:15). Thus in this connection, too, his ideas about history bear the clear stamp of his expectation of the end as soon to come. But the important thing is that the leitmotiv of his conception of "saving history" is identical with the one which governs his doctrine of justification.

LIFE IN FAITH

It may be thought surprising that Paul hardly ever speaks of the forgiveness of sins, though this is central not only to the preaching of Jesus but to the faith of primitive Christianity as well, and closely approximates to what Paul calls justification or reconciliation. Only on the odd occasion does he paraphrase righteousness as forgiveness, in a quotation taken from a Psalm (Rom. 4:7 f.), and explain reconciliation as not counting trespasses (2 Cor. 5:19). The reason for this is that justification does not relate to actual sins committed in the past but to release from sin as a power which makes men its slaves.

But even the term "justification" does not as such render the fullness of salvation, of "this grace in which we stand," however much it may be the basis of believers' "state of being saved" (Rom. 5:1 f.). As a result, to describe present salvation in Christ, Paul often uses schemes of classification not directly stemming from his doctrine of justification. They are not properly forensic, but "existential," terms. Such are sacramental statements

like Romans 6 and Galatians 3:26 ff., "putting on" Christ (Gal.
3:27; Rom. 13:14), the "body of Christ" and its members (1
Cor. 12:12 ff.; Rom. 12:4 f.), and "being" in Christ. These are so
frequent and of such importance that some have regarded them as
actually of the essence of Paul's gospel and theology. Nevertheless, they are not to be played off against his gospel of justification, or separated from it or ranked above it. Influential as these
mystic-ontological concepts and expressions are, Paul hardly ever
uses them unqualified by his doctrine of justification. The latter
serves his purpose of guarding against any naturalism or auto-
matism in the understanding of salvation, whether such thought is
derived from an apocalyptic's scheme of aeons, Jewish speculations about Adam, Gentile-Christian sacramentalism and "enthusiasm," or Israel's unshaken faith in her election.

For Paul, life in faith implies life *at peace with God* who has
reconciled us to himself (Rom. 5:1 ff.; 2 Cor. 5:17 ff.). This does
not mean that the believer is now exempt from sufferings. On the
contrary, it is as believer that he really experiences them. But he
can "boast" of them (Rom. 5:3); for they do not contradict that
for which faith hopes, but accord with it and make a firm link
between it and the glory to be revealed, the final liberation of the
children of God (Rom. 8:18 ff.). Because Christ intercedes for
us, there is no longer condemnation and a barrier of hostility
between God and those who have faith, who meet the world and
its hostile forces as those whom God loves and therefore as conquerors (Rom. 8:31–39). This means that believers' experience
of the world is not now a matter of direct contact, but is mediated
by God's love in Christ (Rom. 8:37 ff.). What this signifies is
made clear by contrast with that alleged immediacy of experience
to which, as everyone knows, the unbeliever lays claim. He pre-
tends to cling without illusion to the things that constitute the
world and life, sets what the Christian says of God's love in the
light, or, rather, in the shade, of these experiences, and finds that
they disprove it. The believer, however, first anchors himself in
what God has said to him of his love in Christ, and then experiences life and the world in the way stated in Romans 8:28: "We
know that everything works for good with those who love God,
who are called according to his purpose."

As justified and baptized into the death of Christ, believers are *dead to sin* (Rom. 6:2). Not that they are no longer liable to sin. The powers which God dethroned *still* want to repossess believers and force them to be their servants. This is the reason why the verb in the indicative mood proclaiming deliverance from their power is followed by a command to resist their usurped dominion (Rom. 6:12 ff., etc.). However, believers no longer go into battle against sin as its slaves and subjects, but as those who have been set at liberty by God and in that liberty bound to him (Rom. 6:12–23). Thus they are summoned to stand fast in the freedom for which they *are* now set free (Gal. 5:1, 13).

Life in faith also signifies *freedom from the Law* (Rom. 7:1 ff.; Gal. 3:1 ff., etc.). However much Paul has to safeguard freedom from abuse, this never makes him call on believers to return to the Law. This would be tantamount to turning the walls of man's prison into a bridge designed to lead to God, when in actual fact he would only built the stones into a dubious foundation for his own presumption and pride.

Galatians 5:6 says that faith *works through love*. This describes the all-embracing importance of faith as entirely determinative of man's whole existence. Here, however, we must guard against the misunderstanding current especially in Catholic theology (though Protestantism is far from exempt) that only faith made perfect in love leads to justification. This represents a serious distortion of the relationship between faith, love, and justification. In speaking of justification Paul never talks of faith *and* love, but *only* of faith as receiving. Love is not therefore an additional prerequisite for receiving salvation, nor is it properly an essential trait of faith; on the contrary, faith animates the love in which it works. Thus love and other "fruits of the spirit" (Gal. 5:22 ff.) are not to be conceived as preconditions of justification: instead, Paul says, justification is their precondition and the root from which they grow. Hence Luther's excellent note on Galatians 5:6 in his commentary of 1535: "Works based on faith are done through love, but man is not justified by love." One must not therefore be too eager to bring Paul into line with James, who makes faith *plus* work the precondition of salvation (James 2:14 ff.). For, justified as James was in inveighing against a "dead" faith, this means abandoning

Paul's leading idea, which is that in virtue of God's grace in Christ the believer is set free for, and summoned to, a new life.

Finally, the new life in faith includes *freedom from death,* even if believers are killed all the day long (Rom. 8:36; cf. 2 Cor. 4:10). But its power to enslave men is abolished (1 Cor. 15:55 ff.).

We have been speaking of faith. Yet faith is based on one thing and one alone, what God did in Christ and what Christ's lordship makes available for men. This alone makes faith what it is.

Paul repeatedly sums up life in the power of God's righteousness in a set of three things, faith, hope, and love (1 Cor. 13:13; 1 Thess. 1:3; 5:8; Gal. 5:5 f.; Rom. 5:1-5; cf. also Col. 1:4 f.; 1 Pet. 1:21 f.; Heb. 10:22-24). It designates a life in which "all things have become new." This formula, which Paul probably inherited, is characterized by a threefold time dimension. First, our past is no longer guilt for which we are responsible, but the act of God who sacrifices his Son for us all. This is the foundation of faith. The present has ceased to be bondage to the law which links us with the past and announces God's future wrathful judgment, but the present is the certainty that God is on our side and that Christ intercedes for us at his right hand. As regards the future it means that: "nor height, nor depth, nor anything else in all creation, will be able to separate us from the love of God in Christ Jesus our Lord" (Rom. 8:38 f.).

IN CHRIST

Among the descriptions of the believers' new existence discussed in the previous section, Paul's often used "in Christ" has a significant place. The fact that it is found in very different contexts indicates that it has a variety of meanings. Often it is simply equivalent to our "Christian," "as a Christian," words which— one might almost say fortunately—were nonexistent in primitive Christianity and for Paul. In this case the term describes a way of speaking, thinking, acting, or suffering, and also the conduct toward others befitting a Christian. Quite often it only expresses membership of the church. Obviously, no profound theological, let alone "mystic," meaning should be wrested from such turns of phrase.

Frequently, however, the term sums up what has come about for believers through Christ and constitutes salvation. In Christ= through him God has given proof of his love (Rom. 8:38 f.); in him=through him believers are called, justified, reconciled, set at liberty, and sanctified (Phil. 3:14; 1 Cor. 1:2; 6:11; 2 Cor. 5:21; Gal. 2:4). In him=because of the saving event Paul is proud of his missionary *work (Rom. 15:17; 1 Cor. 15:31) and knows that believers' labor is not in vain (1 Cor. 15:58).

But "in Christ" can also have the full meaning of the new basic and all-comprehending reality into which believers are transferred once they have been delivered from the power of corruption. Into this category fall statements such as "you have 'put on' Christ" (Gal. 3:27 f.) and "through baptism became members of his body" (Rom. 12:5; 1 Cor. 12:13, 27). Or, from the opposite angle, Paul can speak of Christ or his Spirit as "dwelling" in believers (Rom. 8:9 f.) and say, "it is no longer I who live, but Christ who lives in me" (Gal. 2:20). This does not come about by being caught up into a heavenly sphere, but relates to the believer's earthly existence: "and the life I now live in the flesh I live by faith in the Son of God, who loved me and gave himself for me" (Gal. 2:20).

These and other similar expressions have little in common with mysticism, even where their diction approximates to it. For an essential element in mysticism is the blurring of the boundary between God and man—the two become one. With Paul, however, the qualitative differences of both are preserved. Christ remains Lord; the believer is his property (Rom. 8:7, 14:7 ff., etc.), and the liberating union with Christ comes about in his service (Rom. 6:15 ff.).

The close connection in Paul's doctrine of justification between supposedly "mystical" and "juridical" expressions is eloquently exemplified in Romans 8—the great counter-chapter to what goes before (the fleshly man subject to sin, the Law, and death). We should notice the way in which here the "law" of the liberating, life-giving Spirit is set over against the enslaving law of death, and how it is denied that for those in Christ Jesus there is any "condemnation"—the catchword to which everything leads up (incomparably expressed in Bach's motet, "Jesu, Priceless Treasure," BWV 227). In the matter of the sinner's justification, also, the antitheses in the two chapters link them very closely with one another. Paul can speak of the Spirit only in terms of the coming, life, and work of Christ, through whose offering God achieved for man's lost state that which the Law was powerless to do because of sin—pull down the bastion of man's arbitrary exercise of his own will and break into our hearts with liberating power (Rom. 8:3 ff.). He thereby inaugurated a new and authoritative way of life. It is "Walk in the Spirit" (Rom. 8:9 ff.).

It may seem surprising that though Romans 8 deals expressly with the countermovement to the thoughts and endeavors of the "flesh" and the new start afforded by the Spirit, and clearly outlines Paul's "ethics," it contains not a single verb in the imperative. For the man whose mind is set on himself, both in his most disorderly and in his highest potentialities, the will of the "flesh" is, and can be none other than, a constant campaign against God ("hostility," Rom. 8:7). For the life of which man wants to make himself sure, God spells trouble and danger. This is "atheism" proper: not speculative denial of God's being, but the challenging of God's right to be God. Christ, however, having entered into our realm, death, has brought us into God's realm, life. Thus, his Spirit culminates in "life and peace" (Rom. 8:6).

IV

PRESENT SALVATION

THE WORD

Gospel and confession do not comprise matters of a remote antiquity vanished with the passage of time into an irrevocable past. Nor are they reminders of epoch-making events in the history of mankind. Christ's unique history is the saving event that determines the present and the future: "For we know that Christ being raised from the dead will never die again; death no longer has dominion over him. The death he died he died to sin, *once for all*, but the life he lives he lives to God" (Rom. 6:9 f.; cf. 14:9). The gospel makes the saving event *actual, present*, in the true sense of these words, and itself forms part of it; it is not just supplementary information about it. With its proclamation, the light of a new day of creation shines into the hearts of believers (2 Cor. 4:6). Accordingly, the apostle can also say of God's reconciliation of the world in Christ that he gave the "ministry," the "word of reconciliation" (2 Cor. 5:18 f.). Far from the proclamation's being a mere memory of a past "once," it is the holding out of hopes for a future "then." In it the "today" and "now" that mark the turning point in the ages become event. So Paul cites and interprets words of 2 Isaiah (Isa. 49:8): "At the acceptable time I have listened to you, and helped you on the day of salvation" (2 Cor. 6:2). In the light of righteousness based on faith, he therefore boldly reinterprets words of the Old Testament Law and relates them to the gospel: "Do not say in your heart, 'Who will ascend into heaven?' (that is, to bring Christ down) or 'Who will descend into the abyss?' (that is, to bring Christ up from the dead). But what does it say? The word is near you, on your lips and in your heart (that is, the word of faith which we preach)" (Rom. 10:6–8).

One might take general considerations and theories about word and language in themselves, or analogies from comparative religion, which certainly knows the phenomenon of the word of power, and try on their basis to come to some adequate explanation of Paul's astonishing utterances. But this would lead us nowhere. The sole basis of these utterances is the fact that Christ is near, raised from the dead, and that, as the exalted, present Lord, he "bestows his riches upon all who call on him" (Rom. 10:12). The word is his word (Rom. 10:17). Because his death and resurrection took place "for us" and his lordship applies to all, Paul can, and must, speak of the proclamation in these terms.

But what a word this is! In 1 Corinthians the apostle sums up its subject matter in the one blunt term which excludes all else, "the word of the cross" (1 Cor. 1:18).

One thing is certain: Paul means Christ's death on earth, the death he died in deepest humiliation and shame as a criminal (Phil. 2:8; 2 Cor. 13:4), and not any paradoxical symbol above time. It would never have occurred to any man of the ancient world to exalt into a religious symbol the cross, of all things, the most shameful form of execution, used by Roman justice only for slaves and rebels. But equally Paul did not entertain the idea that has survived down to the present, of a frightful miscarriage of justice, or the modern consideration that if a new trial could not be made retrospective, it might at least lead to rehabilitating the victim. But how is *this* to lead to the conclusion of a once-for-all redemptive significance for the cross? There have been plenty of miscarriages of justice in the history of mankind, and in the ancient world there was nothing of the once-for-all about crucifixion: in the Jewish war of 66–77 thousands died by it.

Nor is the apostle swayed by the concept of a tragedy: God's love, shown to men in his Son, failed utterly, being rejected with hate and blindness. Paul does not think that Christ's death meant the failure of God's love; instead, it demonstrated his power. Again, such a tragedy could evoke only horror and sympathy. Finally, still thinking of Paul, we must reject that motif of sympathy with the Crucified himself which so deeply influenced passion mysticism, particularly in the Middle Ages and later, tremendously absorbed as it was in meditation on Christ's sufferings. It would be wrong to take even Paul's words to the erring Galatians that he "wrote" the crucified Jesus Christ "before their eyes" (Gal. 3:1) in this sense, for the expression does not signify the "picture" of the suffering and dying Christ (Luther's translation "painted before your eyes" is misleading); instead, it is taken from the idea of a public proclamation, a decree promulgated by authority.

Paul expresses his concern in 1 Corinthians through a sharp contrast between "the word of the cross" and the "wisdom of this world" (1 Cor. 1:18–3:20). He never conceives the latter as a wisdom simply wrapped up in itself and excluding the question of God, but sees it, rather, as a wisdom bearing precisely on this question. Among the Jews this world's wisdom manifests itself in a demand for proofs of God's power ("signs"), and among the Greeks in the fact that they expect any statement about God to have the basis of a lofty wisdom, before they are prepared to accept it. A gospel which fails to do either, and is unable to prove its claims according to these standards, is to Jews a "stumbling-block" (skandalon) and to Gentiles "foolishness" (1 Cor. 1:22 f.).

Accordingly, even in the ancient world the Pauline gospel met with scorn. Early opponents of Christianity such as Celsus and Porphyry taunted Christianity with being unreasonable, uncultured, and even fatuous. And, nearer our own day, Goethe disposed of 1 Corinthians 3:19 with the comment: "There would be no point in attaining the age of seventy if all the world's wisdom were folly with God" (Maxims and Reflections 2).

As is shown by the acumen and precision with which Paul puts his case in 1 Corinthians 1–4, here no more than anywhere else does he inveigh against reason as such, and what he says about saving event and faith is not dictated by any secret delight in the absurd. He demands no "blind" faith, and says absolutely nothing about the sacrifice of understanding and intellect. No, what the word of the cross says is that through this "foolish" gospel God turned "the world's wisdom" into foolishness. What characterizes the latter is the desire to measure God by its own standards. It is thus shown to be man's attempt to hold his own with God. However, the unbeliever's verdict on God also determines God's verdict on him—condemnation. On the other hand, in the word of the cross, believers prepared to live on the sole basis of his grace find deliverance. In this very paradoxical way, Christ crucified is God's power and wisdom: "For the foolishness of God is wiser than [the wisdom of] men, and the weakness of God is stronger than [the strength of] men" (1 Cor. 1:25).

The particular audience to which Paul wrote 1 Corinthians should not cause us to tone down the harshness of the term "the word of the cross" and regard it as an exaggerated and incomplete formula dictated by the situation and "of course" requiring tacit supplementation by other "saving facts" such as Christ's resurrection and lordship, about which, too, the letters have a great deal to say. It goes without saying that Paul did not forget resurrection and lordship in this connection either. They form part of the "word of the cross," though not as a second or third adjunct; rather, they are interpreted in these allegedly one-sided brief words. This means that Christ's death is not annulled by the resurrection and exaltation: rather, it is held on to, made operative as saving event in both judgment and deliverance, and so becomes the subject matter of preaching (Conzelmann). The "enthusiasts" at Corinth had succumbed to the attractions of a different theology of the resurrection and believed that, possessing Christ's spirit, they were even now living in a new aeon beyond time and death. This is the reference of the ironic, angry words of 1 Corinthians 4:8: "Already you are filled! Already you have become rich! Without us you have become kings! And would that you did reign, so that we might share the rule with you!" Yet, God has exhibited the apostles, "last of all, like men sentenced to death; because we have become a spectacle to the world, to angels and to men. We are fools for Christ's sake, but you are wise in Christ. We are weak, but you are strong. You are held in honor, but we in disrepute. To the present hour we hunger and thirst, we are ill-clad and buffeted and homeless, and we labor, working with our own hands. When reviled, we bless; when persecuted, we endure; when slandered, we try to conciliate; we have become, and are now, as the refuse of the world, the offscouring of all things" (1 Cor. 4:9-13). For Paul apostleship meant being branded by the "word of the cross" and *not yet* being delivered from the hardships of daily life and death (cf. the section following).

Furthermore, the Corinthians themselves had daily proof of the implications of the word of the cross in their own call and existence in Christ. The social structure of their church was positive evidence of God's no to all human wisdom, power, and worldly status, but also of his free grace in election and of his re-creative, redemptive power. On it alone may believers rest their boasting (1 Cor. 1:26-31).

All that is here said of the power of the gospel of the cross to judge, shame, and bring to nothing (note the accumulation of negatives both in 1:26-31 and in what follows) is nevertheless in reality aimed at a proclamation of the power of the creator and redeemer. Thus, the gospel of faith simply repeats in a new guise the word spoken at creation (1 Cor. 1:28; cf. Rom. 4:17; 2 Cor. 4:6). In so doing, it also elucidates the meaning of Paul's "ontological" terms considered above. They show that authentic existence can only mean indebtedness—as Paul says of himself, "not I, but the grace of God which is with me" (1 Cor. 15:10). God directed that in his weakness and bodily infirmity he should live by it alone: "My grace is sufficient for you, for my power is made perfect in weakness" (2 Cor. 12:9). In the same way Paul also demolishes the boasting of the "enthusiasts" at Corinth, asking, "What have you that you did not receive?" (1 Cor. 4:7), just as in Romans he calls out to the Gentile Christians who want to triumph over fallen Israel: "Note then the kindness and the severity of God: severity toward those who have fallen, but God's kindness to you, provided you continue in his kindness; otherwise you too will be cut off" (11:22). Boasting in the Lord means ceasing to boast of oneself.

This renunciation of all other boasting—even on the strength of the human authorities to whose teaching the Corinthians subscribed—opens up the way from *freedom.* Thus, in the immediate

context of the word of the cross come the strains of Paul's great
hymn on *libertas Christiana*:

> All are yours—
> Paul or Apollos or Cephas,
> the world or life or death,
> the present or the future—
> all are yours.
> But you are Christ's,
> but Christ is God's. (1 Cor. 3:21 ff.)

Does this last ("but you are Christ's") impose a limit on believers' freedom? There might be something to be said for this.
Here, however, it gives the reason for the all-encompassing power
of their freedom.

Amid the important discussions of the cross and wisdom in 1
Corinthians there is a passage which exposition even today finds
considerably more difficult than most (2:6-16). One of the main
reasons is obvious: the apostle is drawing on the style of preaching favored by his "gnostic" opponents in Corinth and taking up a
body of already current ideas; this he does, of course, as elsewhere, in order to amend both and give a different understanding
of them. It is indeed very odd that, having just emphasized and
stressed the crucified Christ as the sole subject matter of his gospel
and standard of his conduct (1 Cor. 2:1-5), he should now
speak of a "wisdom for the mature" apparently transcending this,
a wisdom which he, too, could preach about were not the Corinthians, as their quarreling proved, still unspiritual—only too unspiritual—and not in the slightest "mature." In actual fact, he at
once abruptly breaks off speaking about this kind of wisdom, for
his hearers are still like children needing milk but not yet ready for
solid food (1 Cor. 3:1-3). "Mature"—this was apparently a
haughty way the Corinthian "spirituals" had of describing themselves. It corresponded to a mode of thought and speech both
current in gnosticism and common in the early church, and on
their lips meant those who, by virtue of their exceptional possession of the Spirit, had gone beyond the state of mere faith and
attained to deeper knowledge of divine revelation. Does this mean

that, in spite of all that goes before, Paul did think of a transcending of faith? Was there a wisdom for which the word of the cross did not suffice, and a "spirit," reserved for only the few, which searches and knows everything, "even the depths of God"? Was the apostle not then a traitor to his own deepest convictions? However strongly these questions present themselves, it is clear that an affirmative answer means that Paul is being misunderstood. What he says does not go beyond his gospel of the cross. Admittedly, he here takes up ideas and concepts found in late Jewish wisdom theology which at an early date were appropriated by primitive Christian thought and undoubtedly by the Corinthian "theologians" as well: the gnostics elaborated them into a great redemptive myth. It is certainly no accident that in this very context the apostle cites apocryphal words for which gnosticism has a great fondness (their source is not certain: perhaps the Apocalypse of Elijah): "What no eye has seen, nor ear heard, nor the heart of man conceived, what God has prepared for those who love him" (1 Cor. 2:9). That this "secret and hidden" wisdom of God was concealed from the rulers of this age who are doomed to pass away has been proved by the fact that in their lack of understanding they "crucified the Lord of glory" (1 Cor. 2:7 f.). To us, however, who love God, he has revealed his eternal purpose through the Spirit (1 Cor. 2:9 f.). "Us"—for the apostle these are not just the "spiritual" as distinct from those who only have faith. And the "depths of God" are not his mysterious eternal purposes which none but the mature can fathom, but that which "God's grace bestows" on all believers (1 Cor. 2:12). Paul thus transcends what the Corinthian theology so dubiously emphasized and took as the basis of their pride, the contrast between mature and immature Christians in the church. He also radicalizes it, taking it out of the realm of relativity: rulers of the world=we: spirit of the world=God's spirit; human wisdom=wisdom bestowed by God, given to all of us who as believers have the Spirit of Christ (crucified) (1 Cor. 2:16). This very passage, therefore, in which at the first glance, by trimming his gospel to suit the Corinthian "gnostics" Paul is apparently untrue to himself, makes plain that he knows of no higher or deeper mysteries transcending the gospel than that comprised *in* the "word of the cross." Thus, the argu-

ments which seemed to be taking him beyond himself come back
to where they started, and are not only polemic, but also a very
positive exposition of the gospel of the cross.

THE APOSTLE'S MINISTRY AND SUFFERING

The theme of the work of an apostle plays a remarkably large
part in Paul's life and letters. This is especially true of the letters
to churches in which opponents sought to undermine his authority
and dispute his commission (Gal., Phil., 1 and 2 Cor.). In particular in the months-long correspondence collected in so-called 2
Corinthians, this is the main subject throughout (cf. Appendix
II). This leads one to presume that it was the opponents who
made great play of the question and forced the apostle's hand. But
this impression is deceptive. The prominence given it is not at all
due to situations in which the apostle was involved. All contro-
versy apart, apostleship is of the utmost importance for Paul. In
the superscription to his letters he regularly describes himself as
an "apostle called by the will of God," "servant of Jesus Christ,"
and so on, and long discussions of his apostolic office and conduct
run through his entire correspondence. These are intimately connected with the proclamation of his gospel. The exceptionally long
thanksgiving in his earliest letter, 1 Thessalonians, reminds the
church of its beginnings, at the time when the apostle, driven out
of Philippi, came to them as a stranger and had to work day and
night to earn his living and, with nothing impressive about him,
converted them by the gospel from idolatry: "to serve a living and
true God, and to wait for his Son from heaven, whom he raised
from the dead, Jesus who delivers us from the wrath to come" (1
Thess. 1:9 f.). That they received this word preached in extremely
unpretentious and commonplace circumstances "not as the word
of men but as what it really is, the word of God, which is at work
in you believers," constitutes the reason for and forms the subject
matter of Paul's thanksgiving (1 Thess. 2:13).

The importance of Paul's office on the gospel committed to him
(Rom. 1:1–17). Christ himself makes his ambassadors his
mouthpiece and is present in their preaching (2 Cor. 5:20). Because, as the prophetic statements of Galatians 1:15 f. (cf. Jer.

1:5; Isa. 49:1) say, Paul was set apart and called "before he was born" and "received grace and apostleship for all the nations" (Rom. 1:5), his office forms part of his gospel.

This inseverable connection is expressed in Romans 10 (see above) in a catena of questions, again modeled on the Old Testament: "For 'every one who calls upon the name of the Lord will be saved.' But how are men to call upon him in whom they have not believed? And how are they to believe in him of whom they have never heard? And how are they to hear without a preacher? And how can men preach unless they are sent? As it is written, 'How beautiful are the feet of those who preach good news!'" (Rom. 10:13 ff.).

In its original context the quotation, from Deutero-Isaiah (Isa. 52:7), describes the situation of the few who at the time of the exile stayed on in Jerusalem after it was laid waste and eagerly awaited the return of the exiles from Babylon. Watchmen were posted on the heights surrounding the city and looked forward to seeing the forerunners of the return. At long last the first messenger appeared far off on the mountains. Thereupon the watchers broke out into shouts of rejoicing. These passed from mouth to mouth. The forsaken city resounded with jubilation. These tidings of joy were the dawn of Jerusalem's salvation.

This, as Paul sees it, is the condition of the whole world; the message about Christ which sets men free is to sound to the ends of the earth (Rom. 10:18, with its citation of Ps. 19:5 [EV,6]). This catena—Christ's word, gospel, hearing, believing, confessing —constitutes the messengers' commission and service, in which his own apostolic office forms an indispensable part.

Thus, Paul's appeal to his commission was not the expression of an overdeveloped self-consciousness warped by slanders against him or of a craving (whether secret or not) to justify himself—he remembered that he had once persecuted the church and that later, when he was called to be an apostle, it was in a different way from the rest: it was almost monstrous ("as to one untimely born," 1 Cor. 15:8). While he made no secret of this and insisted that he was the "least of the apostles," he maintained that this did not make his authority any the less. The risen Christ appeared to him as much as to those called before him (1 Cor.

9:1; 15:6 ff.), and the churches he founded were the seal confirming his apostleship (1 Cor. 9:2, 15; 2 Cor. 9:3, etc.). He was their father who begot them through the gospel (1 Cor. 4:15); he looked after them like a mother (1 Thess. 2:7), and suffered birth pangs on their account "until Christ be formed in you" (Gal. 4:19). No one else was so close to them (1 Cor. 4:14 ff.).

But how did Paul conceive of his apostleship and how did he defend it? Interest in the office as an institution and in the external characteristics on which its authority rested, an interest which very soon arose in the early church and later became a vital matter, had no place in his mind. One need only recall his insistence in Galatians on his complete independence from the original apostles in Jerusalem, and on the small store that he set on their persons and status and on the prerequisites of their having been made apostles, namely, that they had been disciples of Jesus and belonged to the Twelve while he was on earth (Gal. 2:6). Further, in respect of his own direct call, much as he insists that it was a sovereign act of God, its supreme importance, he says, was not due to its exceptional circumstances, his vision of Christ, but to the gospel freed from the Law committed to him for the Gentiles. He maintains that this gospel, the one and only gospel, is the standard by which he himself and all others are to be judged— even an angel from heaven (Gal. 1:8; cf. 1 Cor. 4:1).

Philippians in particular showed that while Paul was in prison he was free from anxiety that the tying of his own hands might put the gospel in peril; it did not depend on him personally (Phil. 1:12–18). This feature finds especially happy expression in the numerous passages in his letters in which he commends to the churches his own most intimate fellow workers and other trusted persons, his sole aim being their recognition, he himself withdrawing into the background. To take just one example, here is his testimony to Timothy, whom he hopes soon to send to Philippi: "I have no one like him, who will be genuinely anxious for your welfare. They all look after their own interests, not those of Jesus Christ. But Timothy's worth you know, how as a son with a father he has served with me in the gospel" (Phil. 2:20 ff.: notice the twist the words take. They do not speak, as the beginning would lead us to expect, of Timothy's services to the apostle but of their service in common). His assistants are his partners in the same work and are often mentioned by name at the beginning or the end of a letter. He also repeatedly speaks most emphatically of his own and others' debts to individuals in churches (e.g., Rom. 16:2, 4) and assures his readers that while he may bring comfort to them, he also needs comfort from them and their prayers (Rom. 1:11 ff.; 15:30 ff.; 2 Cor. 1:7, 11; Phil. 1:19). Their relationship to one another is one of give and take (Phil. 4:15).

Paul is not the sole representative of the gospel. Even if, as he writes in 1 Corinthians 3:11, he himself laid the foundation of the church—again he immediately corrects himself and points to the foundation *already laid* by God, Christ—others built upon it. How ridiculous, then, to set too great a store on either his or other people's authority! "So neither he who plants nor he who waters is anything, but only God who gives the growth" (1 Cor. 3:7). "For we are *fellow* workers for God; you are God's field, God's building" (1 Cor. 3:9); the accent is on "fellow." He similarly guards against overestimation of his own personal authority, e.g.: "Not that we lord it over your faith; we work with you for your joy, for you stand firm in your faith" (2 Cor. 1:24), or, "For what we preach is not ourselves, but Jesus Christ as Lord, with ourselves as your servants for Jesus' sake" (2 Cor. 4:5).

These statements and numerous others like them make one all the more astonished at Paul's impassioned vehemence elsewhere, particularly in Galatians and Corinthians, the most emotional in all his letters, as he struggles to force opponents and churches to acknowledge that he is an apostle, rebuts the charges brought against him, and seeks to win back the allegiance of churches which had almost succumbed to the trouble fomented by his enemies. No trace now of composure and unconcern. Instead, he pulls out every stop: pain that makes him weep, anger and indignation, complaints and accusations, bitter irony, utter condemnation of the agitators and rebels, defenses and even commendations of himself, which though expressed against his own will and very out of character are nevertheless moving outbursts of his heart in which his wounded love woos those in danger and misled.

What is the reason for these very different utterances? We should certainly be wrong to regard them as merely the exaggerations of a momentary gloom or to imagine that when he wrote them Paul was provoked and mortified beyond endurance. The whole thing depends on detecting and appreciating the motives which impelled him. Here, if anywhere, it is clear that in this bitter struggle with his opponents what was at stake was not only his commission and conduct as an apostle, which these calumniated, but also the truth of the gospel.

Thus, with Paul in a particular sense person and work go hand in hand. In this conviction he and his opponents were actually at one. In spite of all the keenness of the antagonism, we must not overlook how much he had in common with them, even though both sides conceived of this in a fundamentally different way: only so shall we understand the contentions between them. They, too, call themselves "apostles and servants" of Christ (2 Cor. 11:23) and give themselves out as "servants of righteousness" (11:15). Common membership of the chosen people connects them, too (2 Cor. 11:22 f.; Phil. 3:4 ff.). And both insist that the gospel must be demonstrated in the lives of Christians and apostles. For better or worse, therefore, Paul had to fight it out in the same arena as they and compare himself with them. However coarse and unjustified the reproaches to which he often refers, in particular in 2 Corinthians 10–13 but also in Galatians and 1 Corinthians, there is not the slightest reason to regard his opponents as objects of a senseless veneration. Had they been so, how would they have been able to make their way into the church and find so much understanding there, and why would Paul have taken them so seriously?

We have already considered the kind of men who constituted the "super-apostles" at Corinth. They believed themselves to be filled by the Spirit of Christ with supernatural powers; thus Jesus' death could not mean for them what it did for Paul, not only the end of all earthly and human relationships to him (2 Cor. 5:16), but also of the old aeon of hostility between the world and God. The opponents, on the other hand, certainly did not understand Christ's death as God's reconciling of the world (2 Cor. 5:18 ff.), any more than they understood resurrection as the foundation and beginning of a "new creation" into which "in Christ" we are already transposed (2 Cor. 5:17), though in such a way that the Christian's earthly existence stands under the sign of the cross and of suffering with Christ. To Paul's opponents this union of "already" and "not yet," or to put it in another way, the eschatological tension in Christian and apostolic existence, meant nothing. Their own conduct and criticisms of Paul implied that for them this was a thing of the past. They therefore boasted of their works by the Spirit, zealously danced attendance on people, even armed with "recommendations" from other churches as to the amazing things they had achieved there, and contested Paul's commission by comparison with what they themselves could do.

The Corinthian letters contain several lists of the vicissitudes and acts which in Paul's view legitimatize the true apostle (2 Cor. 4:8 ff.; 11:23 ff.; 12:10; cf. also 1 Cor. 4:9 ff.). It was an age of intense religious and popular-philosophical rivalry. Vagrant popular preachers calling themselves ambassadors of a diety eloquently described the afflictions and tribulations and circumstances (Greek: *peristaseis*) in which as "men of God" they gave evidence of superiority and power, or as truly "wise" withdrew from the pressure of the world into the refuge of the spirit. The lists in 1 Corinthians follow these self-commendations even in points of style. But with Paul of course there is an extremity of paradox. His boast is of his suffering and weakness in which the power of Christ is made perfect (2 Cor. 12:9 f.). In contrast to the contemporary ideal of the "wise" man, he means something more than and different from the confidence that the power of his God enables him to endure even the most adverse vicissitudes. Paul takes a different view of trials: "We are afflicted in every way, but not crushed; perplexed, but not driven to despair; persecuted, but not forsaken; struck down, but not destroyed; always carrying in the body the *death of Jesus*, so that the life of Jesus may also be manifested in our bodies. So death is at work in us, but life in you" (2 Cor. 4:8–12). Thus for Paul the world's experiences and the overcoming of it both have their basis, necessity, and promise in Christ's death and resurrection. The same thing is also said in 2 Corinthians 6:4–10, a related passage: "through great endurance, in afflictions, hardships, calamities, beatings, imprisonments, tumults, labors, watching, hunger. . . . with the weapons of righteousness for the right hand and for the left; in honor and dishonor, in ill repute and good repute. We are treated as impostors, and yet are true; as unknown, and yet well known; as dying, and behold, we live; as punished, and yet not killed; as sorrowful, yet always rejoicing; as poor, yet making many rich; as having nothing, and yet possessing everything."

The series of enumerations of his acts and sufferings, successes and failures in his apostolic work—here and there with echoes of Psalm 118 (Luther's "lovely Confitemini")—right down to their final paradoxical antitheses are not, as with the itinerant preachers, the accounts of the life and fortunes of a hero; they are rather a declaration of the power of God who for Christ's sake brings the apostle into tribulation and death, but also delivers him from dying and changes sorrow into joy and poverty into riches.

This confidence allowed Paul to speak of apostolic and Christian *freedom* in exactly the same terms as used by the contemporary Stoic wise man. But with the apostle this had an entirely different basis and tenor. What he owes to God's grace is something he received, a gift; not merely a postulate and ideals that may or may not be realized, but the reality from which believers derive their being.

The very close approximation of the description of such freedom to the Stoic ideal is also shown in his words written in prison at Philippi: "I know how to be abased, and I know how to abound; in any and all circumstances I have learned the secret of facing plenty and hunger, abundance and want" (Phil. 4:12).

Such words about *autarchia* (Phil. 4:11) might also be found in Epictetus or Seneca. But not what follows: "I can do all things in him who strengthens me" (4:13). The same is true of the words in Romans which conclude the list of sufferings—tribulation, distress, persecution, famine, nakedness, peril, the sword: "No, in all these things we are more than conquerors *through him who* loved us" (Rom. 8:37). We certainly find in Epictetus: "What do money, joy, obscurity, glory, shame, praise and even death matter to the wise man? He can be victorious over them all" (Diss. I, 18,22). Nevertheless Paul and the Stoic understand freedom and its opposite from entirely different points of view. The latter taught that man was not free as long as he allowed all that was "alien," things immaterial to his life (circumstances, vicissitudes), to be in control of him and leave him at the mercy of his passions, whereas the free man withdrew from the things of self and was his own master. Paul, however, says that we are *not* free insofar and for so long as we ourselves control our lives and Christ has not become our Lord. Because of this and in contrast to Stoic thought, he does not start from consideration of man's ideal destiny, but from his actual condition, i.e., his inborn, inescapable, and culpable lack of freedom in God's sight and God's deliverance of him from it.

Paul was convinced that he presented men with Christ crucified both in the gospel he preached and in his own life. Yet, unlike the one who took Paul so much as his model, Ignatius of Antioch (*c.* A.D. 100), this never led the apostle to the further step of longing for a martyr's death and of thinking that unless God's ambassador suffered death in his service he had not done all he had been commissioned to do. Ignatius also believed that martyrdom was a treasury on which the martyr's church might draw for its salvation. This motif is, of course, to be found in the post-Pauline Colossians (Col. 1:24), and ideas of such a kind have been read into Philippians. A prisoner, facing trial and not knowing its outcome—acquittal or condemnation—he did in fact greatly long for death: "For to me to live is Christ, and to die is gain. . . . I am hard pressed between the two. My desire is to depart and be with Christ, for that is far better. But to remain in the flesh is more necessary on your account. Convinced of this, I know that I shall remain and continue with you all, for your progress and joy in the faith" (Phil. 1:21–25).

Death would break down the final barriers between those still alive on earth and Christ. But earthly life, too, belongs to Christ (Rom. 14:8), and only in Christ is there truly "life." Thus the alternative, life in the body or death, is in the last analysis not of ultimate significance: "as it is my eager expectation and hope that I shall not be at all ashamed, but that with full courage now as always Christ will be honored in my body, whether by life or by death" (Phil. 1:20).

The emphasis here is thus not on death by martyrdom: the apostle's whole life and work is "martyrdom." Nor must his possible "being offered up" (Phil. 2:17) be equated with the once-for-all redemptive and sacrificial death of Christ.

Paul's presenting of Christ by means of his own fortunes and
sufferings as well as his preaching certainly meant more to his
churches than anything else. His fate was not, however, to be
thought of as exceptional, but as exemplifying what being a Christian meant: dying and rising with Christ. Accordingly, he identified the lot of the churches at Thessalonica and Philippi, as they
suffered their first experience of persecution, with his own lot (1
Thess. 2:14 f.; Phil. 1:29 f.), and in 2 Corinthians he used similar
terms about his own sufferings in order to show the being brought
to nothing and the renewal that forms part of believers' lives: "So
we do not lose heart. Though our outer nature is wasting away,
our inner nature is being renewed every day. For this slight
momentary affliction is preparing for us an eternal weight of glory
beyond all comparison, because we look not to the things that are
seen but to the things that are unseen; for the things that are seen
are transient but the things that are unseen are eternal" (2 Cor.
4:16–18).

This is also the broad frame of reference within which to view
Paul's confrontations with his opponents, at first sight so odd and
with the appearance of petty, personal commonplace squabbles.
To imagine that the primitive Christians and Paul in particular
lived in an earthly paradise and to refuse to believe that the victo-
ries won under the aegis of the gospel cost hard, bitter fighting will
mean, of course, being profoundly shocked by these passages in
Paul's letters. In actual fact, in these battles the whole being of
both Paul himself and his opponents was at the focal point of
decision between true and false belief, truth and lies, the God of
Jesus Christ and the "god of this world" (2 Cor. 4:4), both sides
(it should be noticed) being convinced that Christ was present in
them. Accordingly, Paul tears away the masks from these "super-
apostles," calls them false apostles, deceitful workmen, servants of
Satan disguised as angels of light (2 Cor. 11:13–15), preachers
of a different gospel and a different Jesus, having received
a different spirit (11:4). But this also makes him stand up
to them and defend himself, though he has the role of a
"fool" thrust upon him (2 Cor. 11:1, 16 ff.; 12:1, 6, 11). He
may seem to "boast" as they did, in a way that is quite out of
character, but on his lips the term means the opposite of their self-

recommendation. For his boast is his weakness, that the power of Christ may rest upon him (cf. 2 Cor. 12:9 f.; cf. also Phil. 4:12). For Paul the "new creation," "the day of salvation" (2 Cor. 5:17; 6:2), is present only where Christ's ambassadors place his cross upon themselves in the concrete experiences of daily life and so attest the reality of God's reconciliation of the world to himself.

Other aspects of Paul's existential understanding and performance of his apostolic work of presenting the saving event and the message of salvation are expressed in an important passage in 1 Corinthians which actually lets us see the subjective presuppositions of his entire work and behavior as a missionary. In 1 Corinthians 9:19–23 he writes: "For though I am free from all men, I have made myself a slave to all, that I might win the more. To the Jews I became as a Jew, in order to win Jews; to those under the law I became as one under the law—though not being myself under the law—that I might win those under the law. To those outside the law I became as one outside the law—not being without law toward God but under the law of Christ—that I might win those outside the law. To the weak I became weak, that I might win the weak. I have become all things to all men, that I might by all means save some. I do it all for the sake of the gospel, that I may share in its blessings" (1 Cor. 9:19–23).

Precise in its composition, uniform structure, and purport, and also a masterpiece of rhetoric, this passage has unfortunately been largely debased on the lips of Christians, being frequently misused to provide cover for all and every accommodation of Christian preaching and conduct to their own day and generation. At best the words are generally taken as a *locus classicus* for the proposition—valid, of course, and one to which Paul himself gave good effect—that if the gospel is to be understood it must be adapted to the speech and thought forms of its hearers. But instead of focusing attention on these truly astonishing statements of Paul, such generalization reduces them to nothing, particularly if and when they are simply conceived as a technique of missionary accommodation.

It is significant and important that these statements, too, come under the rubric of the freedom which we already examined in close conjunction with Paul's understanding of himself as an apostle. As is shown by the whole context (1 Cor. 8–10), freedom is here thought of not as a right, but as renunciation of one's right for the sake of another, this being based on the fateful constraint of the gospel, the content of which is not left to the apostle's own judgment (1 Cor. 9:16). Paul is here taking his own practice in a matter on which the Corinthians were divided, meat offered to idols and joining in cultic meals with pagans, to illustrate the nature of freedom in general. Luther was therefore correct in deliberately modeling the first proposition of his famous "On the Freedom of a Christian Man" (1520) on 1 Corinthians 9:19: "A Christian is a free lord over all things and subject to no one. A Christian is a servant at the disposal of all things and subject to everyone."

Paul's freedom as he dealt with Jews and Gentiles, those inside and those outside the Law, cannot properly be regarded as a thing he might or might not exercise at will, but as obedience to the word committed to him. In this sense he became as a Jew to the Jews, to those outside the Law as one outside the Law, and to the weak person, weak.

What does this mean? None of the contrasted standpoints signifies differences between nations and individuals which from the point of view of enlightened religion and morality had become indifferent to a cosmopolitan sage of Paul's own day. Rather, these contrasts are to be taken seriously, and as sharply and exclusively as every Jew of the day took them; nor had they lost their force for primitive Christianity, either. One way or another they represented religious standpoints which in each case claimed to be a way of salvation. The Judaizers' dogma was the need for Christians, too, to keep the Law and be circumcised. In reverse, as we see especially with the Corinthian "enthusiasts," the counter-party proclaimed as the true proof of being a Christian abandonment of the Law, no law at all ("everything is allowed"). The persons, too, in Rome whom the "strong" contemptuously designated as the "weak" were undoubtedly trying in their way to show the genuine obedience of faith; hence they passed judgment on the others (Rom. 14:9 ff.).

Paul, however, no longer recognized any of these religious standpoints as such. As ways of salvation, preconditions and prerequisites of being a Christian, they were at an end. In his view, to proclaim ways of salvation of such a kind meant destruction of the way now opened by God, which had made an end of all human standpoints, even in religion, and therefore broken down the barriers that separated Jews and Gentiles.

It is important, however, to notice that Paul does not make this insight the basis of a new "standpoint" transcending all these differences; instead, he can say that in his attitude he is one with all of them. The reason for this lies in his acknowledgment—though in an entirely different sense from theirs—that each "standpoint" represents something which cannot be abandoned; they signify the hard-and-fast realities of life which no one may seek to get over and in which the gospel seeks and is appointed to meet each man. To put it more sharply: he does not adopt one or other of the *standpoints* as his own, but takes them seriously as the *place where men actually stand*—on earth and in history—and where all, without distinction though in themselves distinct, *are* as believers already set free: they do not have to change their circumstances before they can put this freedom into operation. Thus, the man born a Jew does not need as Christian to lay aside his mark of membership in the "chosen" people, and the man born a Gentile has no need to assume such a mark. Nor does the gospel call slaves and freemen to seek to change their existing social status, for "in Christ" the slave *has already become* a "freedman" of the Lord's, and the free man (in the social sense) a "slave of Christ's," both alike his property, body and soul (1 Cor. 7:17–24). This is the basis of the apostle's freedom in dealing with Jews and Gentiles, allowing him to become "all things to all men."

There can be no doubt that this did not make it any easier for Paul to approach all the sections and groups which he encountered within his churches and outside them. We can be perfectly sure that it made him a target for criticism: to many he would seem inconsistent, equivocal, vacillating without principle, a time-server, and a flatterer. As we see from Galatians, the Judaizers criticized him for having said nothing of the need to obey the Law and be circumcised, in order to gain easier access for his gospel with the Gentiles. It is perfectly conceivable that the reverse also took place, that many even of those who shared his views sometimes frowned on his readiness to fraternize with Jews and show tolerance toward them and their traditions. Paul, however, rebuts with the utmost sharpness the reproach of pleasing men (Gal. 1:10; cf. 1 Thess. 2:4) and angrily rebuts his opponents who wanted to make observance of the Law obligatory for Christians, too (Gal. 5:12; 6:12), giving as his reason not that they are burdening the churches with unnecessary things, but that they are removing the stumbling block of the cross (Gal. 5:11). Thus, the reason for his attitude toward Jews and Gentiles was not to tone down the "scandal" of his gospel, but to make it stand out in relief. This freedom proclaims his negation of the standpoints on which some men rest their confidence and his approbation of others who, placed as he is, and like himself, become a new creation in Christ.

Examples of how he retained such a freedom are his discussions of and decisions on the controversies within his churches—for example, the party strife in Corinth or the "strong" and "weak" there and in Rome. Characteristically, he never sees the *casus confessionis*, the dividing line between true and false belief, as lying at the point where the contestants saw it. Instead, he summons each side to be responsible for the other on the basis of their common experience through the love of God.

THE CHURCH

The saving event and the lordship of Christ are present realities within the world in the life of the church. Founded by God's saving act, it lives solely by grace. In Paul's view it is a body inaugurated by God and organized by his Spirit. In consequence, if rightly conceived, it cannot be treated in isolation, any more than anything else in Paul, but only indirectly, in the context of his conception of salvation taken as a whole. Accordingly, in our description of his apostolic life and work and of his gospel and theology, we were constantly occupied with it. The basic features of his conception of the church have already been sketched there. But it is in his ecclesiological utterances that the motifs and aims of his thought come to focus: here they are actualized along certain lines and given practical application.

Paul was not the creator and founder of the church. It was in existence before his conversion and initially moved him to zealous persecution. When he first encountered it, it already had a troubled history behind it, not a few traces and effects of which can be seen in his letters.

Ecclesia

While Paul makes abundant use of the church's own term for itself, *ecclesia of God*, this term appeared on the scene before his day. Its specific religious meaning is not immediately derivable from secular Greek; there it is a common technical word for the secular assembly of citizens. In the Septuagint, however, it is the regular term for the chosen people of Israel when assembled before God, as, for example, at Mount Sinai. From there it was taken over by primitive Christianity and became a designation of the new Israel, God's congregation within the world in the last days. The German word *Gemeinde* does not properly bring out the element of time fulfilled and of the end of the world. For the church (*Kirche*) is more and other than the individual congregation or church (*Gemeinde*) or the sum total of local congregations and their members. The church is prior to these in time and as a datum, and is simply given historical form in them, though the word (church) may be used—secondarily—of individual congregations. This is expressed characteristically in the opening words of 1 Corinthians: "To the church of God which is at Corinth, to those sanctified in Christ Jesus, called to be saints together with all those who in every place call on the name of our Lord Jesus Christ, both their Lord and ours . . ." (1:2). Conspicuous here are the numerous ecclesiological turns of phrase, mainly in the passive, also taken over from the Old Testament and in common use in primitive Christianity. They emphasize that becoming a member of the church is something done to a man, not something he does himself. This itself makes clear that, as understood by Paul and primitive Christianity, the "church" is not a man-made organization in which particular religious traditions and convictions are preserved, exemplified, and promulgated.

Significantly, there was nothing sociologically analogous in the religious and political world of the time. The nature of the church cannot be comprehended in the light of either the special features of Jewish national and temple life or the synagogue communities of Diaspora Judaism, or along the lines of the rigidly isolated sects like the Qumran community. This is equally true of the priestly-cultic arrangements in classical pagan temples, of the Hellenistic mystery cults, of the forms in which clubs and associations were organized in the ancient world, and also of political and communal constitutions.

The church did not originate in Jesus' own lifetime, but with the resurrection of the Crucified. Its "founder" is not the "historic" Jesus. The subject of his proclamation was the coming of God's kingdom already being announced by himself in word and deed, and breaking into the present world and its holy traditions and standards with liberating and judging power. The power of the coming kingdom was the basis of Jesus' own authority, of his gospel for sinners and outcasts, his struggle with the scribes and Pharisees, his word of healing, and his summons to discipleship. Jesus' mission was for all; unlike many other contemporary movements, he did not gather a "holy remnant," nor did he found a separated community of the righteous. His earthly life has no room for what, after his crucifixion and resurrection, is called the church. Even the famous isolated *logion* to Peter as the rock on which he was to build his church (Matt. 16:18 f.) cannot be claimed as representing the foundation of the church by the historic Jesus. There are good reasons for believing that it was put into his mouth by the post-resurrection church.

But the appearances of the risen Jesus and the Easter gospel evoked among the disciples the conviction that what in men's sight appeared to be utter failure and the end signified a new beginning on the part of God. From this arose the primitive church, united by faith in Jesus as the promised Messiah and the expectation of his speedy return in salvation and judgment as the Son of Man. This is the origin of the church as the community of the age of salvation, as a company of those made "saints" by God and "chosen," as *ecclesia*. To this end its proclamation began, believers were cleansed by baptism for the coming kingdom, received and experienced the Spirit, and with joy at the approaching end and prayer for the Lord's coming celebrated the meal after the Jewish fashion, as Jesus himself had done with tax collectors and sinners and, before his death, with his disciples. But this community did not separate itself from Judaism; it joined in the worship of the temple and remained true to the Law as hitherto. The promises made to Israel had now reached fulfillment in Jesus. Thus, the primitive church's duty to preach was also initially restricted to Israel.

The bursting of the limitations of Jewish religion took place only with the appearance of the "Hellenists"—though it happened early and on the same soil: Jerusalem. In the course of the book we have repeatedly spoken of this dramatic story. It led to bitter conflicts with Jewry and to clashes with the legalist wing of the primitive church. But in addition it led to new experiences of the presence of the exalted Lord and of the workings of his Spirit, and so to a new conception of salvation and of the church. Gentiles, too, now had access to salvation and the church. God's dealings and promises as authoritatively recorded in the Old Testament were not abandoned by Hellenistic Jewish groups of Christians, or by the Gentile churches. The authority of the Scriptures was not in dispute. Here, too, there was celebration of the Lord's Supper and baptism. Further, the realization that, as the eschatological people of God, the church by its very nature was and had to be *one* remained definitive for the whole body of Christians, though there were changes in the conception of it, the expression of its traditions, and the forms of its worship and organization.

A vivid picture of this variety is given in the sources for early Christianity, especially in the traditions collected and elaborated in the New Testament. They present no uniform and normative doctrine of the church. Everything is still in flux. Nevertheless it would be a mistake to think of a vague variety of churches instead of the one primitive Christian church. Rather, a distinction should be made between the reality and superiority of the one church and the variety in the manifestations and concepts of it. At the same time this directly explains why even in the earliest days the unity

of the church was bound to present a problem and become a
matter of struggle within the first decades. To this Paul is among
the oldest witnesses, as he is certainly the most conspicuous of
them. His life and gospel show that his ideas about the church
have their roots in Hellenistic Christendom. Nonetheless, his own
force and consistency meant a rethinking of what he took over,
and gave it greater effect than it ever had had before.

The Spirit

In Paul's view, the promises made to Israel applied to all Jews
and Christians who believed in Christ. The Gentiles, too, are now
Abraham's offspring and heirs (Gal. 3:29), no longer children
enslaved under the law of the earthly Jerusalem, but children of
the free, heavenly city (Gal. 4:23–31); the true Israel of God
(Gal. 6:16), his "field" and "building" (1 Cor. 3:9). In this
sense he wrote to Corinth: "Do you not know that you are God's
temple and that God's spirit dwells in you?" (1 Cor. 3:16 f.). In
predicating the church in those terms he was thinking not of the
numerous heathen shrines and temples throughout the world in
honor of a deity, but of the one unique temple in Zion; here alone,
as the Old Testament and Judaism well knew, God has his dwelling place and let himself be found in the world. The metaphor was
taken up in other parts of the New Testament (cf. 1 Pet. 2:4 ff.),
and it implies that God is present for the world in the church, no
longer of course tied to an earthly holy place, but active by means
of his *Spirit* alone, the manifestation of his presence, the power
behind a new world.

The whole of primitive Christianity shared this eschatological
conviction with Paul. As a result he shared even with the Corinthian "enthusiasts" the experience of God's Spirit as an impelling
force breaking in on believers. He did not even fight shy of re-
minding the Corinthians of the ways in which they were moved by
the Spirit when they were still pagans (1 Cor. 12:2). But this very
thing made him aware of the equivocal character of such phe-
nomena. The sole mark of genuineness in connection with the
Holy Spirit is the confession that Jesus is Lord (1 Cor. 12:3); but

this means confession of the One crucified. The Spirit dwells in the church and makes it God's temple, because the church hears the word of the cross which discredits all human wisdom (1 Cor. 3:18 ff.), just as all striving to gain righteousness by the works of the law founders on it (Gal. 3:1–5). Thus, for Paul God's Spirit is not the supernatural power that enables a man to transcend his earthly life and its limitations: instead, it is the power of God who shows himself mighty in lowliness and weakness.

Paul's directions about worship (1 Cor. 14) best show how vigorously the apostle had striven to restrain the spirits and prevent them from causing chaos without at the same time quenching the power of *the* Spirit and replacing it by reason and order. The wording of the chapter might suggest the latter because, when approached by the Corinthians themselves as to a point of view on "gifts of the Spirit," he repeatedly drew a sharp distinction between "speaking in the Spirit" and "speaking with reason," and accordingly gave a fundamentally lower rank to what was for the Corinthians the supreme manifestation of the divine Spirit, ecstatic "speaking with tongues," than to prophecy and other "reasonable" forms of utterance. However, here Paul is merely using the popular concept of "Spirit" and "gifts of the Spirit" current also in Corinth, as elsewhere in primitive Christian language, in order to correct it, in a new content, and make it into a new standard. In actual fact he regarded prophecy, too, as a gift of the Spirit, all the higher because it could be understood by everyone present at worship, by outsiders and even unbelievers, so that, convicted and conscience-stricken, they had to fall on their faces and confess that "God is really among you" (1 Cor. 14:24 f.). Hence his critical reserved attitude to all forms of ecstatic discourse in public worship (proclamation, prayer, hymn, and blessing) by means of which the believer might well edify himself but not the church. His guiding principle was responsibility toward others, even for the least of them who as yet had not been caught up in the Spirit. Thus it was not a simple matter of opposition between God's Spirit and reason. In Paul's view these were in no sense abstract principles. This point of view would be more opposite to the "enthusiasts'" way of thinking and consciousness. For the apostle, on the contrary, the only subject matter and standard was the word of salvation which is for all, and which all may understand.

Spirit and Law

Paul's utterances in 1 Corinthians 14 furnish important hints toward answering a much debated question: What is the relationship between Spirit and law in the church as he conceived it? Here again, thinking in terms of basic principles and efforts to adjust and link the two by developing the ideas of office, hierarchy, succession, and so on came about only in the post-Pauline period. By that time the church had also become institutionalized and, the other side of the coin, various forms of "enthusiasm" made their appearance as a countermovement. Modern discussions of the history of canon law, which continue today with vigor, still start from the alternative, spirit or law (Sohm). For Paul, however, there was no such alternative. Law and spirit were not opposed: each demanded the other; for "God is not a God of confusion but of peace" (1 Cor. 14:33). Many of his apostolic directions are thoroughly legal in character. Yet he does not give them in order to concede and preserve a function of limitation and correction for law *in addition to* the free play of the Spirit, regarding it as necessary in the earthly community for good or ill. Rather, his intention was to establish on a firm basis the law that was already *in* the proclamation and *in* the operation of the Spirit. Thus, when he opposes the Corinthian "enthusiasts," he claims that he, too, has the Spirit: "If any one thinks that he is a prophet, or spiritual, he should acknowledge that what I am writing to you is a command of the Lord" (1 Cor. 14:37). "And I think that I have the Spirit of God" (1 Cor. 7:40).

This law inherent in the power of the Spirit, of which he himself was the fountainhead, was admittedly exceptional in kind. The elements which elsewhere form indispensable concomitants of law and the bases of a community founded on it—a fixed law, an authoritative court that makes the law or interprets it in mandatory fashion, authorities which possibly enforce it and punish offenses against it—these either play no part at all or at best have a subordinate and indefinite role. True, in extreme cases Paul could remind the church of its spirit-given duty and authority to exercise discipline, even to the point of excommunicating notorious offenders (1 Cor. 5:3 ff.), and threaten that as apostle he might come "with the rod" (1 Cor. 4:21). Nevertheless, the church had as yet no uniform and binding constitution to regulate its legal functions and competences. We certainly sometimes read of overseers whom members are to respect and not make their work more difficult (1 Thess. 5:12), of "overseers and deacons" (Phil. 1:1), and of the charisma of "leadership in the church" (1 Cor. 12:28; Rom. 12:8). But the terms are rare, and not fixed; they suggest *ad hoc* service and can nowhere be brought within a hierarchical gradation of institutional offices. Even patriarchal government by elders, stemming from the synagogue, was, on the showing of Paul's genuine letters, unknown to his churches; it made its appearance only after his day. Admittedly, Acts and the post-Pauline Pastorals take it back to Paul himself, but this is wrong. The same thing holds, of course, for the subsequent monarchical episcopate.

What then are the sources of law and the principles on which the apostle based his advice? Just once or twice he brings forward *words of the Lord*. Their authority is unconditional. But are they of the nature of legal maxims? Among the few which he cites, one at most, Jesus' prohibition of divorce (1 Cor. 7:10), is legal in character, but only contingently. For while Paul cites the saying as canonical, he nevertheless allows divorce when it is insisted on by the unbelieving partner in a mixed marriage. In another place he gives Jesus' words to the effect that the laborer is worthy of his hire (1 Cor. 9:14), but his mention of it comes in a series of other rules on the same subject designed simply to establish his right to maintenance from the church—a right which, however, he himself chose not to exercise. Nor is the *Old Testament* a source of law. Naturally, for Paul and his churches, it was Holy Scripture, and he frequently adduced it in rabbinic fashion. But it did not exist in its own right. It had been "written down for our instruction, upon whom the end of the ages has come" (1 Cor. 10:11; cf. Rom. 15:4). To the extent that the Old Testament pointed beyond itself to its fulfillment and to the eschatological "today" in which the Christian church was now living its life, Paul acknowledged that it had an important function to fulfill, but at the same time, he made its importance as a norm for believers' living very relative indeed. As binding law it had been done away with by Christ; at best it could serve only to shed light on the believer's own situation and confirm what he has already been told in the gospel. This was also the case with the arguments which Paul quite often adduced from the order of *nature* and universal *morality* and with his references to what obtained throughout the churches as *use and wont*. But these, too, only help the argument along: they are not the church's basis, themselves establishing law. Rather, in certain cases they serve the purpose of putting the church to shame by making it aware of what is accepted as law and order throughout the world. Thus, of a man's marriage with his father's wife (i.e., stepmother; cf. 1 Cor. 5:1 ff.) to which the Corinthians turned a blind eye, Paul says that it is an arrangement not tolerated "even among pagans."

All these sources are important, some more so than others. However, they are always merely coordinated with the real fountainhead which gives Paul's directions their force, the *gospel and the new being in Christ*, into which believers have been transposed by God's grace without any additional action on their part. This is the new life from which they derive, irrespective of whether or not they conform to the gospel which they have heard. Paul can bluntly ask the Galatians, "Whence did you receive the Spirit?" (Gal. 3:2): similarly, in 1 Corinthians he can give thanks—and this not simply in the sense of a *captatio benevolentiae*—that the church had been greatly enriched by God's grace, and that the testimony of Christ had taken root among them (1 Cor. 1:4 ff.), even though in Corinth there had been dreadful moral lapses. Nevertheless, the Spirit performs his work with them. All the more resolutely does the apostle stretch out his hand and seek to put the church in order again. Nor does he ever write off a church or even one of its members, though he does his utmost to make them aware of the immovable barriers erected by God's Spirit against all transgression, and of the judicial power which he himself possesses as much as the church, and to which he gives expression by conjuring them and even calling down curses upon them (1 Cor. 3:17; 14:38; 16:22; Gal. 6:7 f.).

The most important source of Paul's directions, the basis of all else, is the church's *remembrance* of its origin, God's saving acts in Christ as proclaimed in the gospel. Distinguished neither by culture, power, and noble birth nor by their own righteousness, believers were "called" and given by their creator, who summons "even things that are not to life" (1 Cor. 1:26 ff., etc.), a new existence in Christ. Delivered from the power of the world which is passing away (Gal. 5:1, 13; Rom. 6, etc.), they are no longer in bondage to men and themselves, but belong to God (1 Cor. 6:19 f.; 7:23 f.; Rom. 14:7 ff.). Formerly pining away in night and darkness, they are now children of the light and the day (1 Thess. 5:5 f.; Rom. 13:11 f.), "washed, sanctified, justified in the name of the Lord Jesus Christ and in the Spirit of our God" (1 Cor. 6:11), "in Christ a new creation" (2 Cor. 5:17). This is the church's position *even now*, in virtue of the grace offered in the gospel and accepted by faith. This is also, Paul knows, the basis of his own apostolic authority (1 Cor. 4:15; Rom. 12:1, 3, etc.).

Tied to the word of the cross, the Spirit constitutes an extremely stern court of law to judge all the visible manifestations and guarantees on which men try to base their confidence. In this respect Paul regarded his churches as in mortal peril from both Judaism and "enthusiasm"; hence the war on two fronts throughout his life. At first sight, the two look very different, but in reality they are clearly connected and could therefore, as shown by Paul's opponents in Corinth, Galatia, and Philippi, actually act in combination. On the one side was the temptation to seek union with the chosen people by accepting the Law, circumcision, and ritual observances and so retreading Judaism's hopeless, prospectless path. On the other side was the apparently opposite effort, to break with all earthly ties—even going so far as sexual libertinism shamelessly proclaimed and practiced—and to make a great parade of the new life "in the Spirit." Both alike, relapse into the Law and advance into the headiness of experience in the Spirit, are described by Paul as profanation and annulment of Christ's cross (Gal. 5:11; Phil. 3:18; 1 Cor. 1:17), at any rate as an attempt to transcend the present, both in place and time, in which the gospel seeks and meets believers and holds them fast, and to pass over to a fancied past or a fanciful "perfection." In both cases his opponents and critics for whom his gospel was not sufficient had fallen victim to a hopeless anachronism and robbed the word of grace both of its true here-and-nowness and of its counterpart, mankind in whom its liberating word should bear fruit.

Worship

It is no accident that many of Paul's directions in 1 Corinthians have to do with worship. Primarily and pre-eminently the Ecclesia is in fact the church assembled for worship. In worship the church proves what it is, though worship also reveals and exemplifies disorder and confusion. Here again, what the apostle discusses in his directions and what he regards as unessential are both insignificant. Though we gather more about the worship of primitive Christianity from him than from any other New Testament writer, we hear practically nothing of things which formed part of Jewish or pagan worship; sacred places and seasons, rites and priestly functions. We are certainly told of proclamation of the word, blessing, the church's answering Amen, invocation of the Lord and acclamations affirming his presence and power, and hymns in his praise and acts in the context of worship such as baptism and the Lord's Supper. We can also clearly see that worship in Paul's churches had been influenced by the worship of the synagogue in Diaspora Judaism and also by various rites and concepts of the mystery religions. But to many questions no answer is furnished, and there is no prospect of success in attempting on the basis of his letter to reconstruct anything like a tolerably uniform liturgical formulary. Even the question of whether the Lord's Supper was always and everywhere accompanied by preaching is given no firm answer. It generally was, in all probability, but the two may also have been separate. The incidental note in 1 Corinthians 16:2 lets us see at most that the church observed the first day of week, the day of Christ's resurrection. By and large we have to reckon with great freedom and diversity. But many of the elements normally and elsewhere of the essence of worship certainly had no place in the worship of Paul's churches.

On the other hand, the apostle's statements about the meaning of acts of worship and the criterion by which they are to be evaluated are eloquent and clear. The sole standard is *"edification"* of the church. In 1 Corinthians 14, to which frequent reference has been made above, the word occurs no fewer than seven times. Paul, we may recollect, was being obliged to define his attitude to Spirit-inspired demonstrations and their effects, which were threatening to swamp the church at Corinth, and to express his opinion on the tempestuous activities in their worship. The word "edification" keeps cropping up. Unfortunately, in our traditional churchly speech it has become so narrowed down, emptied of meaning, and twisted away from its significance in Paul that we must first recall its original meaning. With Paul it does not refer to *individual* subjective religious experience. This must have been the way in which it was taken by the Corinthian fanatics. The apostle, however, speaks critically and with irony of "edifying oneself" (1 Cor. 14:4; cf. also 8:10) and recognizes only the edification of the church (1 Cor. 14:3-5, 12, 17, 26). Is the man who is not distinguished by particular gifts of the Spirit, and so the church in general, edified? This dictates the crucial test question Paul poses in evaluating speaking with tongues and prophecy. Paul also describes his own founding of churches and the work of his successors as building and continuing to build (1 Cor. 3:5 ff.; 2 Cor. 10:8; 12:19; 13:10). But each and every church member has the duty of edifying the rest (1 Thess. 5:11; 1 Cor. 8:11-12; 1 Cor. 14; Rom. 14:19; 15:2), following the standard set and the example given by Christ, who even died for others (1 Cor. 8:11 f.; Rom. 14:15) and welcomed all (Rom. 15:7). Self-surrender and service in renunciation of one's own rights is now the law of the church's "edification." In this sense Paul describes himself as "one outside the law—not being without law toward God but under the law of Christ" (1 Cor. 9:21)—and summons the church to "be imitators of me, as I am of Christ" (1 Cor. 11:1; cf. Gal. 4:12; 6:2; Phil. 3:17; 1 Thess. 1:6; 2:14).

These statements show that Paul's directions for worship are simply a practical application of the "theology of the cross." But at the same time they also show that in his view worship was in no sense merely an arrangement for the discharge of certain cultic obligations. It bears on every part of believers' lives: "I appeal to you therefore, brethren, by the mercies of God, to present your

bodies as a living sacrifice, holy and acceptable to God, which is
your spiritual worship" (Rom. 12:1). This exhortation introduces
the parenetic part of Romans. The term "a living sacrifice" is
frequent in post-classical mystic-religious texts. In contrast to the
common people's sacrifices and rites, the enlightened among the
Greeks evolved the idea that true religion consisted in the proper
exercise of reason. Hellenistic mysticism, however, went further
and said that the supreme form of worship of God lay in ecstatic
hymns in honor of the deity, in the suppliant's union with the all-
embracing living principle. It is in this sense—not only of the
intellectual attitude of reason, but also of the attitude brought
about by the Spirit of God—that Paul takes up the motif, though
he gives it a fundamentally different and critical application: you
yourselves, body and soul, in your everyday lives are the only
sacrifice pleasing to God.

In this way the apostle takes the "enthusiasts," who thought of
themselves as already transposed into a realm beyond time and
history, back into the temporality and historicity of human existence, where each is responsible for his neighbor. For the church is
not living in the new aeon of perfection, but in the tense last days
between the resurrection of the Crucified and his second coming,
still under the auspices of his death on the cross in weakness, and
yet already in a life deriving from the power of the Risen One (2
Cor. 13:4). In this way, to the vaunted and admired manifestations of the Spirit which Paul, too, knows from his own experience
and which he does not simply forbid in the church, he denies the
character of ultimate perfection; he evaluates them by the standard of the word of the cross and the commandment to love one's
neighbor as oneself.

Baptism and the Lord's Supper

Similar ideas reappear in what Paul says about baptism and the
Lord's Supper. Here again he was able to link up with what the
church already knew (Rom. 6:3; 1 Cor. 10:15). But how did he
conceive of both? The theological term "sacrament" under which
we range the two was unknown to Paul, although he sometimes
does mention them together (1 Cor. 10:1-4). Nor is the term

altogether a happy one, since it can easily focus interest on ritual practices which he did not properly have in mind. To be sure, he did not regard the sacraments as human devices, either, but as acts efficacious through the power of grace, presupposed as such both throughout primitive Christianity and in his own churches, and of great importance. At the same time he adduced them rather as exemplifications and illustrations, and from them gained insights which elsewhere he derived directly from the gospel itself and, frequently, from confessions of faith drawn up before his day, without appeal to the "sacraments."

His statements about baptism are initially of the nature of reminder and existential appeal. In the primitive church from the very beginning baptism in the name of Jesus was practiced and conceived as a sacrament, that is, an act giving rise to actual results which made its recipients over to the Lord, mediated their forgiveness of sins, bestowed the Spirit, put them under the protection of the Kyrios, and thus made them members of the eschatological community of the redeemed. Paul, too, speaks of it in just the same way and uses terms already current in primitive tradition: wash, sanctify, justify (1 Cor. 6:11); establish in Christ, anoint, seal (=mark with a seal), gift of the Spirit (2 Cor. 1:22). The degree to which he, too, regarded baptism as having actual results is shown, among other things, by his reference in passing to the odd custom at Corinth of vicarious baptism (1 Cor. 15:29). This implies that the Corinthians were having themselves baptized as representatives of and on behalf of pagans who had died unbelievers, in order to procure for them a portion in salvation. Paul can hardly have introduced or commended this custom, found also in gnostic mysteries, yet he did not reject it either. His purpose in mentioning it was to make clear to the Corinthians that if they denied the resurrection of the dead they also made nonsense of this custom of theirs.

The terms for the saving event conveyed by baptism which are listed above do not exhaust its full meaning. Other Pauline expressions, such as "putting on" Christ (Gal. 3:27) and "being baptized into the body of Christ and made to drink of one Spirit" (1 Cor. 12:13), more intensively and specifically convey the full union of the person baptized with Christ. This is pre-eminently

true of the idea found in Romans 6:3 that baptism affords participation in Christ's death and resurrection. Parallels from other
religions, not numerous indeed but enough for the purpose, indicate that this idea arose in the Hellenistic churches under the
influence of pagan mystery cults in which initiates were given a
share in the fortunes of their deity and, by means of a ritual dying
and rising along with him, attained salvation, deliverance from
their own appointed death. Significantly, however, though Paul
utilizes the idea, he applies it in a different way from what might
lead us to expect the mysteries, just as it is clearly different from
the conception of it in his churches. For the latter, baptism signified an already accomplished transposition, in virtue of Christ's
resurrection, into a new, supernatural life beyond death. Paul, on
the other hand, his mind on the present state of baptized believers,
speaks only of their being crucified, dead, and buried with Christ.
Rising with him, life, is an object of hope (in Rom. 6:2–8 note
the contrast between the past tense in the verbs and the markedly
future terms). Thus their present state is under the auspices of the
cross. As crucified with him, believers still wear a "body of
humiliation" (Phil. 3:21; cf. also 3:10; Rom. 8:17, etc.). But
this already signifies eschatological existence, for the baptized are
delivered from the destroying power of sin: they have left it behind. Since they are dead with Christ, death no longer faces them
but is at their back. They come from death—not, however, in the
physical sense of bodily resurrection; instead, they are now for the
first time set free and called to a new form of being, life, "so that
as Christ was raised from the dead by the glory of the Father, we
too might walk in newness of life" (Rom. 6:4). In this sense, of
course, it can be said even of the present state of those baptized,
"so you must consider yourselves dead to sin and alive to God in
Jesus Christ" (Rom. 6:11).

In thus differentiating between death and resurrection, present
and future, already and not yet—closely connected as they still
remain—Paul made a radical break with baptism not only as
conceived in the mysteries, but also as popularly and commonly
conceived in the Hellenistic churches where this all-important
dialectic had been leveled down and canceled out.

Quite the same motifs are to be found in Paul's treatment of the

Lord's Supper. There is no need here to go into the origins and prehistory, now somewhat obscure in detail, of this observance of the primitive church's, and to follow up its further development in the early church. There can be no doubt that it goes back to Jesus' last meal—when Paul himself cites the words of institution he appeals to a tradition deriving from the Lord (1 Cor. 11:23). But it is equally clear that, particularly among Hellenistic Christians, the form and meaning attached to the observance changed to no small extent. Here, too, the apostle is in a position to remind the church of a well-known tradition and appeal to a conception of the Supper of which he himself was not the author (1 Cor. 10:15). The tradition signifies that, in virtue of the blessing of the cup and the drinking of the wine those present "participate" in the blood of Christ, just as in virtue of breaking and eating the bread they "participate" in his body given up to death on our behalf (1 Cor. 10:16 ff.; 11:23 ff.). This presupposes that the "Lord's Supper" (1 Cor. 11:20) was an actual common meal with the breaking of the bread accompanied by thanksgiving at the beginning and the presentation of the cup at the end "after the eating" (1 Cor. 11:25). The two acts, presentation of the bread and of the wine, separated by the meal and probably accompanied by the citation of the Lord's words of institution, were of supreme importance in the expressly "sacramental" sense of 1 Corinthians 10:16 ff. This does not contradict the formula of the institution, "this do in remembrance of me," but rather is in harmony with it; for the words do not indicate a mere memorial meal in memory of a man now dead, but strictly mean "making present reality" of Christ's saving death.

The sacramental significance indicated by the term "participation" is not, however, specifically Pauline—whatever the derivation of the words of institution, also given in the Synoptics (Mark 14:22 ff. and parallels), "participation" is of Hellenistic Christian origin. What is Pauline is the turn he gives to the sacramental act. He concludes that "because there is one bread, we who are many are one body, for we all partake of the one bread" (1 Cor. 10:17). Here the word "bread" is used in two different senses. Corresponding to Jesus' words about the bread, "this is my body for you," Paul first means Jesus' body in the bread offered,

mediating salvation to those who ate it and received it as such.
But by receiving, they are, and show themselves to be, the body of
Christ, though now in a new but not less real sense, the *corpus
mysticum ecclesiae*, the church. This is not mere metaphor: the
"real" statement in the words of institution, "this is my body,"
and the "reality" of the others, "we are his body," correspond.

In Paul's conception of the Lord's Supper, both things, the
believers' saving reception into the sphere of Christ's lordship and
their unity one with another together with its obligations, are
conjoined. This dictates the leading motifs and arguments in his
sharp reproof of the church in the matter of abuses in its observance of the Supper (1 Cor. 11). In Corinth, too, it was celebrated
within the framework of a common meal. But, as we may see, the
two sacramental acts of breaking the bread and drinking from the
common cup, originally separated by the meal, had come to be
placed at the end of the whole proceedings and so given pride of
place. This usage had evolved at an early date in other places as
well as Corinth, for the old phrase preserved in Paul and Luke
(Luke 22:20), "after the eating," disappears in Mark 14:22 ff.
and Matthew 26:26 ff. Nor had Paul any interest in reintroducing
the former liturgical order. He did, however, come sharply out
against the way in which this development had led to a devalua-
tion and travesty of the common meal, and against the misunderstanding of a truly sacramental Lord's Supper. For in Corinth had
arisen the abuse on the part of the sophisticated of eating the meal
right away in cliques, the rich doing themselves well and finding
no need to wait for the poorer (e.g., laborers and slaves), who
were not able to come at the proper time for the evening celebration. The supper had thus degenerated into a shocking exhibition
of the cleavages within the church, with the result that Paul was
obliged to complain bitterly that "it is no longer possible to eat the
Lord's Supper" (1 Cor. 11:20). One has to imagine that the
Corinthians themselves were not really aware of the implications
of their behavior: indeed, they may still have believed that the
latecomers were not excluded from the sacrament proper. But
Paul had no mind to put up with this, for as he saw it, there could
be no breaking of the connection between the body of Christ
received in the sacrament and the church as the one body of

Christ and, on the other hand, participation in the blood, that is, the death of Christ, and the "new saving order" (the new covenant, 1 Cor. 11:25), manifesting itself in the church. However, because of their lack of consideration for one another the Corinthians had made a mockery of the Supper and thereby incurred divine punishment (1 Cor. 11:27 ff.). Paul was thus forced to appeal to them to celebrate the meal "worthily," that is, according to the intention of its foundation, and not to begin "without discerning the body" (1 Cor. 11:29), that is, respecting it as the body of Christ who joins us to his body.

It follows that the Corinthians had not, as is often asserted, simply forgotten the sacramental significance of the Lord's Supper and turned it into a jollification having nothing to do with religion. On the contrary, they must have been tremendous, exaggerated sacramentalists, and convinced that, through the participation in the risen Christ mediated in the sacrament, they were already translated into the higher sphere of the redeemed. To counter this error, Paul already in 1 Corinthians 10:1–3 had presented them with the picture of Israel in the wilderness, blessed with God's gifts, yet hardened in heart and terribly punished. "Therefore let any one who thinks that he stands take heed lest he fall" (1 Cor. 10:12).

Thus, as speaking in tongues and prophecy, Paul's treatment of the Lord's Supper is a piece of actualized theology of the cross: "For as often as you eat this bread and drink the cup, you proclaim the Lord's *death* until he comes" (1 Cor. 11:26). The observance which the fanatics translated into a fanciful Beyond is given its place *within* time and history between Christ's death and his coming again and instead of an illusion the church becomes a highly realistic earthly togetherness in brotherhood.

The Body of Christ

In the context of what Paul says on worship and specifically on the sacraments, we have several times encountered the designation of the church as the *body of Christ*. Here Paul took over a sociological figure well known and much used in the ancient world and employed by himself for purposes of illustration (cf. 1 Cor. 12:14

ff.). But we soon see that this common metaphor of a unified yet many-membered organism in which each member has its function and the whole could not remain alive without each is far from exhausting Paul's idea. Important passages, particularly in the context of the sacraments (1 Cor. 12:13; 10:17), speak not just metaphorically of the church: it is not something *like* a body, but—in a real and actual sense—it *is* Christ's body (1 Cor. 12:27; cf. also 12:12), *one* body in Christ (Rom 12:5), something which cannot be compared with any other earthly community and yet is of the earth, founded in the One who gave his body to die on the cross and is present in the church. It has its being as "body" primarily in this One, and not in the multiplicity and variety of its members. In it human, earthly boundaries and barriers are now irrelevant—Jew and Gentile, bond and free, man and woman (1 Cor. 12:13; Gal. 3:28). Accordingly, it is not an organism in the strict sense of the word, but rather—though this, too, is open to misconception—an organ, a means and tool through which Christ himself organizes his lordship and gives it effect by the Spirit. The church is not just to become this: it *is* so already, in virtue of Christ's death and resurrection, released and endowed by him, all members without exception. It is for this reason that Paul will not permit what was happening at Corinth, the church's being turned into a playground and battleground for religious virtuosos, fascinating for some but depressing for others, a terrain for Spirit-inspired excursions from the earthly and historical realities of human existence into a supposedly divine world beyond. To Paul the Spirit was not the privilege of individuals, and its manifestations were far from being attested only in these exceptional utterances, which in the Corinthian church had obviously given rise to feelings of superiority on the one side and despondency on the other. The Spirit was given to all, and is at work in all in very varied ways, even in the apparently trivial, very matter-of-fact duties and functions of everyday living together which the Corinthian assembly did not include in the "gifts of the Spirit." Accordingly, alongside prophecy, speaking with tongues and their interpretation, the ability to distinguish between spirits, apostolic preaching and teaching, and the gift of healing the sick, Paul ranges as gifts of the Spirit or, better put in his own terms, "gifts of grace," leadership of the church and comforting and caring for one another. In all his lists of these "gifts" there is no trace of any ordering by merit, and there are gifts other than those enumerated (cf. 1 Cor. 12:9 ff., 28 ff.; Rom. 12:7 ff.). The important thing is that no one is without a gift and that, however different the form it takes from person to person, the effect of grace is in every case concrete, to each according to the measure of faith assigned by the one God, the one Kyrios, and the one Spirit (Rom. 12:5; 1 Cor. 12:4 ff.).

Only in this context of the effects and gifts of grace does the apostle utilize the ancient world's figure of the one body and the variety of its members. This second metaphorical use of the body motif is subordinated to the first and does not of itself define the nature of the church. But with the statements about the body of Christ, meant to be taken literally, as his basis, Paul makes use of the figure of an organism to overcome the dramatic, almost surrealistic devastation of the church painted in 1 Corinthians 12:15 ff.—the hypertrophied and atrophied members rivaling one another in contention, some inconsiderately parading themselves, others feeling that they are being given a back seat or even shut out. Therefore, in criticism of the one side and to give heart to the other, Paul calls on the members to give a welcome not only to themselves but to the rest, each in his station, his potentialities, and his limitations, not to do violence to another or to ask too much because of an arbitrarily adopted pattern, and so, recognizing their dependence on one another, to fulfill what was the basis of the church's life, the "law of Christ" (Gal. 6:2). Where this law reigns, suffering no longer repels or makes indifferent, nor do honor and brilliance excite envy. When one member of Christ's body has pain or joy, so do all the rest (1 Cor. 12:26).

V

FUTURE AND PRESENT

(ESCHATOLOGY AND ETHICS)

THE TIME OF FAITH

As Paul conceives it, the time of faith cannot be calculated according to the world's scheme of time: What was? What is? What will be? In the preceding chapters we were occupied with the extent to which his proclamation declares that what was done for the world in Christ is present reality. But we were no less concerned with the future which this opened up; Paul continually inculcates the "not yet" element in earthly existence. Nevertheless, we must now consider the relationship between future and present more precisely. The question is posed by what appears to be the absolutely contradictory juxtaposition in the Pauline ideas on this: because Christ is soon to come, Paul summons the Philippians to rejoice (Phil. 4:4 f.); he reminds the Corinthians that this world is passing away (1 Cor. 7:29); he gives teaching about the imminent resurrection of the dead and how those who are still alive will be changed (1 Cor. 15:50 ff.). Yet this same Paul proclaims that the time is fulfilled (Gal. 4:5), that the "new creation" is present reality in Christ (2 Cor. 5:17), and that "the end of the ages" has come upon believers (1 Cor. 10:11). Is this really no more than an unresolved juxtaposition, due perhaps to change of mood or situation, or is the contradiction in fact resolved in, as it were, a quantitative sense: the one is already vouchsafed to faith, but the other has not yet appeared? Though Paul repeatedly speaks in

these terms, and was obliged to do so particularly when confronting "enthusiasm" (cf. 1 Cor. 4:8–13; 15; 2 Cor. 13:4, etc.),
there is nevertheless a much closer bond of union between the two
sets of statements, and the formula, "yes-but," "yes-although," is
hardly adequate to describe the basic thought pattern. The actual
facts demand a "because-therefore" (cf. Rom. 5:1–11 etc.): because the testimony to Christ was confirmed in the Corinthian
church and they had become exceedingly enriched in him, therefore they await his future revealing (1 Cor. 1:4 ff.). Because Paul
was apprehended by Christ, he can say of himself, "not as though
I have already apprehended this, either were already perfect; but I
follow after, if that I may apprehend" (Phil. 3:12, A.V., slightly
altered to suit the German). "For in this *hope* we *are* saved"
(Rom. 8:24). This is in fact what is also implied in the passage
quoted earlier dealing with the present saved condition of those
who are baptized into the death of Christ and wait for the life
which only the future will give (Rom. 6:1 ff.), a passage in which
the apostle is manifestly referring to the church's confession of
Christ (Rom. 6:8 ff.). Similarly 1 Corinthians 15: here the apostle takes the events connected with Christ on which faith rests
(15:3 ff.) as the basis of his argument in substantiation of the
expectation of the future resurrection of the dead.

Eschatology has left such a deep impress on Paul's gospel that
it will not do—as was very common in the later church—to gather
together his teaching "on last things" into a body and then make
out of it a kind of summary appendix assembling all that the
apostle ever said or thought about the death of the individual and
the end of the world. Even the traditional term, "of the last
things," is not in place with Paul; in principle they are the "first"
things. We are therefore faced with the question whether it would
not be more pertinent to place his eschatology as a coherent body
of ideas at the beginning, because without it the rest is inconceivable, his teaching on the Law, his doctrine of justification and
salvation, and all else he has to say on the word of the cross, on
baptism and the Lord's Supper, on the working of the Spirit and
the nature of the church. Yet even were we to do so, we should
just as little strike the right note in respect of the distinctive eschatological basis of his thinking and activity. This would all too

easily give rise to the impression, erroneous though fostered by
not a few "Lives of Paul," that his eschatology was a sort of
framework taken over, though perhaps with modification, from
Jewish and primitive Christian apocalyptic, into which as into an
already given fixed system he set the Christian gospel. Even if the
impression finds some support in comparative religion, and even if
in fact there is a co-relation between apocalyptic inheritance and
Paul's gospel, the truth is the reverse: the eschatology which Paul
took over he conscripted into the service of the gospel; he did not
reinterpret the gospel in the light of tradition, but the latter in the
light of the saving event. There cannot be even the slightest watering down of the force of what Paul says about the present. His
statements are not the exaggerations of "enthusiasm." "If anyone
is in Christ, he is a new creation; the old has passed away, behold,
the new has come" (2 Cor. 5:17)—this is absolutely true. That
which Jewish and primitive Christian apocalyptic awaited in the
future and described in a great variety of pictures (cf. Rev. 21:5),
Paul, because of God's reconciling the world to himself in Christ,
proclaimed as accomplished fact. This does not mean that eschatology is abandoned and replaced by an immanent theology
and philosophy of history. It was in this Hegelian sense that the
great historian of primitive Christianity, F. C. Baur (1792–1860)
of the Tübingen school, commented on Galatians 4: "Just as . . .
it is of the essence of human nature for the child of tender age and
the youth to grow into an autonomous mature man, to become his
own master after having been under tutelage, to be son instead of
slave, so, at the appointed time, i.e., at the time when mankind
was ready for it, Christ came into its midst as son. Thus viewed,
Christendom is a stage in the development of religion proceeding
from an inner principle [sic] immanent in man, the advance of
the spirit to the freedom of self-consciousness" (Neutestament-
liche Theologie, 1864, p. 173). But Paul does not mean that the
time had ripened automatically, and that the saving event was, as
it were, its harvest in world history, or that at the moment of
Christ's coming man's need of salvation had grown so great that
Christ could in fact be called a *deus ex machina* for world history.
Rather, the hour of deliverance is the hour of God's free grace. "It
was not the time that occasioned the sending of the Son, but the

reverse: the sending of the Son brought the time of fulfillment"
(Luther). But what does this make of eschatology? Obviously it
does not just mean that the world's clock has run down. Paul
certainly shared with late Judaism and primitive Christianity very
definite, indeed singularly fixed, concepts of the end of the world.
Yet his is a very different concept of an event beginning in the
world which God alone put into operation and is to bring to
completion. It bursts asunder the horizons and potentialities of the
world's and mankind's history and brings it to an end—God's
history as a radical countermovement to earthly history. When
Paul thought in this way, he was working with a conception of
time, the world, and history different from the modern one. For
the latter these are verifiable human observation of and reflection
upon perceptible data: time in its billowing, fluctuating ebb and
flow of present, past, and future, history as that which is in constant change in time, the world as the lasting structure enfolding
both. Apocalyptic also conceived of them in just the same way
(though from a theological angle), observed the lapse of time,
divided the course of history into periods, and interpreted the
world in terms of its end and of God's opening up of a new
world.

The language and concepts of apocalyptic deeply influenced the
Pauline theology as well as that of the primitive church, but were
radically changed there. Apocalyptic's speculations, panoramas,
and concepts fall away or are even expressly rejected (1 Thess.
5:1 ff.), and as a rule occur only in fragmentation and with no
coherence. The most fundamentally new thing in Paul's eschatology is his insight that the sending, death upon the cross, and
resurrection of Jesus constitute the turning point in the ages. Al-
lied to this as closely as may be is the other insight which he
reasoned out and developed as never before, that man, in God's
sight lost, sets his seal on the world, and that this man is the
recipient of God's act of release *in* time. The time of faith has thus
become the time between Christ's death and resurrection and his
future.

In so doing, Paul went beyond and left behind not only Judaism's and primitive Christianity's apocalyptic expectation, but also
the standpoint of faith represented by the fanatics in his churches.

These had only too eagerly caught hold of the tidings of the time's being fulfilled and the dawning of salvation, and believed that they were showing forth the new aeon in their own lives. They were not, however, ready to take up the provisionality of Christian existence in humiliation and suffering. A considerable number of polemical utterances in the letters shows us the extent to which the "enthusiasts" construed as weakness and inconsistency the apostle's factor of "at the same time" and "together with" in the salvation already realized and its still future completion, and how greatly they impressed the churches with the presumed force of their one-sided high-flown thinking and behavior. In their sight Paul's way of thinking must have seemed a relapse into a meaningless "interim" and an obsolete "vacuum." They therefore believed that they on their part could go beyond his gospel and leave it behind. Nevertheless, Paul's conception of still-continuing temporality was not primarily dictated by a deficiency, but positively by the Christian gospel; it was not an awkward relic of earth which believers had to endure, but the condition of salvation to which the crucified and risen Christ gave meaning and content. Time and history are the field in which faith exercises and verifies itself.

This insight is expressed, certainly not solely, but in a particularly characteristic way, in what we commonly call Pauline *ethics*. The term is open to misunderstanding and easily gives rise to what is not in place with Paul, the idea of a system of maxims and directions for the correct conduct of Christians as distinct from his "theology," the two perhaps even being arranged under the catchwords "theory" and "practice." Though exhortations often have a place and even a form peculiar to themselves in his letters, the above would result in a fundamental misconception of Paul. It would be equally false to construct a "Pauline ethics" on the basis of this or that idea of his about man, the state, society, or the cosmos as in Platonic, Stoic, and modern ethical systems. Nor are his exhortations oriented, as in Judaism, on a fixed Law expounded to meet all of men's various relationships and situations and applied to these. On the contrary, with Paul it is: "You are not under law, but under grace" (Rom. 6:14).

LIFE BASED ON GRACE

To live on the basis of grace means that from first to last the believer's every action is oriented on God's antecedent act in Christ. The initial factor is not abstract, ideal potentialities, but an existing datum to which the believer has nothing of his own to bring, but which, accordingly, he has all the more to receive and accept, obediently surrendering his own existence. Thus, the apostle's exhortations are simply another mode of his gospel. In consequence, the parenesis (exhortation) in Romans (12–15) begins with the summons (see p. 211) which is the deduction from the message of the whole of the previous part of the letter, and once most solemnly appeals to his readers to remember this: "I appeal to you therefore, brethren, *by the mercies of God* . . ." (Rom. 12:1). Another classic example is to be seen in Philippians 2:1 ff. in an exhortation to self-renunciation in love for others (humility). Paul introduces a hymn on Christ taken from the hymnody of the early church (the oldest extant church hymn). Its subject is Christ's renunciation of divine majesty, his self-emptying and humbling himself in obedience, entering to the full into man's lot and even dying on the cross, for which very reason God appointed him Lord (Kyrios) over powers and authorities (Phil. 2:6–11). It is this action on Christ's part, and not the historic Jesus' exemplary humility of mind, to which the opening words refer—they mean more than Luther's translation suggests ("Let each have the mind that Christ Jesus also had"): "Direct your mind on what applies in Christ Jesus," that is, in him as the reality encompassing us.

Reception and acceptance of this reality, though not achievement and a work, is nevertheless supremely an act—the operation of grace on the believer is not a physical compulsion, nor is its recipient an object with no life of its own, as stone is for the sculptor. Because of this Paul paradoxically follows the hymn up with, "Therefore, my beloved . . . work out your own salvation with fear and trembling; for [sic] God is at work in you, both to will and to work for his good pleasure" (Phil. 2:12 f.). Note that the action is not divided up between God and men, making the two propositions supplementary to each other. Nor is the sense:

Bend all your endeavors on this, and God will add his and crown it. Nor: He has made the beginning; see to it that it comes to a successful issue. No, each proposition substantiates the other: Because God does everything, you too have everything to do. "With fear and trembling"—in the Old and New Testaments this characterizes the dismay and disquiet of the man whom God encounters or who, brought within the sphere of his mighty workings, is overwhelmed with anxiety to keep up with him and not make his grace in vain (2 Cor. 6:1). Thus, with Christ as starting point, Christians are on the way to his "day," called "to be blameless and innocent, children of God without blemish in the midst of a crooked and perverse generation," as "holding fast the word of life, shining as lights in the world" (Phil. 2:15 f.).

The interrelatedness of word of salvation and calling on the one hand and obedience, summons, and demand on the other has a particular significance for Paul. It is often described in a formula which, while not wrong, is certainly threadbare: "gift and task," or "become what you are." Many forms occur in Paul's letters of this collocation and conjunction of indicative and imperative (cf. Rom. 6:2 ff./11 ff.; 8:1 ff./12 ff.; 51:1 ff. Gal. 5:1, 13, etc.). The interrelatedness is also brought out in the fact that statement and summons often agree in subject matter: "You have put on Christ" (Gal. 3:27)—"Put on the Lord Jesus Christ" (Rom. 13:14); "We died to sin" (Rom. 6:2)—"So you also must consider yourselves dead to sin and alive to God in Christ Jesus. Let not sin therefore reign in your mortal bodies . . ." (Rom. 6:11–12). Or 1 Corinthians 5:6 f., where, making the link with Passover and the Jewish custom of eating unleavened bread, Paul says metaphorically: "Cleanse out the old leaven [of malice and evil] that you may be a new lump [of sincerity and truth], as you really are unleavened." Or the classic formulation in Galatians 5:25: "If we live by the Spirit, let us also walk by the Spirit." The orbit of the admonitions is everywhere the same as that of the statements expressing salvation. The new life does not go beyond what grace bestows on faith. Accordingly, it is not sufficient to think of the new life to which the admonitions summon the Christian as a mere supplementary effect of faith; in itself it is a mode of faith, an appropriation of what God has already assigned. The believer's actions derive from God's act, and the decisions taken by obedience from God's antecedent decision for the world in Christ. Thus the two come together in equilibrium: to live on the basis of *grace*, but also to *live* on the basis of grace.

In the apostle's admonitions, the source of faith is all-important, but it is important as the origin of action having an end in view. It is no accident that in describing life in obedience Paul repeatedly uses expressions already current in Judaism for "stepping out" ("that we too might walk in newness of life," Rom. 6:4): teaching and direction can also be described as a "way" or "ways" (1 Cor. 4:17, etc.).

In the process, and with a renewed urgency and single-heartedness, the many varied modes of human conduct are reduced to an either-or—or, more frequently, with God's saving act in mind, to a once-now—that drives a wedge between the "old" life and the "new" (cf. Gal. 5:19 ff. and 1 Cor. 6:11, etc.). This once more shows that when the apostle admonishes, he does not begin with choices open to the Christian, but with powers and dominions from which he is delivered and for which he sets out: law and grace (Rom. 6:14), sin and righteousness (Rom. 6:16 ff.), flesh and spirit (Rom. 8:5 ff.; Gal. 5:16 ff.), death and life (Rom. 8:6).

In enumerating the practical implications of such Christian life in "obedience," "service," and "indebtedness," Paul in his admonitions quite deliberately employs current concepts and expressions which everyone understood, and makes no effort at all to work out a new, specifically Christian, scale of values. This is particularly apparent in the numerous loose and not systematically ordered lists in his admonitions, which in form and content have direct parallels in the catalogues of "virtues and vices" in the Jewish tradition as found in Proverbs and in Hellenistic popular ethical teaching (cf. Rom. 1:29–31; 12:8–21; 13:13; 1 Cor. 5:10 f.; 6:9 f.; 2 Cor. 12:20 f.; Gal. 5:19–23). In Romans 12:8 ff. he strings together material taken from Proverbs and other Old Testament books and also uses primitive Christian tradition. But without break and distinction he can also have recourse to moral maxims taken from pagan rationalistic ethics—for example, in the parenesis of Romans he takes up the well-known Greek concept of sobriety and makes a kind of artistic summary formulation: "For by the grace given to me I bid every one among you not to think of himself more highly than he ought to think, but to think with sober judgment, each according to the measure of faith which God has assigned him" (Rom. 12:3). Equally characteristic is the good Greek compendium of directions: "Finally, brethren, whatever is true, whatever is honorable, whatever is just, whatever is pure, whatever is lovely, whatever is gracious, if there is any excellence, if there is anything worthy of praise, think about these things" (Phil. 4:8). Tradition here implies that what is to be realized in practice is known to all, or that all can know it and in any case ought to know it. God's will is directed to what always has held and always will hold, what is inscribed on conscience, heart, and reason and has constantly to be tested and verified afresh as "what is good and acceptable and perfect" (Rom. 12:2).

The new thing here is not the subject matter, but rather the context of the admonitions: the whence and whither of the road on which Christians are under way; the grace from which they derive their lives and in virtue of which they are summoned to a new service and obedience, and the coming day of Christ, for which they are "called" "to obtain salvation" (1 Thess. 4:7; 5:9). They, too, have to give account of themselves before God, the just judge, on that "day" (Rom. 14:12; 1 Cor. 4:5; 2 Cor. 5:10, etc.).

Going through the parenetic sections from letter to letter, it is amazing to see the variety of and differences in the apostle's *argumentation* in each case—absolutely no set form or clichés; in other words, he appeals to his hearers' and readers' understanding and does not simply proclaim and decree. His arguments are in the best sense of the term "motivations," reasons for "moving." To be sure, certain central motifs recur frequently and are intertwined, while others are more in the nature of supplements and confirmations. Nevertheless, there is no mistaking the number of different ways in which Paul expounds the meaning and significance of God's act in Christ, and seeks to make it bear fruit in believers' lives, relates it to their baptism into Christ's death (Rom. 6:3 f.; 1 Cor. 6:11) and their membership in the body of

Christ (1 Cor. 11:17 ff.; 12:12 ff.; Rom. 12:5 ff.), and summons them to use their freedom properly, the freedom, that is, which does not stand on its own rights but is ready to renounce self for the sake of others, the weaker ones (1 Cor. 8:1 ff.; 10:23 ff.; cf. also Rom. 14:15). Or else he warns the church against esteeming itself too highly and being complacent (1 Cor. 10:1 ff.) and appeals to its common responsibility for the impression made by the message of Christ's lordship on the Gentile world and its acceptance there (Rom. 15:7 ff.), or reminds them of the Lord's approaching advent (Phil. 4:5; Rom. 13:11 ff.).

Alongside these main ideas Paul also ranges motifs which are not strictly theological, appeal to what is seemly (1 Cor. 11:13; 14:34), to usage (1 Cor. 11:17), to what "nature teaches" (1 Cor. 11:14 ff.; cf. Rom. 1:26; 2:14), or to practice accepted in all churches (1 Cor. 11:16). On occasion, of course, as in the oddly obscure passage in 1 Corinthians 11:2–16, where the apostle is opposing "enthusiastic" tendencies in the direction of the emancipation of women, these are combined with personal speculations about the order of creation.

Whatever way Paul chooses to substantiate his exhortations in detail, even recourses such as the above to what is everywhere acknowledged, he does not think of them as conforming with the world. On the contrary, it is in one of these very passages that we find the direction: "Do not be conformed to this world, but be transformed [note, an imperative in the passive] by the renewal of your mind" (Rom. 12:2).

This is the source of the apparent contradiction that Paul's directions are based on eschatology and at the same time on what is past and permanently present in the world. The lines of the Christian's relationship to the world are laid down by both of them.

CHRISTIAN ENGAGEMENT AND DISENGAGEMENT

In Paul's view, Christian life is as far removed from fallenness into the world as it is from flight from it. Faith releases the Christian so he can be independent of the world and at the same time puts him under obligation to stand up to its testing. Paul's letters have many expressions of this Janus-like relationship. In virtue of the new life opened up for them, believers no longer belong to this world with its powers and entanglements (Gal. 1:4), but to the crucified and risen Lord (Rom. 14:7 ff.). By the cross of Christ the world is crucified for Paul and he for it (Gal. 6:14). One must no longer fall victim to it in the way of the Galatian Judaizers with their performance of the works of the Law. But falling victim to the world is no less a threat in the guise of one's day-to-day concerns and dealings with it. Hence the apostle's summons to detachment from all earthly conditions:

> From now on, let those who have wives live as though they had
> none,
> and those who mourn as though they were not mourning,
> and those who buy as though they had no goods,
> and those who deal with the world as though they had no dealings
> with it.
> For the form of this world is passing away. (1 Cor. 7:29–31)

In themselves these words could be described as a classic paraphrase of the Cynic and Stoic ideal of severance from all earthly ties and detachment from all that fortune and circumstances may bring, whether good or evil. Whatever the wise man's surroundings or experiences—native land, friendship, family, health and sickness, respect or contempt, riches or poverty, the pleasures of love and death—these do not affect the truly wise man's inmost being; he is independent of all things and does not get lost in them (Epictetus).

Like the wisdom-teaching of proverbs, 1 Corinthians 7:29–31 bases its argument on the transience of all earthly things. Yet it scarcely needs saying that here there is more than a voice of mankind's universal experience of the swift passage of time. The reason why time is foreshortened and running out is that Christ's imminent coming again and the end of the world are at the very door—so near that many in Paul's own generation would live on to experience them (1 Thess. 4:15 ff.; 1 Cor. 15:51 ff.; cf. Phil. 4:5). Even though no one knows the day and the hour, and the "day of the Lord" will come "like a thief in the night" (1 Thess.

5:1 f.), this makes no difference to Paul's conviction that it is near. This is also the context of the directions and counsels in 1 Corinthians 7, and they may not be divorced from it. Nevertheless, for Paul this implies—far from a general cosmic *memento mori*—that believers in Christ *have already been* called to a new existence (1 Cor. 7:17 ff.), and that accordingly their only concern is with the Lord, now present in the Spirit and soon to come in judgment and salvation.

The questions about marriage which the apostle discusses in detail in 1 Corinthians 7 in a time perspective thus eschatologically and Christologically foreshortened have been put to him by the Corinthians in a letter (1 Cor. 7:1), the occasion clearly being the "enthusiastic" and ascetic views propagated by a certain section in the church. Here again we have the same tendency toward emancipation, the dissolving of all earthly and human relationships, and the realization of a new super-earthly mode of life; appeal may even have been made to Paul's own words: "There is neither Jew nor Greek, there is neither slave nor free, there is neither male nor female; for you are all one in Christ Jesus" (Gal. 3:28; cf. 1 Cor. 12:13). The conclusion drawn was dissolution of marriage and abstention from all sexual intercourse. Note the diametrically opposite results of which this "enthusiasm" was capable: abandonment to unbridled satisfaction of sexual desire with prostitutes, because of course inferior things like this could not possibly affect the Christian's inmost being (1 Cor. 6:12 ff.), and, in the case before us, rejection of all sexual relationships. The oddly hesitant answers as to whether Christians should enter into marriage or not, whether and how existing marriages were to be continued or dissolved, and whether a father should still give in marriage a daughter already betrothed all go to show the difficult position in which these questions placed the apostle: we today find them very hard to understand, though on the assumptions of primitive Christianity they are perfectly comprehensible. Paul personally was inclined to an "ascetic" answer, as is shown by the very first sentence in the chapter: "It is well for a man not to touch a woman" (1 Cor. 7:1, 8), like himself to remain unmarried (1 Cor. 7:8, 26 ff.; cf. also 7:36 ff.). But such conduct presumes a "gift" not bestowed on everyone (1 Cor.

7:7); because of the drive of natural instincts Paul absolutely
refuses to lay down a law (1 Cor. 7:2, 9). To marry or to remarry
after the death of one's partner is no sin (1 Cor. 7:28, 36, 39 f.).
And certainly, in accord with Jesus' teaching, existing marriages
should not be dissolved (1 Cor. 7:10 ff.), unless the non-Christian partner insists upon it (1 Cor. 7:12 f.). However, this does
not alter the fact that, in a total view, Paul regarded marriage and
married life as an emergency measure, even if sanctioned by God,
in face of the overwhelming power of the sexual urge in man and
as a safeguard against unchastity and the temptations of Satan (1
Cor. 7:2, 5, 9, 36 ff.); in particular, he thinks of marriage as
bringing with it necessary involvement in "worldly troubles" (1
Cor. 7:28) and "anxieties" (1 Cor. 7:33 f.) from which, in view
of the imminent end, Paul would like to see the members of his
churches spared (1 Cor. 7:28).

No one can deny the one-sidedness and the eschatological fore-
shortening of time in Paul's view of marriage, which means nothing to us today. In the detailed discussions of 1 Corinthians 7 one
looks in vain for a positive appreciation of love between the sexes
or of the richness of human experience in marriage and the family.
Paul does speak of the "sanctifying" power which the Christian
partner in a marriage may unconsciously exert on the unbelieving
members of the family, the other parent and the (unbaptized)
children, but this is only in passing, where in words which sound
almost like a magical spell he advises the Christian partner not to
demand a dissolution of the marriage (1 Cor. 7:14).

Nevertheless, one should not be blind to the very sober realism
of Paul's judgment and should remember in particular that, unlike
the ascetic "enthusiasts" in Corinth and widespread tendencies in
the later church, Paul did not utterly reject marriage and sexual
life because of any dualism held on principle. In distinction to
such views, the apostle's concern is not with *relationships* which
first have to be changed—as such they are without significance for
salvation—but with the *relations* of Christians within them. The
sole leitmotiv and criterion in Paul's counsel is the believers' relationship to the coming Lord. Paul does not take from the individual his right to decide for himself as to how he is to give
practical effect to his being a Christian and approve himself as

such. He only points out the necessary criteria, though at the same time uttering a warning against any self-deception in regard to one's powers. Hence the odd hesitancy in his counsel. It does not indicate that the questions put to him perplexed him; rather, the reason is a very definite aversion, based in the nature of the case, to making a pronouncement in legal terms on a matter in which, after self-examination, decisions must be taken "in the Spirit" (1 Cor. 7:40) and in the light of faith: "I say this for your own benefit, not to lay any restraint upon you, but to promote good order and to secure your undivided devotion to the Lord" (1 Cor. 7:35).

After all, this very chapter of 1 Corinthians—so bound up with its own time in the truest sense of the term—is important as exemplifying the Christian's relationship to the world. However strongly the apostle stresses the *disengagement* from the world required of the believer, given classic formulation in the five variations of "Have . . . as though they had not" (1 Cor. 7:29–31), he at the same time attaches a fundamental importance to the individual Christian's *engagement* in it. The clearest indication of this comes in the short passage inserted into the discussions on marriage, the subject of which is a further question, whether Christians are not also under urgent obligation to prove themselves Christian by abolishing religious and social relationships within the church, that is, should former Jews disguise the mark of the covenant, their circumcision, or Gentiles be circumcised, or should even the differences between slave and free be done away with (1 Cor. 7:17–24)? The apostle's answer is remarkably "conservative": "Everyone should remain in the state in which he was called" (1 Cor. 7:20); indeed, even when offered the chance of release, slaves should not take it (1 Cor. 7:21). In order to understand this strange counsel we have of course to notice, first, that it bears on relationships within the church and not on questions of the structure of society in general, and second, that our modern term "engagement" inevitably but falsely imports ideas deriving from a different context. The Greek word, which, as in nonreligious Greek linguistic usage, may in fact here be rendered "engagement" is the same as used elsewhere in Paul's letter for (the divine) "call" (*klesis*). In 1 Corinthians 7:17 ff., however, the accent clearly falls on the actual religious or social situation *in* which, each in his own way, believers encountered God's "summons" to faith. Paul thus brings two things to bear equally: in themselves all outward circumstances whatsoever are no longer of importance; as regards the salvation of believers, they have basically ceased to be absolute and do not enter into religion. At the same time they are, and continue to be, of supreme importance because they denote the specific place on earth and history where Christ *has* already made believers free for a new existence: the slave has already become a "freedman of the Lord" and the "free man" "a slave of Christ" (1 Cor. 7:22 ff.). This will be proved "in the state in which he was called" and is to "remain."

BE SUBJECT TO THE POWERS THAT BE!

The apostle's much-discussed admonition to be subject to the governing authorities (Rom. 13:1–7), the only one of the kind in his letters in respect of form and subject matter, has played a more active part in history than most biblical texts. Even with this encumbrance, however, it touches upon an important sphere of the Christian's relationship to the world. In subject matter it is nothing more or less than the plain demand that Christians, like everyone else, should render obedience to the powers of the state. That is to say, it is an admonition to uprightness as citizens.

The text itself demands that we put the point in this "old-fashioned" way and do not forthwith import into it all the ifs and buts that immediately come to mind, as well as the much debated problems of the limits of Christian obedience and the possibility and moral justification of revolution. These, one might almost say, were almost deliberately brushed aside by Paul. It is also remarkable that he refrained from mentioning any of the specifically Christian arguments for the relationship to the state that is laid down here. Nowhere at all do we find even the name of Christ or the word "faith." Instead, the apostle imposes on Christians absolutely the same obligation as he lays on all: "Let *every* person be subject to the governing authorities" (Rom. 13:1). Our knowledge of the vocabulary of Roman-Hellenistic law and administration is sufficient to show that these "powers" and their representatives are the *potestates* (*imperia*) and *magistratus* functioning in the empire and the municipalities. They maintained order and prevented rebellion. They bestowed—as many other contemporary texts also tell us—"praise" on citizens' good behavior and punished the refractory, "good" and "evil" being here used in a generally accepted sense requiring no further explanation (Rom. 13:3 f.). Accordingly, the governing bodies were vested with the "power of the sword" (*jus gladii*), that is, the power of life and death resident above all in the emperor but also exercised by his governors (Rom. 13:4). On the other side of the picture Romans (13:6) mentions "taxes" and "revenues" to be paid by citizens, as well as "the respect" due to the governing classes (13:6).

Like pre-Christian and contemporary Judaism, Romans 13 speaks of the civil power as an "order" instituted by God. How much this term "order" dominates the admonition can be seen from the numerous Greek expressions of which it is the focus: "be subject," "instituted by God," "appointed by God," "resist the authorities." Accordingly, the person in authority is "God's servant for your good . . . to execute his wrath on the wrongdoer" (13:4, 6). Officials are due obedience not only out of fear, but "for the sake of conscience" (13:6).

Paul says all this without the merest suggestion that the authorities, who were pagan, might also misuse their powers and force a Christian to obey men rather than God (Acts 5:29)—not a problem to which Christianity first gave rise (see *Antigone*). Thus, because of its "unproblematic" character, Romans 13 has largely become a problem—good reason for beginning with a close examination of the special features of the text and what it was trying to do, and for restraint over our own problems.

In regard to form and subject matter it is a typical piece of parenesis originating in Hellenistic Judaism and taken over from there by Paul. The purport of the almost self-evident statement is not instruction for the governing classes, as in a "Pattern for Princes," on the proper discharge of their office. Rather, the people addressed are the Christians in Rome, and they are given counsel which, on the model of other classical and Christian parenesis, gives no discussion of actual situations or cases of conflict, in order the more strongly to inculcate simple and ever valid rules of conduct. Once this is recognized, it follows that Romans 13 is not to be expanded into a general doctrine of the state and society and a theology of the orders of creation and preservation, a process of which, unfortunately, church history furnishes abundant examples. This idea of Paul's admonitions sets them on a false course, distorts their aim, and sacrifices them to a religious and metaphysical system of thought entirely alien to him.

With Romans 13, too, the context preceding and following is of the utmost importance: first, the admonitions already mentioned, the key note for all that comes after (Rom. 12:1 f.), that as Christians they are to "present" themselves to God and "not to be conformed to the world"; and, second and equally, the summons appended to our passage to recognize the "time" and the "hour" of the approaching last "day" and accordingly to "put on the armor of light" (Rom. 13:11 ff.). These two circumscribe the counsel to be subject to the governing authorities and not to resist "what God has appointed." With this eschatological perspective Paul would scarcely have made his demands on Christians for obedience less than absolute or played down their relationship to the state as something insignificant. Yet, without having to say it in so many words, he does assign political life its place, one limited to this world. But at the same time, by recognition of the "time," he gives to the proving of one's being a Christian in the workaday world—the same for Christians as for all men—a fresh urgency and a deeper substantiation which goes beyond the content of the admonition itself (Rom. 13:1 ff.). This again shows how keenly and exclusively his field of vision here is the life of Christian people and not the institution of the state as such or the question of the proper discharge of their duties by officials.

It may help us to appreciate the chapter historically if we remember that up to the time when Romans was written, there had been no systematic persecution of Christians on the part of the empire. No doubt by Paul's day spontaneous and merely local outbursts of hatred and pogroms had broken out here and there, instigated often by the Jews, but also with the cooperation of imperial and municipal officials. The apostle himself was given a taste of some of them (cf., for example, 1 Thess. 2:2; 1 Cor. 15:32; 2 Cor. 1:8 ff.; 11:26; Phil. 1:12 ff.), as were also his churches in Philippi (Phil. 1:29 f.) and Thessalonica (1 Thess. 2:14 ff.). Even Paul's own last imprisonment and martyrdom at the hands of Nero and the latter's appalling treatment of the Roman Christians (probably a few years later, A.D. 64) are not definitely to be termed "persecutions," since after the fire of Rome the Christians suffered not because of their faith, but for alleged arson. Nowhere is there the slightest indication that Paul regarded the emperor and the state power as "Antichrist," as did the author of Revelation in the time of Domitian (A.D. 81–96), in one of his great visions (Rev. 13). Even this development, which Paul could not foresee, would hardly have confounded his conviction that in virtue of the duty laid upon them the state powers were obliged to fulfill the will of God in their functions as named in Romans 13. Certainly he would scarcely have retracted a word of his admonition. Significantly, subsequent early Christian authors, also, did not feel called upon to step out of their obligation to be loyal to the empire and thus become its foes (Acts, 1 Pet., 1 Tim., Heb., 1 Clem.).

Just because of their literary category, parenetic passages do not allow inquiry into the occasion of their writing or into specific situations in a church. This is also true of Romans 13. Yet the fact that this admonition has no parallel in the rest of the letters justifies the surmise that, exceptionally, the Roman church was in danger, if not of open rebellion, at least of taking some other way of showing that it stood aloof from the empire and neglected its civic obligations. There may be a connection between this and the fact that, some years before Romans was written, and owing perhaps to the advent of the Christian gospel, there had been turbulence among the Jews which led to the emperor Claudius' issuing his decree expelling them from Rome (A.D. 49). In the interval the membership of the church had of course become preponderantly Gentile Christian (see p. 89). While this fits in with the historical background of Romans 13, it remains a hypothesis: Paul could have written in similar terms to any church.

Paul's counsels in this chapter, clear and precise, yet oddly undifferentiated and one-sided, exercised an influence on later Christianity that was in many respects enigmatical. This is seen in the very fact that the famous chapter was divorced from the context of the Pauline ethic, made authoritative in itself, and given a weight to which the isolated passage has no right. In view of the importance of the problem which it discusses in church history, down to the present day, one can understand this. But the dubious results are plain to see. As is well known, Romans 13 widely evoked thinking in terms of a blind submission, just as, conversely, it also kindled the fire of impassioned protest; and at any rate, it has raised more questions than it has answered. At the present day it is especially disputed in a world that has turned against Paul, where the Christian's responsibility to join in the shaping of political life has been elevated into a self-evident requirement. In the face of such reactions, we must remember that the apostle's counsels were directed to his own time. This means that it is as inappropriate to make them the basis of a perennially valid attitude of unconditionally preserving the state as, conversely, to demand of them answers to questions which Paul never knew in their present form.

It is only as we take into account the historical circumstances of Romans 13 that we can see the fundamentals of Christian life with which Paul was concerned. In a kindred matter, paying tribute, when the Pharisees pertly put their captious question (Mark 12:13–17) about what was due to the emperor, Jesus first asked what was due to God. Paul acted in the same way, and so anticipated all tendencies toward a political or social rebellion. Admittedly, this gives the question of the Christian's life and conduct an absolute primacy over all questions of perhaps indispensable alterations in world affairs. Nevertheless, this will be felt as "taking the Christian faith out of public life" only by those who cannot or will not make out the revolutionary, world-changing force in the saving event, even as Paul conceived it. As in 1 Corinthians 7, the apostle thus validates both the independence of the world bestowed on the believer, that is, his "disengagement," and his "engagement" in it, in the everyday sphere in which he strives to prove his faith. Paul produces neither a program nor a casuistry to show how the two are to be brought into harmony in specific instances. But in all events, neither a general glorification nor the demonization of the state is open to the Christian; rather, he is to show respect to it in its limitations in time and space as a divinely

instituted order—in modern terms, his attitude is neither an ideo-
logically obsessed engagement nor a supercilious disengagement
on the basis of "spirituality."

A number of expositors of Romans 13 point to the final admonition, "Owe no one anything, except to love one another" (13:8),
and describe the commandment to love one's neighbor as oneself
as the leitmotiv of Paul's counsel. Since with Paul love is truly the
determining factor of the Christian's new life (cf. Rom. 12:9 ff.),
it must certainly have at least some bearing on the believer's relationship to the state. Nevertheless, it should not be imported as
the chief leitmotiv into this sphere where the issues are subjection,
citizens' attitude to the law, official measures, conscientiousness,
taxes, revenues, and respect. Instead, Paul conceives political life
as a sphere in which it is the Christian's duty not to lag behind or
get himself entangled in unfulfilled obligations. To deal duly and
promptly with one's obligations in order to be free for the never
ending duties imposed by love, which is far more important than
this transient world and its responsibilities—this is Paul's aim in
giving his admonitions.

This is confirmed by the apostle's attitude to a grievance that
was splitting the church at Corinth, members' resort to pagan law
courts to settle their disputes (1 Cor. 6:1-11). Here Paul sees
conduct that puts Christians to shame, and in arguing against it he
uses ideas and words taken from Jewish apocalyptic: what an
absurdity for Christians who, as "the saints," are someday to
judge the world and even the angels to have recourse for their
petty, earthly concerns before the judgment seats of "unbelievers"
and "unrighteous"! If you Corinthians are at odds among yourselves, why do you not appoint members of the church as judges?
He goes even further: Why do you insist at all on your own rights
and not rather as Christians suffer wrong? In spite of the familiar
depreciations, stemming from Jewish tradition, of "unbelievers,"
"unrighteous," and "those who have no status in the church,"
these utterances of Paul are not directed toward questioning civil
courts in general, but apply to Christians who as such have been
called to be sharers in the divine eschatological sovereignty and
are already set free for a new life. The repeated, emphatic appeal
here to "brotherhood" (1 Cor. 6:5 f., 8) amid the wrangling and

strife is a defeat—no matter who is in the "right" and who is not (1 Cor. 6:7). The summons to put up with injustice rather than insist on one's own rights, the concluding reminder of the new being which believers owe to grace and which puts them under obligation (1 Cor. 6:9–11)—all of this is in principle just another way of putting the commandment to love one's neighbor as oneself. In this way, this passage in 1 Corinthians comes close to Romans 13, where the commandment similarly takes in and goes beyond the admonition respecting the Christian's conduct toward the state (Rom. 12:9 ff.; 13:8 ff.). The difference, of course, is that the one case has to do with conduct which is right and proper for "everyman" in political life, the other with the life of the Christian society which is given its norms by the saving event it experiences and which breaks through the frontiers of mere citizenship.

LOVE

What does Paul mean by love? His letters give ample reason for considering the question, especially since this word, almost more than any other, has entered into the vocabulary of Christians and —used and misused—has largely lost its meaning and force.

In Romans 13:8 ff. Paul sums up the whole law in the commandment to love one's neighbor as oneself: "He who loves his neighbor has fulfilled the law" (cf. also Gal. 5:14). Here, again, the apostle is the heir of a tradition which, while not immediately derived from the Old Testament Torah, probably comes from Hellenistic Judaism, in which the Old Testament sense of "neighbor" as restricted to Israelites had been extended to include other people in general. This is the way in which Jesus and the primitive church after him also interpreted the commandment (Matt. 5:43; 19:19; 22:39; Mark 12:30 f.; Luke 10:27; James 2:8).

The words "to love" (agapan) and "love" (agape), taken over by Hellenistic Judaism of the Diaspora, were not entirely unknown in classical Greek, but they were of no great significance and lagged far behind other lofty terms such as eros and philia (friendship). It was only in the Greek translation of the Old Testament (the Septuagint), in the literature of Hellenistic Judaism, and, to crown all, in primitive Christianity that these little-esteemed words were given their momentous relationship to God and man (the two factors in Jesus' commandment) and, accordingly, their central importance. Only as we are aware of this background can we estimate Paul's contribution to the concept of "love."

The basis of love is the fact that in Christ's coming and his sacrifice God showed his love to us men who are absolutely unworthy of love, godless, and God's enemies (Rom. 5:8 ff.), and thereby made us "justified," and "reconciled" to him as victors amid the pressure of the powers of the world. Nothing can separate us from his love (Rom. 8:31 ff., especially 37-39). It is God's act upon us, but at the same time his power at work within us: "God's love has been poured into our hearts through the Holy Spirit which has been given to us" (Rom. 5:5). The same thing is said in: "For the love of Christ controls us" (2 Cor. 5:14). It reaches out beyond the individual and takes in others as well. This feature and operation is of the essence of love and makes it the field in which faith has its being and goes to work; "in Christ Jesus being a Jew or a Greek [circumcision or uncircumcision] counts for nothing, but faith working through love" (Gal. 5:6). Similar teaching had been given before Paul's time in liberal Hellenistic Judaism, upon which Paul obviously models himself in another place: "For neither circumcision counts for anything nor uncircumcision, but keeping the commandments of God" (1 Cor. 7:19). Nevertheless, in the form found in Galatians 5:6 above and later in Galatians 6:13 f., an important change is made in the words; obedience to God's commandments is replaced by faith active in love and the "new creation" (in Christ). Thus a possibility which man had first to realize has been made into a reality inaugurated and opened up by God: love as the distinguishing mark of the new existence.

1 Corinthians' great hymn in praise of love (chap. 13) occurs in the context of the apostle's discussion of the "gifts of grace" (chaps. 12-14). Love is described as the incomparably higher way, a "still more excellent way" (12:31); love is greater even than all conceivable "gifts" which in the thought of primitive Christianity represented the highest possibilities open to its mem-

bers possessed of *charismata*. Ecstatic speech through the operation of the Spirit—without love meaningless, futile noise; prophecy, faith that works miracles, giving up house and home for the
sake of the poor, and preparedness to suffer the death of a martyr
—all are useless without love (13:1–3).

It is more than poetic convention that makes Paul speak here of
love itself and not the loving man as the subject. He conceives
love as a divine power. Its workings are set in complete contrast to
the natural man's acts and go far beyond what he can ever achieve.

Accordingly, it is no accident that in the second part of the
hymn (13:4–7) we find pointed antitheses (eight negatives),
though the passage is summed up at the beginning and end by
positive statements as to what characterizes love in its nature and
its actions. Yet, brief as this second section is (only fifteen verbs),
it shows love working out in men's everyday relationships with
others: it is "patient," lasts the course, and waits for others; it
does not boil over in passion; does not swagger or puff itself up;
does not ignore the limits set by good manners; does not let
offenses come between man and man; is full of joy—not the
venomous, crypto-Pharisaical sort which loudly laments the evil in
the world, perhaps in order to put its own self in a better light; it
rejoices in the truth, particularly the truth that benefits others. Its
force is a confidence that nothing can destroy ("believes all things,
hopes all things"); it never lets the other man down ("bears all
things"), and it never itself falls into resignation and despair
("endures all things").

The chapter ends on a note of praise for love's imperishability
over against the "imperfection" of even the gifts inspired by the
Spirit (13:8–13). What Paul has in mind is not a timeless contrast between earth's imperfect realities and a never attainable
ideal, but an eschatological contrast between "now" and "then" in
time, comparable to that between the speech, aims, and thoughts
of the wishful, dreaming child and the illusion-free thoughts of the
man (vs. 11) and—even more clearly—the contrast between par-
tial, mediated knowledge "as in a mirror" and knowledge "face to
face" (vs. 12), the one confused and unable to pass beyond the
frontiers of temporality, the other breaking through this—the
coming perfection reserved to God alone (cf. 2 Cor. 4:18; 5:7;

Rom. 8:24). Significantly, Paul says nothing of the idea of a gradual process of deification as propounded by the contemporary mystery religions and Hellenistic mysticism. He no doubt speaks their language in talking of a "change from one degree of glory to another" (2 Cor. 3:18), and approximates to it when he describes the future perfect knowledge as "being known by God." But, as shown by the tense of the verb, this means "having been chosen" by the grace of God (cf. 1 Cor. 8:2; Gal. 4:9).

Man's knowledge of God and his being known by God cannot be harmonized within the life of faith in space and time. God alone may, and will, bring them into accord. Even when in the perfected state, however, man will not cease to be dependent on God. Accordingly, faith and hope, too, are to "abide" when the frontiers of temporality are left behind—but love abides "as the greatest of these" (vs. 13). This is not to be understood as implying a scale of values with love as the supreme value at the head overlapping even the religious modes of behavior, faith and hope. Love is greatest, not as a value and virtue in itself, but as a coordinate of faith, based on God's past action, and hope, directed toward his future. It is the present part of salvation that does not pass away. In this sense, the triad of faith, hope, and love is the quintessence of the God-given life in Christ (cf. also 1 Thess. 1:3; 5:8; Gal. 5:5 f.; Cor. 1:4 f.). No one is excluded from it; it is therefore greater than the "gifts of the Spirit," which are bestowed on some but withheld from others.

HOPE

Not only in the hymn in praise of love in 1 Corinthians 13 and the triad faith, hope, and love, but in Paul's gospel and instruction as well, love's constant and indispensable concomitant is an expectation for the future. As already shown, eschatology cannot be written out of Paul's theology, and at this point its special features demand closer examination. When we review these eschatological sayings referring to the future as a body, we at once see certain characteristic traits which it is important to understand. As was said above, they are found dispersed throughout the majority of his letters, differing from one to another in form and content,

often in fragmentation, terse even if weighty utterances, generally
with no concepts to illuminate them and only on the odd occasion
developing into apocalyptic imagery; in every case they are firmly
planted in a definite context of teaching or parenesis. But one can
never put them together to form a total picture. Their subject
matter is too varied for this, and they seldom reveal any effort on
Paul's part to relate them to one another. This is not to be taken
as implying that they should be estimated as, so to speak, the
apostle's tentative steps and attempts to speak about what lies
beyond the experiences of time and space, attempts he made bold
to use in one or another situation only to reject them as inept.
This is the very department in which more often than not the
terms are emphatic and precise: "but we know . . ." (Rom. 8:28;
13:11); "I consider . . ." (Rom. 8:18); "for I am sure . . ."
(Rom. 8:38); "for this perishable nature *must* put on the im-
perishable . . ." (1 Cor. 15:53). Here we also have the prophetic
style of discourse in which Paul proclaims a quite definite divine
saving decree referring to the future (Rom. 11:25; 1 Cor. 15:51),
or grounds his comfort on "a word of the Lord" (1 Thess. 4:13
ff.).

Many of these eschatological sayings merely draw in brief the
conclusions for the future which lie beyond all earthly and human
history and which follow from belief in Christ's death and resurrection. They thus express the hope whose firm foundation is
God's antecedent act in Christ for believers and the world. These
extremely numerous statements are spread, as we said, over practically all Paul's letters, and one or two examples are sufficient
here. As those given over with Christ to death "we shall live"
(Rom. 6:5 ff.; Phil. 3:10 f.; 2 Cor. 4:10 f., 13:4, etc.). Transferred into the new status of sons and endowed with the Spirit as
"earnest" ("security") (2 Cor. 1:22; 5:5; cf. Rom. 8:23), we are
"heirs" and "fellow heirs" and "will be glorified with him" (Rom.
8:17). Justified and reconciled by the death of his Son, we shall
be delivered from the "wrath" (to come) (Rom. 5:9–11; cf. also
8:11; Gal. 5:5).

Other passages, though there are not so many of them, expand
the expectations for the future and develop them into larger-scaled
apocalyptic pictures and concepts. Wherever they occur, we find

Paul having to write in reply to questions, anxieties, doubts, and even other ideas that have arisen in his churches; as a rule he makes use of ideas and imagery taken from Jewish and primitive Christian apocalyptic, though he goes his own way in putting the accent differently and quite often makes modifications in the light of his understanding of Christ. The concepts and world pictures clearly belong to the times in which they arose, are often strangely crude, and have practically nothing to say to us today. Take, for example, the consolation which, on the basis of an apocryphal word of the Lord which certainly came into being only in the post-Easter church, the apostle gives the Thessalonians in an effort to allay their disquiet about the fate of those who may die before the Parousia, and to remove their anxiety that those who fell asleep may have no part in the coming redemption. They will not, he promises, be preceded by those who are still alive, but at the Lord's descent on the last day they are to rise first, and together with the rest to be "caught up in the clouds in the air to come up with the Lord" (1 Thess. 4:13–18).

Similarly, in 1 Corinthians, in reply to denials of the resurrection of the dead, Paul defends the idea that they will arise "in groups": "Christ the first fruits," then believers, thereafter the final end of the world (1 Cor. 15:23 f.). It is not a "fleshly" but a "spiritual," "heavenly" body into which the living, too, are to be "changed" (1 Cor. 15:51 f.). These ideas had their antecedents in later Judaism, and the influence of the religion of the Parsis is obvious. But Paul took them quite literally, as is shown by his not altogether successful attempt, inconsistent with his own presuppositions, to answer the Corinthians' doubts as to "how" the dead are raised, and to make the idea of resurrection plausible by analogy from persons and things terrestrial and celestial (1 Cor. 15:35–49). This shows that he thinks of the future existence, too, as not uncorporeal. He also means to be taken quite literally when he speaks of the concomitants of Christ's second coming (cf. 1 Thess. 4:16; 1 Cor. 15:52). A further aspect of these views is the definite expectation that, before the imminent end, the conversion of the Gentiles will be followed by the return to belief of the whole people of Israel which is at present obdurate in unbelief (Rom. 11:11–32).

As was said above, the character of Paul's statements about the future and the differences in them, specifically, in the "apocalyptic" ones, make it impossible to even them all out and gather them into one uniform picture. To attempt to do so would be to fail to appreciate not only how closely they are tied to a general world picture and to their own time, but also how they developed and changed with the passage of time. Admittedly, the sources do not allow the reconstruction of anything like an unbroken evolution of Pauline eschatology. Yet we can trace some stages and modifications, at least in outline. They mark themselves off as we seek in each context to answer the question as to the occasion of Paul's writing them and the specific situations—whether problems and emergencies of a church or the slogans and view of his opponents, the "enthusiasts"—to which they were addressed.

Paul's earliest letter, to the Thessalonians, has much to tell us. It introduces us to a church whose whole expectation had been directed by the apostle himself toward the imminent coming of Christ (even if its day and hour could not be calculated) and the end of the world (1 Thess. 5:1 f.). This church apparently thought that the end would suddenly arrive and believers be redeemed within the lifetime of the generation then alive (1 Thess. 5:1 f.). Otherwise there would have been no sense in its worry about the death of some members before the Parousia. At the start, then, the idea of a general resurrection must have been still alien to this church of Paul's. In order to meet such a situation, it is clear that a word of the Lord had been coined and put into the mouth of an inspired prophet, and to this Paul had recourse in order to comfort the church. Thus here the concept of the resurrection of the dead, derived from Jewish apocalyptic, is used to give a definite assurance that life and death, "waking" and "sleeping" (1 Thess. 5:10), constitute no unbridgeable gulf: both alike, those still alive and those fallen asleep, will soon be forever united with the Lord (1 Thess. 4:17; 5:10).

A mere eighteen months later, in 1 Corinthians, Paul has to defend the resurrection of the dead on another front. While he still maintains his conviction that "we shall not all sleep" (15:51), the accent has shifted, and the apostle now feels obliged to describe the consummation, to come but still delaying, as an entirely new creation of the whole of mankind reserved for God alone. Here the distinction between those still alive and those fallen asleep is completely broken down because in both cases they are to attain to life only through a change. As we have already seen, Paul grounds this idea in the creed, well known in Corinth as elsewhere, of Christ's death and resurrection (1 Cor. 15:1–11). He does this with such intensity that he describes the gospel and faith itself as altogether meaningless (15:12–19) if those who deny the future resurrection of the dead are right.

The conviction of Paul's opponents should not be equated, as often happens, with the Greek idea of the immortality of the soul. Nor was its basis denial of the resurrection of Christ from the dead. Rather, this was common ground between Paul and the "enthusiasts." The radical difference lay in the conclusions drawn by the two sides: the people who denied the resurrection of the dead believed that in their spirit-inspired experiences they were already possessed of the consummation as present reality (cf. 2 Tim. 2:18). Paul opposed this overhasty and premature identification of their experiences in the Spirit with God's new creation, to come in the end time but still delayed, in 1 Corinthians 15, with the utmost vehemence, and indeed with biting irony (cf. earlier, 1 Cor. 4:8 ff.). He emphasized that he himself was the last to have seen, and the last who would see, the risen Christ (1 Cor. 15:8). Accordingly, he rejects the "enthusiasts' " criticism of his teaching and gospel as illusion, and says that he would rather choose again and forever to be with the unbelievers and pagans who at least have the experiences of "sound understanding" on their side and do not twist these into pious illusions, if there is to be no such thing as the future resurrection of the dead.

What does all this mean? Obviously that faith never lives from itself and its emotion, but from what God has done and will do for believers and to the world, outside its own and beyond man's potentialities. Thus while all Paul's utterances go beyond the individual's human experience in time and refer to the divine "beyond," they serve the purpose of pinning believers down within the confines of the "here," "this side," the "not yet" of their temporality and historicity. To put it in another way, the purpose of the apocalyptic concepts and imagery is to maintain the qualita-

tive difference between "faith" and "sight" (2 Cor. 5:7): the
announcement of the "day" of Christ prevents men from con-
founding it with their own days in time and from evening out the
difference between God and man by means of the very matter of
faith and religious experiences. To counter the far too narrowly
individual and subjective "pneumatic" experience of the "enthusiasts," in which they lost all grip of God's saving action past and
future, the apostle explains in "objective" apocalyptic utterances
of cosmic range the saving event which, while only to be com-
pleted with the Parousia and the resurrection of believers, is
nevertheless already on the way because of Christ's resurrection
—Christ's lordship and conquest of the powers of the world until
the work of subjugating them is achieved and he delivers to God
the world which is his as creator and lord but which as yet still
bears the marks of death, "the last enemy." Then "God will be all
in all" (1 Cor. 15:20–28, A.V.).

Similarly, though with different concepts and imagery, 2 Corinthians 5:1–5 says that believers live on the basis of what they are
not yet, but what awaits them. Whether directly or indirectly, this
remarkable passage, too, is obviously polemic directed against a
gnostic and dualistic longing for deliverance from all the things of
the body. Over against it Paul sets the hope of a new, heavenly
"house" to which we are to be transported, and of a new "rai-
ment" with which we are to be clothed, that is, a new kind of
body, a new creation of the whole man, into which those still alive
will be transformed at the Parousia and into which those who
have fallen asleep will rise. Here again Paul maintains the tension:
because of the saving event God is assuredly with us; yet the other
side is also true—we are not yet with him, "at home with the
Lord" (2 Cor. 5:8).

It is impossible to reduce all Paul's statements about the Christian hope to a system. They are too diverse and dispersed, and
some are offset by others. Further, in view of what the apostle was
trying to effect by their means, any such attempt would be beside
the mark. Above all, there is a disjunction between the apostle's
cosmic expectations of the end, of which the announcement of the
"day" of Christ and of the world judgment also form part (1 Cor.

4:5; 2 Cor. 5:10; Rom. 14:12, etc.), and other passages speaking
of a consummation directly following upon the individual's death,
effected by final union with Christ (Phil. 1:23). Yet in this very
same letter he speaks of the "day" of Christ (Phil. 1:6, 10; 2:16)
and shows no interest in offsetting the one against the other to
form a coherent world picture and conceptual system.

Remarkably enough, although Paul's last great letter, Romans,
takes up a whole series of central theological ideas found in other
letters and meditates on them afresh, it has no parallels to the
utterances on the resurrection as in the letters to Corinth and
Philippi. Not that the expectation of the nearness of the coming
salvation and the last judgment is extinguished or has even become less intense (Rom. 13:11 ff.; 2:3 ff.; 14:12; 5:12 f.). But
here a fuller exposition of eschatological and apocalyptic motifs is
directed into an entirely different channel: first, the discussion of
Israel's final destiny (Rom. 9–11), in which the motifs are
transposed and applied to a hope to be fulfilled in time and history, and second, the channel of the redemption of the whole
creation (Rom. 8:19–23). Paul does not regard creation as dis-
sociated from mankind. Like the latter, it is subject to futility,
while at the same time sighing and longing for the final liberation
of the children of God in which it, too, is one day to have part. It
is groaning and in travail, but gazes into the future: the time is
now within sight, and the banner is hope.

However diverse all these statements in the Pauline letters
about the future and whatever their application, they again reveal
fixed basic motifs in the apostle's theology viewed as a whole: the
sovereignty and final victory of God, who alone is to bring the
work he began to completion. Accordingly, 1 Corinthians 15 ends
with a cry of victory over death, the bold, challenging tones of
which no man would presume to utter—on a man's lips the words
would soon turn into a vainglorious illusion. But the faithful,
themselves spoils in God's victorious hands, are to join in with
it:

> Death is swallowed up in victory
> O death, where is thy victory?
> O death, where is thy sting? (1 Cor. 15:55)

All such eschatological ideas in Paul, even those which at first
sight seem to get lost in the apocalyptic speculations of his own
day, are universally related to man and the world: they pin down
man and the world within the frontiers of their temporality and
debar believers from passing over not only suffering and death,
but also responsibility for others, in their enthusiasm. Nevertheless, all of them, whether comforting or admonitory, are stamped
by the hope which is based on God's acts in salvation and experiences affliction not as a contradiction to the divine salvation, but
as a comparison to it, so that it is as if a firm chain is formed—
suffering, endurance, character, hope (Rom. 5:3 ff.). For in the
scales, the "sufferings of this world" do not prevail against "the
glory that is to be revealed to us" (Rom. 8:18). Even afflictions
become a source of boasting, praise given to God (Rom. 5:2,
11).

Accordingly, by constituting reminders of God's action and the
new being into which believers are transposed, Paul's eschatological statements become a motive force in his parenesis: to be
watchful as those who stand in the light of the dawning day and
belong no more to darkness; to be sober and not to get drunk like
the children of night, in view of the advent of Christ, whenever its
hour may come (1 Thess. 5:1–11; Rom. 13:12 ff.). As a result
Paul's eschatological preaching, above all, opposes anxiety and
faintheartedness and indolence (Phil. 4:4–9), and clearly and
simply issues in the summons to "manliness" (1 Cor. 16:13), to
"standing immovable," to "being strong"—being confident even in
everyday things that "your labor is not in vain in the Lord" (1
Cor. 15:58). And this not only with regard to the individual
existence of each believer and his personal yesterday, today, and
tomorrow, but also with regard to God's time, which reaches beyond the individual, and to God's future, which, in the vistas he
has opened up, does not leave the world to itself or futility but
rather embraces it along with the individual and directs it to the
liberty that awaits it (Rom. 8:18 ff.).

On looking back over the presentation of Paul given here, some
may be surprised and regret that, in spite of the apostle's revolutionary insight into the liberating power of grace that breaks down
the frontiers separating men and men and nations and nations, we

have not drawn much more forceful and definite conclusions for the questions which press upon us today as to the shaping of our own lives and that of the world. But anyone who wants to wrest from Paul's theology a direct program and blueprint for these tasks will find no reward for his labor. Such effort would of course be not only an unhistorical, anachronistic, and therefore fruitless undertaking, one which fails to realize what has repeatedly come up for discussion here, the involvement of Paul's thinking in his own day and age; it would also represent a theological misconception of the apostle's gospel. The world in which he preached Christ is not to be equated offhand with our own. However, present in his faith are insights and forces which are for every generation to rediscover and develop. By his gospel of liberation in Christ, Paul of course gave the death blow to the presumptuous and indeed deliberate illusion that man's efforts can put the world to rights and turn it into a paradise. With the ardor that characterizes him, he thereby averted the ever present danger of relapse into bondage to this or that law of the world. Equally, however, on the basis of freedom, he revealed potentialities and standards which are to be proved in the very matter of men's living together in the power of the Spirit and in a changed world. He did not decide for all time how and where this was to be realized, but he trusted, and encouraged the man liberated by faith to test and form his judgment. This is what he means when he says that nothing else is of avail but the faith that works itself out in love.

CONCLUSION

PAUL AND JESUS

It is the virtue of Protestant research at the beginning of the century that it put the comparison between Jesus and Paul in the context of the theological question of the relationship between the two, and indeed of the question of the very nature of Christianity, even if the answer that it gave was problematical. It therefore compared the two not simply as historical figures—in this case figures in the history of comparative religion—as, say, did Plutarch of Chaeronea (c. A.D. 45–125; very nearly a contemporary of Paul) in his classic *Parallel Lives* (biographies in pairs), who set over against each other two heroes, statesmen, generals, orators, etc., of the Greek and the Roman worlds. This kind of approach is, of course, still popular today and used not only for thinkers and artists, but also for founders of religions, reformers, and leading figures in church history. It can undoubtedly facilitate the understanding of important people in history and sharpen our verdict as to which of the two compared achieved more. In our case, however, such an attempt would mean no more than coming to the outskirts of the matter represented by Jesus and Paul, and would block rather than open up access. We should fail to bring their coordination and relationship within our view.

Admittedly, the results of critical Protestant research were largely negative. Above all, it revealed the deep gulf between Jesus and Paul and ended by saying that Christianity was founded not by the Jesus of history who, in spite of all his uniqueness, is to be understood in the light of Judaism, but by Paul, who turned it into a religion of redemption, the influences on him being Jewish modes of thought, but also, and especially, Oriental pagan views and myths, as these had spread mainly in the Hellenistic mystery religions. The elements of truth in this, as well as what calls for correction, cannot be discussed in detail here. We also refrain from any full debate of the previous generation's theological positions based on its studies in comparative religion. The strictures with which the majority of them, in freely criticizing the church's dogmatic tradition, confined themselves to their own chosen department of history was a crucial factor in throwing into bold relief the question of the historical necessity, perhaps indeed the intrinsic legitimacy, of the development from Jesus to Paul, or even of the misfortune and decline involved in this. At that time the discussion of these questions of theological research was not confined to the armchairs of scholars, but became a very widespread topic among the laity as well. Since then the much debated slogan "Back to Jesus, away from Paul" has never settled down. Periodically it has died away and become a matter only for the theologians, but it has been kept smoldering at least underground. Often it has been no more than an unexpressed, secret line of demarcation between those still attached to the Christian tradition and those alienated from and hostile to Christianity. And most recently it has again become an open battle cry.

The question of how Paul and his gospel are to be assessed is, of course, extremely old. As we have already seen, even in his own lifetime his opponents considered him as an apostle without legitimation and a perverter of the Christian gospel. In the subsequent history of the early church, too, there were two very different judgments. For a considerable period he continued to be sternly rejected by Jewish Christians as antagonistic to Peter and James the brother of the Lord; in these circles people did not even stop short of ranking him with Simon Magus, the chief of heretics (Pseudo-Clementine). It is true that from the end of the first century onward there are a few ecclesiastical writers who hold him in high esteem and quote from his letters (1 Clement, Ignatius of Antioch, Polycarp). Apart from these, however, very soon it was the Gnostics and leaders of sects, in particular Marcion, who

claimed him as theirs, thereby making him suspect in the eyes of
the church. Accordingly, for decades we hear absolutely nothing
about him or else, as in the spurious 2 Peter (written in the middle
of the second century), he is mentioned as "dear brother," but
with reserve because, since his letters were hard to understand,
"ignorant and unstable people have twisted" his teaching "to their
own destruction" (2 Pet. 3:15 f.). Even when, as in Acts, he was
hailed as a great missionary or, as in the Pastorals, an attempt was
made to preserve his teaching, and when in other parts of early
Christian literature voices were raised in his honor, the lines along
which theology evolved were different from his. Then, unequivocally and finally, the great church wrested his theology from the
heretics and requisitioned it as its own—but in a tamed and modi-
fied form.

Since the last century, however, the debates between Christianity and its opponents have been the occasion of much loud and
open talk declaring war on Paul, talk which, while thoroughly anti-
ecclesiastical, still unites with it a high regard for the person of
Jesus. Thus, De Lagarde, the champion of a "German religion"
and "national church," traced the disastrous development of
Christianity back to the fact that "a man with no call whatsoever
[Paul] attained to influence in the church." With even greater
ferocity and commanding force Nietzsche in his *Antichrist* summarized the whole history of Christianity as one of "unflagging
corruption": "basically, there was only one Christ, and he died on
the cross. The 'good news' *died* on the cross. What from then on
passed for 'good news' was already the opposite of what *he* lived;
an 'evil gospel,' 'bad news,' a *dysevangelium.*" "The 'good tidings'
were followed hot-foot by the *most evil of all*, that of Paul." Paul
carried through this process right to the end, "with the logical
cynicism of a rabbi." "He embodies the antitype of 'the messenger
of good tidings,' the immense creative power of hatred. . . . Of
what *holocausts* to hatred has not this preacher of bad tidings
been the cause! Above all, the sacrifice of the Redeemer: he
nailed him to his cross. His life, example, teaching, and death as
well as the meaning and right of the whole gospel. Nothing remained when this counterfeiter conceived in hatred that of which
he alone could make use." It would not be hard to augment this

chorus of voices with the names of lesser spirits down to a book now painful to recall, Rosenberg's *Myth of the Twentieth Century*.

In recent days the slogan "Jesus, not Paul" has become virtually a slogan in the discussions between Jews and Christians, very tersely marking out the line of separation between them. The fact that this discussion was resumed at all after the Second World War—and this actually thanks to Jewish initiative—is most certainly the reverse of a foregone conclusion, considering the share in the unspeakable sufferings of the Jewish people of which the Christian church has been guilty for almost a thousand years, though the ghastly outburst of hatred in the last decades took its motive force not only from "Christian tradition" but also from many other dark non-Christian and anti-Christian sources. Accordingly, when things were revealed in their true colors, in the furious attack on religion which, oddly enough, both unites and separates them, both parties, Jew and Christian, became companions—though of course there was no comparison between the suffering of the two sides—in being treated as scum. This is the basis on which the dialogue, piecemeal at the start, developed under the influence of the hope expressed by Buber in one of his last books, that both had things unsaid to say and an almost unimaginable mutual assistance to render.

We cannot here enter in detail into the problems of this latest phase of the discussion. However, what chiefly characterizes it is manifestly the fact that the Jewish representatives (Buber, Baeck, Schoeps, Shalom ben Chorim, etc.) designate Jesus as one of the great Jewish prophets and their brother, though not as Messiah, whereas Paul, they say, fell victim to an illegitimate, apocalyptic, and Hellenized Judaism and, more important, to Greek and Oriental myths and ideas: he therefore bears the real responsibility for the fateful opposition between Jews and Christians and the alienation of the teaching of the church from Jesus' own preaching and from genuine Judaism. In the process, many well-known arguments of the past are remarshaled, though with differences in detail and entirely changed presuppositions: the abrogation of Law and circumcision, the perversion of the faith *of* Jesus into faith *in* Jesus Christ; the proclamation of the eschatological time of salvation already present in him (a thing daily contradicted by all experience in the world and history) and, consequently, the abandonment of the hope of Israel; finally, the severing of the individual from the sheltering embrace of nation, history, and the world, and indeed the nonrecognition of these as creation and their conversion into demonic powers.

The Jewish background of Paul's theology and the apostle's zeal and love for his nation are not disputed; but instead of the reproach brought against him earlier of "re-Judaizing" the gospel of Jesus, he is now charged with breaking out of Judaism's strictly maintained frontiers; it is alleged that for the sake of the Gentiles this made him fall victim to heathen syncretism.

Most recently, this band has been joined by Ernst Bloch (*Atheismus im Christentum*, 1968), not of course as faith's champion, but as its impassioned challenger. He, too, bases himself on the Bible and indeed makes an emphatic appeal to "the rebel and arch-heretic" Jesus as an agent of the subversive powers still scarcely revealed in the two Testaments, which, for the benefit of man and the world, revolt against "Jahweh" and the theocratic traditions and orders preserved by the priesthood. Bloch is the definitely atheist spokesman of the apocalyptic utopia to be realized on this earth in the sense of Karl Marx—ingenious in many of his formulations and when tracing the eschatological basis of Jesus' preaching of the "coming" of the kingdom of God; but also violent in his ideas and interpretations. As might be expected, what we find is not, as with Jewish thinkers like Baeck and Buber, a wisdom and moderation of his own. Rather, along with the lack of moderation characteristic of Marxist philosophers and accompanied by a gross distortion of the facts, the vials of wrath are poured out on Paul; on his primitive idea of a Moloch-like God who demands the sacrifice of his Son for the quitting of man's death for sin; on his replacing of Jesus' socially dangerous apocalyptic expectations by an illusionary salvation already present and pushed off the proper course by being related to the inner life and the life beyond, a salvation that is in addition cultic and sacramental, thanks to his theory of a sacrificial death and a resurrection mystery borrowed from a pagan nature myth. Thus, Bloch says, Jesus' gospel of the kingdom was brought to nothing and robbed of its power. Now, under the sign of the cross, believers are summoned only to patience, patience and in particular submission to the governing authorities—the whole thing a "Christianity" in which eschatology was "strangled" at its source, which makes itself at home in this world's vale of tears and concludes peace with its political, social, and economic conditions "in an odd mixture of transience and changelessness." "The will to sally forth or force the way into the kingdom" was broken, Bloch alleges, by Paul's conservatism, the "Son of Man" was replaced by "The Son of God," and so, thanks to Paul, was inaugurated a pagan and ultimately Byzantine lord—and "court theology around, over, and against Jesus."

This is the situation in which the question "Jesus or Paul" has once again been raised today. Within the limits of this final chapter it would be both impossible and hopeless to attempt a detailed apologetic discussion of either the criticisms of Paul and the attacks on him just mentioned or those previously enumerated. If the picture of Paul we have given has not already disarmed some at least of the arguments marshaled against him and corrected notorious distortions, such an apologetic effort would in any case come too late. In all events, the unending polemic against Paul, moderate or abusive, should be all to the good in keeping steadily burning the flames of unease which he himself kindled, and in making us aware of the disquieting character of the Christian gospel in general and of the Pauline "word of the cross" in particular, "a stumbling block to Jews and folly to Gentiles" (1 Cor. 1:23), and along with these of the odium to which in any case the gospel is always exposed. This polemic demonstrates, of course, that faith cannot be proved, and that the gospel's foundations are in themselves and in nothing extrinsic. Everything depends on the question to which for Paul and primitive Christianity the answer was the Crucified and Risen One—the question as to the significance of the figure of Jesus Christ and the events connected with him as the once-for-all efficacious act of God which decided and decides the destiny of the world and our own.

As is at once apparent, to adopt the definitely post-Easter formulation just given means perpetuating the difference between the preaching and works of the historic Jesus and the gospel of the later church mentioned in our introduction to Paul's theology. From the beginning, Paul's critics have had all the facts on their side in taking their stand on this difference and using it again and again as the basis of whether the Christian faith in general is or is not legitimate. For its basis and justification faith can seek its standing ground only at the place where its right is challenged by lack of faith. The difference between Jesus' gospel and the later church's kerygma is plain to see, though of itself the tradition about him which the Gospels assembled and worked up is ample proof that in retrospect many kerygmatic elements were subsequently imported into the preaching of the historic Jesus.

To any view oriented primarily and exclusively on a body of timeless ideas and concepts in the preaching of Jesus and that of the later witnesses to him, this change must inevitably seem a dire process of falling away and perversion. Yet, self-evident and natural as such a way of thinking may seem to us who have been so long accustomed to it, it comes to grief on the "historic" Jesus himself. For, according to the ideas expressed in his preaching, in his revolutionary criticism of both the dominant traditions of his nation and its doctrines and religious observance, Jesus is much nearer than was for long believed to what is echoed in the message of the prophets before him and in the wisdom teaching of later Judaism. Recognition of this has quite justifiably led representatives of present-day Judaism to claim Jesus as a prophet who is one of themselves. Matthew very appropriately expresses the fact that Jesus had very close connections above all with John the Baptist—whose message, authority, and importance he himself expressly acknowledged in more than one of his sayings without demoting him to the rank of a mere "precursor"—by summing up the message of each in identical terms (cf. Matt. 3:2 with 4:17). This shows that the two of them, Jesus and the Baptist, were in agreement on this very subject of the announcement that the kingdom of God had drawn near and of the summons to repentance. But the Baptist found this message far from being angrily rejected: rather, his nation listened to it. Of itself, it would not have involved Jesus, either, in deadly hatred and the cross. What obviously kindled the hostility was his proclamation that in him, his word and his acts, the era of judgment and salvation was already dawning here and now. The stronger one was already present, who destroys the power of Satan and strips him of his booty (Mark 3:27); already it was true that "if it is by the finger of God that I cast out demons, then the kingdom of God has come upon you" (Luke 11:20). As demonstrated by later Jewish apocalyptic, the message that the end of the world and the kingdom of God were near was elaborated in grandiose theological blueprints, but brought none of its representatives under a cloud. Even the concept and doctrine of a gracious God could very easily be fitted into the theology of contemporary Judaism. But if the word and work of Jesus, "My son, your sins are forgiven," should become and pass for reality as an "authority" not in the hands of or guaranteed by any priestly or scribal ruling body, the result was blasphemy. Now no longer a matter of mere preaching but of accomplished fact, the truly revolutionary questioning of all hallowed traditions and orders, the blotting out of all the lines drawn between clean and unclean, righteous and unrighteous, and the proclamation of this "today" and "now" against the horizon of the approach of the world-transforming, eschatological kingdom of God summoned Jesus' opponents to battle and involved him in condemnation as a rebel. (This subject is exceptionally well discussed, with characteristic vehemence, in Bloch, though his atheistic and utopian interpretation violently distorts it.)

For Jesus' enemies this "here" and "today" very soon became an irrevocable "yesterday" and "there," a mere item, an annoying incident for Jews and Romans, not worth worrying about. But, as the story of the journey to Emmaus shows, for Jesus' disciples it was a bitter question (Luke 24:13 ff.), the end of a cherished hope, the setting of their nation's star. Israel's redemption had not after all come to pass; instead, the world and its inexorable course still went on. To this experience Easter, the crucified, risen, and present Lord himself, supplied the answer.

We cannot enter into detail here about the honorific Christological titles in which this came to expression in the confessions of the later church, or the steps and stages by which the life and preaching of Jesus changed into the post-Easter gospel, into which he himself has been taken up and made its basis and subject matter. Nor can we say anything about the concepts and categories of thought in which primitive Christian faith was variously expressed and developed, whether they were adequate or open to criticism. They are time-conditioned and almost incomprehensible to us, however relevant and necessary for their time, and in every case constantly require fresh interpretation and elucidation. Paul's life and gospel have shown, as does the history of theology down to the present time, the large part played in this process of understanding by the apostle himself as an interpreter of the primitive Christian kerygma. But it also shows how he himself, in and with his theology, always calls for fresh exposition and appropriation. The questions about the right understanding of the saving event, both those with which he found himself faced and those of his own which he raised for the future, have never been settled, and it is terrible to think that they should ever be. It is therefore not surprising, and indeed all to the good, that even today the waves of critical debate still beat upon him: it is to be hoped that they always will.

So far, the justification and point of a comparison of Jesus' preaching and Paul's gospel have not been in dispute. However, such a comparison will now have to inquire whether and to what extent a similar body of ideas recurs and is preserved both in the apostle's gospel and in the preaching of Jesus. On general principle we have to take into consideration the standpoint in history and the new situation in time and the world brought about by Jesus' death on the cross and the presence in the Spirit of the living Lord, a change whose implications Paul thought out and developed to a greater extent than any of his predecessors or successors in the primitive church. In spite of all the difference in subject matter, mode of thinking, and language, the message of both agrees in being directed to man and his world, that is to say, to man and the world in God's sight and God's relation to the world.

In the Pauline gospel man is not simply conceived as a moral leper, any more than the world is degraded in terms of gnostic dualism into the domain of the devil. To oppose such tendencies, of which he had ample experience at the hands of his "enthusiastic" opponents, the apostle, himself, upheld the world as God's creation bound up with man, man's past, present, and future, for good or ill. But Paul was well aware that man is "godless" (*asebes*), yet without getting quit of God, summoned by him to live, yet incapable of true life. According to Paul, the Law, summed up in Jesus' preaching in the commandment to love one's neighbor, says this to all men, even and precisely those who mistakenly believe that they can manage by means of "works" or "wisdom." But the point of his gospel is that God has not abandoned, but has found and liberated, these men—in faith, provided that they renounce their own greatness and "boasting": he does not lay down antecedent conditions or insist that they should first have something to show, such as firm convictions about the existence of God and a Jewish or Christian *Weltanschauung*.

This makes clear that Paul's gospel of justification by faith alone matches Jesus' turning to the godless and the lost. In neither case is it a *concept* of God, the *idea* of the God who forgives, but the establishment and, in the full sense of the term, the bringing home to men of what is now happening and what the hour has proclaimed; the kingdom of God "in the midst of you" (Luke 17:20), "the fullness of time" (Gal. 4:4). As with Paul, in Jesus' preaching and work salvation means deliverance as event and miracle. The men who surround Jesus and encounter him are, for all their differences, alike characterized by an abysmal lack of freedom: illness, demon possession, guilt, as well as being prisoners of their religious conventions and traditions, their religiosity and dreams for the future. Only as Jesus encounters them does their lack of freedom become revealed, and only as he speaks his word and does his mighty works is deliverance effected both from the burden of their past and that of the future, the object of their anxieties and strivings. The coming kingdom of God—on earth, not beyond it (here Bloch is absolutely correct)—is therefor already breaking in. Accordingly, in Jesus' message as well as Paul's, the people who are really in danger and lost are the "good" who need no repentance, the Pharisee in the temple (Luke 18:9 ff.), the lost son's grumbling elder brother (Luke 15), the laborers in the vineyard who calculated with their master the greater amount of work done and, in consequence, their claim to bigger pay (Matt. 20:1 ff.).

Paul made no direct reference to these and similar words of the earthly Jesus. Indeed, everything suggests that they were unknown to him. One may confidently affirm what many may find surprising and a paradox, that in spite of the almost two thousand years' interval, we today probably know more about the Jesus of history than did Paul. At the same time, on the basis of what Paul did know of him, his death on the cross and resurrection, he proclaimed Christ's liberating work and conceived his person as the "Yes and No" confirming God's promises (2 Cor. 1:17 ff.). Jesus, by his turning to sinners and tax collectors, and Paul, by his gospel and missionary work among the Gentiles, alike broke through the limits imposed by achievement and supposed privileges.

In the gospel of both Jesus and Paul, the "freedom of the sons of God" is still a hidden one; the consummation has yet to come. Accordingly, their respective preaching is shot through with the summons to be watchful, prepared for suffering and trouble. However, this is watchfulness and preparedness not for what is uncertain, not because of the sketch of an apocalyptic utopia, a hope that "raises [men] even from the grave," but in view of the new day which has dawned with Jesus Christ.

All this makes it practically unnecessary to add that Paul is absolutely misunderstood when he is reproached, as he often is, with having by means of his theology forced his way between Jesus and Christianity and by reason of his "complicated" doctrine of salvation having erected a new barrier between God and man. The author of Ephesians had a much truer estimate of what the Pauline gospel was trying to do. It aimed at nothing less than the proclamation that Christ "has broken down the dividing wall of hostility" (between God and man, and also Jew and Gentile) (Eph. 2:14).

It would be naïve to suppose that the thoughts expressed here give a simple and complete résumé of Paul and his theology. Enough and more than enough in both is still obscure and perplexing. One may cite and emphasize this or that: many of the ideas in his doctrine of the law and salvation that were due to tradition and his age; the oddness of his expectations for the near future that were unfulfilled; the often unfathomable forward thrust of his theological thinking; and his exposition of Scripture, sometimes verging on the recherché, let alone the abstruse (here again, of course, he is the child of his age). In addition, there are the very embarrassing traits of his personality: the hard, bitter, and inexorable resoluteness of his decisions; the impassioned outbursts in his letters; the fact that the judgments he passed on his opponents were probably in more cases than one unjust; the forcefulness with which he pressed onward; the almost fantastic scope of his aims, and so on. With this apostle in particular, his greatness and limitations go, as always, hand in hand. These rough edges leave no place for clichés or for the traditional picture of the "saint." Yet all of it simply manifests the truth of his own words: "But we have this treasure in earthen vessels" (2 Cor. 4:7). Both are equally true: earthen vessels—treasure.

APPENDIX I

AUTHENTIC AND INAUTHENTIC

PAULINE LETTERS

In the present state of research, the authenticity of the Pauline letters on which the present volume is based needs no defense. They were each and all written during the apostle's six or seven years of missionary work in Galatia in the province of Asia Minor, in Macedonia, Greece, Ephesus (Asia), and again in Macedonia and Greece (Corinth). Their *order of writing* (in part certain, in part probable) is as follows:

1. During Paul's first stay in Corinth: 1 *Thessalonians*. Cf. 2:17–3:8 (spring of 50).
2. At the time of his work in and around Ephesus:
   a. *Galatians*. Addressed to churches in the *province* of Galatia, but scarcely in the districts mentioned in Acts 13 and 14 (conjecturally A.D. 54);
   b. the greater part of his *correspondence with Corinth* (cf. Appendix II; date: probably 54/55);
   c. the Imprisonment Epistles, *Philippians* and *Philemon*. Both presuppose an animated exchange of news, and therefore relative proximity between the place of Paul's imprisonment and the home of the recipient, which suggests Ephesus, not Rome or Caesarea. Though Acts gives no account of any arrest of Paul in Ephesus, and the letters do not expressly name the place of his imprisonment, 1 Corinthians 15:32 and 2 Corin-

thians 1:8 ff. tell of persecution and mortal danger in Ephesus
(Asia). Date: 54/55(?).

3. During Paul's last stay in Macedonia and Greece (Corinth): the
last part of the correspondence with *Corinth* (2 Cor. 2:13; 7:5 ff.;
8; 9), *Romans* (15:25 ff.), and *Romans* 16 (cf. Appendix II).

There are several traces in the early church of *inauthentic* letters
composed in Paul's name, for example, one to the Laodiceans and a
third Corinthian letter. Paul was not the only authoritative figure in
primitive Christianity to have letters composed in his name (1 and 2
Peter, James, and Jude). This phenomenon of pseudonymity is not
without more ado to be judged by present-day standards. The ancient
world had no idea of things like "intellectual property," "authorship
and copyright." Accordingly, we must look in detail before we leap to
the derogatory term "forgery." In ecclesiastical writings especially, the
fictitious authors are primarily the custodians of an authoritative
doctrinal tradition, particularly in the battle against false teaching and
for the securing of the church's faith and order.

In this book the following are regarded as Deutero-Pauline for the
reasons detailed in each case (listed not in chronological order, but
according to the consensus of opinion as to their genuineness or
otherwise in present-day research):

1. The *Pastoral Epistles* (1 and 2 Timothy, Titus): circumstances in
   Paul's life which cannot be verified from the rest of the (undisputed) letters; the post-apostolic ordering of the church; the
   characteristics of the heresy; vocabulary and theological evidence.
   Date of composition: in the first decades of the second century.
2. *Ephesians*: place name not certainly attested by textual evidence;
   no relationship to a particular church; a theological treatise rather
   than a letter; not Pauline in style; theological differences from
   Paul (cf. in particular the church as a cosmic body, of which
   Christ is the "head"; world view influenced by gnosticism; dependence on the ideas of Colossians, though developed independently. Date of writing: about A.D. 100.
3. *Colossians*: the very close stylistic and theological affinities (in spite
   of certain dissimilarities) align Colossians with Ephesians and at
   the same time set it out of line with Paul himself (differences in
   conceptions of Christology, of the church, baptism, the apostolic
   office, and eschatology). Although the writer clearly uses genuine
   Pauline ideas and is acquainted with the apostle's situation in

prison, there are already traces of further theological work on the
part of a "Pauline school" (cf. above, p. 86). For details see
Lohse, *Die Briefe an die Kolosser und an Philemon* (Meyer Commentary, IX, 2, 14th ed.), 1968; contains full bibliography.

4. *2 Thessalonians*: closely dependent on 1 Thessalonians (even in
insignificant matters of phraseology). The (imagined) situation is
the same as there; if genuine, it must have been written immediately after 1 Thessalonians. But the use of a previous letter is unlike
Paul himself, and above all, the very different answer to the question of the end of the world and Christ's Parousia, involving
detailed apocalyptic teaching, is odd (enumeration of the events
that must precede the eschaton and delay the end; cf. 2:1–12).
Further, there is polemic (2:2) against letters "purporting" to be
from Paul (1 Thess. ?), announcing the nearness and imminence
of the day of the Lord, and the apostle's own signature to letters
is adduced in support of the "authenticity" of 2 Thessalonians.

APPENDIX II

CRITICAL PROBLEMS IN 1 AND 2

CORINTHIANS, PHILIPPIANS,

AND ROMANS

The evaluation of these epistles here is based on the following findings of literary criticism:

In any case Paul's correspondence with the *Corinthians* (see above, p. 68) amounted to more than just two letters (1 Cor. 5:9; 2 Cor. 2:4; 7:8). By means of arguments which deserve consideration but are not in my opinion convincing, several scholars have maintained that the letter mentioned in 1 Corinthians 5:9 (A) was not simply lost, but that important fragments of it were later worked into the canonical 1 Corinthians (B) and are preserved there. This book, on the other hand, assumes that 1 Corinthians is a unity. The question may be left out of account for the further reason that A and B must have followed so closely the one on the other that a possible division would scarcely yield any substantial historical information.

In the case of 2 Corinthians, we are on much firmer ground in assuming that it was not composed as one continuous letter: several fragments of letters written at various times and to meet very different external and internal situations are set alongside one another, in an order not corresponding to the course of events.

1. The discrepancy is at its clearest in the relationship between the last four chapters, 10–13, and chapters 1–2 and 7. The latter were written when Paul was looking back on the very troubled story (see above, p. 77) of the beginning of fresh agitation against him on the part of his opponents and continue it right up to the time of

his complete reconciliation with the church. The situation is entirely different in 10–13. Here Paul's battle with the Corinthians for the legitimacy of his apostleship is at its height (ruthless unmasking of the "super-apostles"; very sharp words about the church they led astray; bitter, ironic self-defense). In the two parts of the "letter" there are differences not only in tone and mood but also in the actual situation of the author and the church. If 10–13 are in their right place, it would mean that the effect of 1–2 and 7 had gone for nothing. Accordingly, for a century many scholars have assumed, in my opinion correctly, that the last chapters contain the most important parts of the "painful letter" (D) mentioned in 1 Corinthians 2:4 and 7:8 (four-chapter hypothesis).

2. As is often pointed out, a second striking break can be seen between 2:13 and 14. After Paul has told of his departure from Troas to Macedonia in order to meet Titus, for whose arrival back from Corinth he was waiting impatiently, 2:13 breaks off abruptly and the narrative is not resumed until 7:5. The two parts (2:12 f. and 7:5 ff.) fit together "like the fragments of a ring" (J. Weiss). Between them suddenly appears the first great defense of Paul's apostolic office (C), without any relationship whatsoever to what precedes (1:1–2:13) or what follows (7:5–16). This section, too, can hardly be in its original position. While its subject matter is akin to that of D, C obviously reflects an earlier phase in the battle between the apostle and his opponents or the church, when things had not as yet gone to the full length. Accordingly, C must have been written when news had reached Paul of the new agitation against him, but while he still counted on the church's insight and loyalty (cf. 6:11 f.; 7:4 with 11:16–21; 12:11 ff. etc.); that is to say, before his flying visit and the painful letter.

3. The two chapters about the collection, 8 and 9, were also evidently not written at the same time. Admittedly, the subject in both is the collection for Jerusalem, but each is a unit in itself, neither refers to the other, and they were written in different situations. Chapter 8: along with others Titus is again sent to Corinth to continue with the gathering of the collection and is recommended to the church. Paul's complete reconciliation with it is presupposed. Thus, chapter 8 (F) is to be regarded as a short personal letter of recommendation for Titus, or as an appendix to the letter of reconciliation, 1:1–2:13; 7:5–16 (E), which he was taking with him. Chapter 9: composed later, and the

apostle's final writing in the matter of the collection. Paul remains in Macedonia, but asks the Corinthians to have the collection, a successful one, complete before he himself comes to Corinth in the immediate future (G).

There is not the slightest reason for doubting the authenticity of any of these parts (with the exception of 6:14–7:1, a few parenetic verses characteristically non-Pauline both in vocabulary and in theological content; they also break the connection. This passage, which has close affinities with Qumran texts, must be a later insertion).

If our 2 Corinthians is therefore a collection of various letters (C to G), the question then arises as to the reason for this and the time when it was done; above all, why did the collector put the fragment of the "painful letter" (D) at the end, and so cause the impression made by the letter of reconciliation (E) to appear illusory? His method of composition is, however, explained by a law of "form" of which there is ample evidence elsewhere in early Christian literature: since heresy had been announced as one of the perils of the time of the end, warnings against it were placed at the end of writings or documents. Quite obviously the collector wanted Paul's polemic against the "false apostles" and "servants of Satan" to be taken in this sense and accordingly placed it at the end. For the rest, he took E as the foundation document, worked into it the oldest and particularly important fragment C, and then followed this unit, consistently with date and subject matter, by F and G.

The hypothesis of subsequent collection is supported by the fact that the apostolic fathers in the last years of the first century and the first of the second (1 Clement, Ignatius, and Polycarp) frequently quote from the canonical 1 Corinthians and it alone, never from 2 Corinthians. The various pieces were possibly gathered together toward the end of the first century and, in the nineties of it, joined together as an apostolic didactic writing in Corinth, whence it spread, at a time when, on the evidence of 1 Clement, the Corinthian church was again threatened with rebellion (see further G. Bornkamm, "Die Vorgeschichte des sogenannten Zweiten Korintherbriefes," *Sitzungsberichte der Heidelberger Akadamie der Wissenschaft*, 1961; bibliography given there).

Philippians, too, (see above, p. 60) is conjectured to be a collection of at least two, and probably three, letters. In point of time 4:10–20 should come first: it is a short letter of thanks to the Philippians who, while the apostle was in prison, sent one of their members, Epaphroditus, to minister to his need, giving him a gift to take with him (A). Here there is no sign of an arrest stretching over any considerable period. This is only presupposed in 1:1–3:1(B): Epaphroditus proved himself true, but had been ill, near to death, causing anxiety to the Philippians: he was now well again, but longing to be home, and the apostle sends him back, hoping that he himself will soon be released and able to come to Philippi (2:19–30). This is also the situation in chapter 1: Paul's imprisonment has been protracted, its outcome is imminent but still uncertain (release or execution), 1:12–26; 2:17. Nothing more—or should we say nothing as yet?—is heard of all this in the very sharply polemical section of the book, 3:2–4:9(C), which begins abruptly and ends with a greeting: "and the peace of God will be with you." It presupposes the apostle's own release, but also, as compared with A and B, the danger owing to the recipients' church situation, as before (recent research in G. Bornkamm, "Der Philipperbrief als Paulinische Briefsammlung," in *Neotestamentica et Patristica, Freundesgabe für O. Cullmann*, 1962, pp. 192–202).

For some time now, and for the reasons given on p. 79, many critics also regard the long list of greetings in *Romans* 16 as misplaced at the end of Romans and originally a fragment of a letter to Ephesus: it also presupposes information about a heresy threatening the church, of which there is no indication elsewhere in Romans (16:17–20, closely connected with Phil. 3). If this assumption is correct, this is part of a letter to *Ephesus* composed about the same time as Romans, before Paul's final journey from Corinth to Jerusalem. We cannot here enter into the question whether the list formed part of an independent letter now lost or had been attached to a copy of Romans which Paul sent to Ephesus (T. W. Manson). In my opinion our hypothesis explains Romans 16 more convincingly than does the fanciful idea of a fresh return to Rome on the part of persons domiciled in Ephesus and the east (owing to Nero's perhaps having revoked the edict of Claudius); it would be like a small-scale "migration of nations." If we remember the time at which the apostle wrote Romans and Romans 16 (see above, pp. 79–80), the situation makes the unusual length of the list perfectly comprehensible: Paul was taking farewell of the Ephesine church in which, until a short time previously, he had worked for a longer time than anywhere else.

Romans 16:25–27: as shown by the uncertain textual witness and especially by the un-Pauline terminology, Romans 16:25–27 is recognized as an ending not coming from Paul himself.

APPENDIX III

CHRISTOLOGY AND JUSTIFICATION

(on Romans 1:3 f. and 1:16 f.)

Romans 1:13 f. and 1:16 f. (cf. above, pp. 116–17) give two very different summaries of the content of the gospel.

1. There are the following reasons for assuming that Romans 1:13 f. is a pre-Pauline credo: (a) the use of participles, characteristic of propositions in primitive Christian confessions, and the (synthetic) parallelism; (b) the Christological scheme: according to the flesh— according to the Spirit (cf. 1 Tim. 3:16; 1 Pet. 3:18; Ign. ad Eph. 18:2; Try. 9; Sm. 1:1); (c) the motif of Jesus as son of David, found nowhere else in Paul; (d) un-Pauline turns of phrase ("designated as . . ."; "Son of God in power"; "Spirit of holiness"; "since [his] resurrection from the dead"). Cf. R. Bultmann, *Theology of the New Testament*, Scribner/SCM Press, 1952, p. 82; E. Schweizer, *Jesus Christus*, Siebenstern Taschenbuch, 1968, pp. 72 ff., id, arts. "pneuma" and "sarx" (*Theol. Wörtb.* 2 N.T., VI, 415; VII, 125 f.); F. Hahn, *The Titles of Jesus in Christology*, Lutterworth, 1969; W. Kramer, *Christ, Lord, Son of God;* SCM Press/Allenson, Studies in Biblical Theology 50, pp. 108–112. In itself the credo reproduces the Christology of the early (Jewish Christian) church: Jesus, legitimated by his Davidic descent, is by his resurrection exalted as "Son of God." The formula does not speak of the significance of his death for salvation, nor is it oriented on the gospel of justification.

2. Romans 1:16 f. is primitive Pauline and, unlike the purely Christological credo, is formulated in soteriological terms ("the power of God for salvation for everyone who has faith"; "God's righteousness through faith for faith"; "he who through faith is

righteous shall live"; no honorific Christological titles such as Son of God, Kyrios, not even the name Christ). Both formulations are full and complete statements of the faith; they do not select from the gospel, the one the one thing and the other the other.

How are they related? The idea that Paul quoted the traditional formula only in order to prove his orthodoxy to a church which did not know him before going on to *his* gospel is hardly adequate. It fails to do justice to the indissoluble connection in the Pauline theology between Christology and the doctrine of justification. What is the bridge leading from the content of the first summary of the faith to that of the second, and what is the way back from the second to the first? The answer is not to be found in the (traditional) motif of Jesus as son of David, which plays hardly any part in Paul (cf., however, the quotation from Isaiah in Rom. 15:12), but rather in the honorific title "Son of God" which, while strictly speaking not in conformity with the credo itself (because it covers only the second half), Paul emphatically puts at the beginning ("concerning his Son," 1:3; cf. 1:9); at the end (1:4) he replaces it by his most usual title for the Kyrios ("Jesus Christ our Lord"). Though less frequent in the letters, "Son of God," too, is important and significant with Paul. He does not use it as in the church's confession given here. For Paul the Son of God is the *pre-existent* Christ, whom God "sent" into the world for its redemption (Rom. 8:3; Gal. 4:4). He has no thoughts to offer on Christ's divine being in itself before time began, nor does the title imply Jesus' supernatural birth (so also in John and Hebrews). Instead, it points to the redemptive event, not something immanent in the world itself, but commencing in the act of God: "God did not spare his own Son but gave him up for us all" (Rom. 8:32); Paul declares that "God is for us" (Rom. 8:31). For Paul this means all men: now there is no restriction to Israel as the only nation privileged to be saved. This allows us to understand why the honorific title is firmly implanted precisely into Paul's doctrine of justification (Gal. 1:15 f.; 3; 4; Rom. 8) and connotes both Christ's significance for salvation and his death and resurrection (Rom. 5:10; 8:29). The soteriological significance of Christ's sonship with God also comes out in the fact that sonship of the believers is based on the sending of the "Son" and attested to them by his Spirit. He does not call them to be "Christs" and "Kyrioi," but "sons" and "heirs" (Rom. 8:14–17; Gal. 4:4–7). While these connections are not made explicit in Romans 1, as Paul understood it, 1:3 f. points forward to 1:16 f., and conversely, 1:16 f. points back to the credo as Paul reinterpreted it.

INDEX OF REFERENCES

D. Nonbiblical Sources

INDEX OF SUBJECTS AND NAMES

(supplementing the Contents)

71 72 73 10 9 8 7 6 5 4 3 2 1